MASS MEDIAURAS

Form, Technics, Media

Samuel Weber

Edited by
Alan Cholodenko

Stanford University Press
Stanford, California
1996

Stanford University Press
Stanford, California

© 1996 Power Institute and Samuel Weber
Originating publisher: Power Publications,
 Sydney, Australia
First published in the USA by
 Stanford University Press 1996
Printed in Australia
Cloth ISBN 0-8047-2675-2
Paper ISBN 0-8047-2676-0
LC 95-70817
This book is printed on acid-free paper.

CONTENTS

Introduction

'Where in the World are We?'

In May and June of 1992 I spent several weeks in Australia giving a series of lectures, seminars and interviews. Out of the intense and exhilarating exchanges that marked my visit came the idea of collecting the various talks and discussions into a volume. The result is *Mass Mediauras: Form, Technics, Media*. The book is a collective effort, if ever there was one. But it is a curious collection, in more ways than one. First of all, the persons involved in its production came from highly divergent backgrounds and, to some extent at least, were moving in equally divergent directions. What made the exchange of views fruitful and exciting was the fact that, despite, or rather, because of, such divergencies, everyone was willing and able to put themselves, their projects and their premises into question. This, however, is easier said than done. For questioning is never innocent. No question can ever be asked without some sort of answer being anticipated. One can, however, distinguish between questions asked primarily to reach an answer and a questioning that is after something else, something that can not be measured in strictly cognitive terms.

Such is the questioning that traverses this book. This might not be immediately evident. For the essays and discussions collected in it often take the form of statements, propositions, declarations. And yet such assertiveness knows better what it is challenging than where it is going. One of the beliefs being so challenged is nothing less than the touchstone upon which much of modernity has relied in defining itself: the notion of its radical distinctiveness from all that has come—or gone—before. Nothing is more modern than the idea of the radical break, separating the 'new' decisively from the 'old'. A classic articulation of this sentiment is the declaration with which Rousseau introduces his *Confessions*: 'I feel my heart and I know people. I am made like no one existing. If I am no better, then at least I am different'.

It is precisely the nature of this *difference* that is in question in this book. In place of the perspective that construes difference in terms of an interval or interstitial break—*either* something is different *or* it is the same—the essays gathered in this volume display difference more as a structuring fissure or fracture, in the sense of a Heideggerian *Riß*, potentially dividing and fracturing individual works, brushing them against the grain, as it were, deforming and dislocating them and in the process making way for a spaciousness in which the remote and the intimate uncannily converge.

This convergence is both a very old story and yet surprisingly new. It confounds the still prevalent conception of history as a more or less linear, if not developmental, process. Instead, the figure of history that emerges from the readings undertaken in this book is one of conflict, compromise and negotiation, resulting not so much in *breaks* as in *shifts*, that is, in a movement that is never simply irreversible.

The terrain upon which these shifts play themselves is demarcated on the one side by the aesthetically oriented notions of art and reality, form and work, and on the other by that of media. If the word 'media' is used here without a definite or defining article, it is because one of its singular characteristics is to undercut the ostensibly clear-cut oppositional relationship between singular and plural, general and particular, genre and work, and in so doing, to call attention to the irreducible significance of the space in-between—and outside of—such polar oppositions. To retrace mediatic articulation at work within the boundaries of the individual *work* is to call attention to the way in which what had hitherto been considered to be accessory and intermediary—the program, its transmission, reception, storage, recycling, retransmission, etc.—infiltrates the inner integrity of the work, revealing it to be inscribed in, and as, a *network*.[1]

It is not that the idea of a radical discontinuity—the break—thereby disappears or is invalidated. Far from it. Rather, such discontinuity is shown to be itself continually at work within the work itself. As network, the work reveals itself to be what it has probably always been: a relational process which depends as much upon what it is not as upon what it is.

Such dependency or relationality brings with it an important corollary, one that again goes against the idea of a radical break separating the old from the new, the other(s) from the Self. As the passage from Rousseau's *Confessions* indicates, the radicality of the New can ultimately be measured only in terms of the emergence of a unique and distinctive subject, and ultimately, of an *I*: 'I may be no better, but at least I am different (*au moins je suis autre*)'. What diverges from the past decisively and definitively is ultimately *an indi-*

---

1 See, in this context, the pioneering work of Friedrich Kittler, and in particular his *Discourse Networks 1800/1900*, 1990. Kittler's work, despite its unquestionable qualities, remains informed by the notion of the radical break alluded to above, which in turn reintroduces the traditional hermeneutics of the subject and of meaning by the back door of technological determinism.

vidual (even if that individual can come to be identified with a *collective*). The 'break' becomes the setting for that which is supposedly *unbreakable*: in-dividual. One nation, indivisible... *E pluribus unum*.

By contrast with this scheme, the following essays tell the story not so much of the individual Self as of its highly divisible *Settings*. This is a book about *places* and *positioning* rather than about human beings. Or rather, it suggests that the *being* of human being has had more to do with *setups* and *sets* than with *subjects* and *objects*, unified in and through self-consciousness. By focusing upon an emerging crisis in the definition of space and place, the essays here collected retrace how the development of aesthetic theory can be understood as a (perhaps ultimate) effort to defend the notion of the indivisibility of place as a condition of the individuality of the subject. This effort to establish a concept of place as self-contained and unified, as well as the problems it encounters, can be traced back to the earliest stages of Western philosophy—to Plato's discussion of the *chora* in the *Timaeus*[2]—and there is every indication that the task has become one of the most powerful forces driving the modern period. For without the unity of place, the unity of the subject becomes difficult to conceive. It is the function of aesthetic theory, as it is developed by Kant, to help secure this ever more problematical unity of place by introducing the no less problematical notion of *form*. That Kant's effort, in the Third Critique, is more significant in coming undone than in succeeding 'sets' the scene for the following essays, which explore the unraveling of form as the 'setting' for the rise of the media.

The relation of form, place and media is, to be sure, highly complex, conflictual and dynamic. It is above all a relation of

---

2   See the remarkable text of Jacques Derrida, *Khôra*, 1993. See also my discussion of the *chora* in 'The Parallax View', *assemblage* 20, 1993.

forces rather than of substances, subjects or entities. Two recent events can serve as indications of how this relation shapes the contemporary situation.

Shortly after the January 17, 1994 Northridge earthquake, a front page article appeared in the *Los Angeles Times* under the heading, 'Where in the World are We?'. It introduced its readers to the story of the emergence of a new technology: a worldwide satellite system developed by the Pentagon for purposes of military surveillance, and which now was being increasingly adapted to civilian uses. The system bore the acronym GPS, for *Global Positioning System*. Through its intervention, movement on the earth could now be located with a precision heretofore impossible. It was GPS that enabled geologists to determine the movements of the Los Angeles basin following the January earthquake with unprecedented accuracy and speed, just as the same technology had allowed the Allied military commanders to locate, and annihilate, units of the Iraqi Army in the so-called 'Gulf War'.

'Where in the World are We?' One answer is that we are in a world overseen, in its planetary totality, by GPS. Small black-box GPS-receivers are now showing up in taxies and trucks, permitting drivers to determine their location instantaneously and precisely. In that sense, at least, we—or others—can soon hope to know *just exactly where we are*. As mobile as we may be, or become, we are even more *localizable*. We are, as it were, on call—and from this call it is difficult to imagine any escape.

This brings me to the second incident. It was the televised spectacle of O.J. Simpson, invisible in a white 'Bronco', returning to his home after an unsuccessful attempt at escaping arrest for the brutal murder of his former wife and her friend. Sports and its practitioners have long been a cultural paradigm for American society, and the power of that paradigm is inseparable from the advent of the media. The one 'mirrors' the other,

in complex and intricate ways. Certain aspects of that relationship are interpreted in this book, in particular at the end of the
essay 'Television: Set and Screen'.

The prime-time spectacle of O.J.'s Homecoming brought to
the fore another decisive element in the fascination sports exer-
cises upon America in the Age of Media. O.J. Simpson made his
athletic reputation above all as a running back. His most mem-
orable sporting achievements involved precisely what the final
cortege both recalled and mourned: the ability to *break out* of
what seems to be—and what in reality generally is—an inextricable confinement and to *break through* what appear to be—
and in reality generally are—insuperable obstacles. To *break
out* and *break through*, however, one must first be enclosed,
embedded, in a firm and fixed location (the sort of location that
GPS appears at long last to offer and to confirm).

It is this ambivalence, between the desire to occupy a place
of one's very own and the desire to break out of a place in
which one is caught, that is raised to incalculable proportions
in the modern period generally and in the Age of the Media
more particularly. Hence, the pathos that *riveted*—the word is
hardly fortuitous here—millions of viewers to their TV *sets* at
dinnertime, as that 'white Bronco', escorted by a phalanx of
LAPD vehicles, with countless television helicopters whirring
overhead, made its slow, ceremonious way along the Los
Angeles 'free-ways', past the cars slowed down on the opposite
side of the road, past the throngs gathered on the overpasses,
towards an uncertain but inevitable destination: 'home'.

The hero comes home, but the sport goes on. The essays in
this volume recount the sport of homecoming and the homecoming of sport as a movement that is reducible neither to
escape nor to return, to breaking out nor breaking through. A
movement difficult to name, and surely impossible to name
univocally, it nevertheless emerges, in the following pages, as

having something to do with what an older form of discourse called: *coming-to-pass*.

In the age of the media, things, people and places *come to pass*, in an *event* more sportive than any sporting event, and more spectacular than any spectacle. It is the coming-to-pass of such an event that these essays seek to stage. Such a staging opens onto questions far richer than any imaginable answers: how do 'technics', film and television, the 'setup' and the 'set', change our relation to *places, positions* and *emplacements?* What is left over when *forms unravel* and *works* come undone? What happens to reality when our traditional access to it—sense-perception—is no longer restricted to the individual body? What comes *after deconstruction?* What is *coming to pass?*

So many questions, so few answers. If a book is measured by the answers it gives to the questions it raises, then this is not a book, or—what amounts to the same—not a very good one. But despite the need for reassurance that, understandably, has become increasingly insistent over the past years, questions do not go away simply because they seem to have been 'answered', any more than problems disappear when they seem to have been 'solved'.

We live in an age of increasing uncertainty, when the solutions and answers that were taken for granted until recently no longer seem viable. It is an age in which the technology and media that were supposed to bring about the 'global village' have contributed to the revival of 'ethnic cleansing' and religious fundamentalism. It is an age in which economic competitiveness goes hand in hand with mass unemployment, when 'prosperity' means growing economic inequalities and when the much heralded end of the Cold War coincides with spreading social and political disintegration.

One of the few advantages of this strange and dangerous age is the possibility not just of asking questions but of letting them make their way, without feeling obliged to provide definitive answers. This is a book of questions, then, and of curious conclusions, for readers who can confront problems without demanding recipes of salvation.

It is also a way of saying thanks to those participants and interlocutors in Australia whose hospitality demonstrated what seems to be increasingly overlooked in our age of identificatory constraint: that the encounter with the other need not be simply a threat to oneself.

A special word of thanks goes to Alan Cholodenko, Head of the Power Department of Fine Arts, whose initiative is responsible both for my visit to Australia and for this book. Without his tireless efforts and incisive editorial input none of this would have been possible.

Samuel Weber
Los Angeles, July 1995

The Unraveling of Form

I

> Enough of the subjects of poetry: let us now speak of the style; and when this has been considered, both matter and manner will have been completely treated.
>
> I do not understand what you might mean [...]
>
> Then I must make you understand; and perhaps I will be more intelligible if I put the matter in this way. You are aware, I suppose, that all mythology and poetry is a narration of events, either past, present or to come?[1]

I interrupt a scene that is doubtless familiar to many of you: a wise teacher explaining to some of his students and admirers what might be involved in constructing a just society. The teacher is, of course, Socrates; and the particular episode from

---

1 Plato, *The Republic*, 1982, III, 392. Future references are given in the body of the text using the abbreviation *REP*.

which I have quoted is to be found in the Third Book of *The Republic*, where Socrates is in the midst of discussing the nature of poetry with regard to its social and political effects. Having just reviewed a number of different instances in which Homer represents gods and human beings in ways that can only sap the morale of the impressionable, including those who are destined to lead the fortunes of the State, Socrates turns from questions of theme and of content to that of poetic 'style' and in particular to that of *narration*. He distinguishes between two types of narration: the one is characterized by direct discourse, in which 'the poet is speaking in his own person; he never leads us to suppose that he is any one else' (*REP*, III, 393). In the other form of narration, by contrast, the poet no longer speaks for himself. Rather, 'he takes the person of' one of his characters; 'and then he does all that he can to make us believe that the speaker is not' the author but the fictional figure. This is what Homer does at the beginning of the *Odyssey*, Socrates remarks, and indeed 'throughout' the poem: 'The poet speaks in the person of another' and thereby, through 'imitation', 'assimilates his style to that of the person who, as he informs you, is going to speak' (*REP*, III, 393). This latter form of narration Socrates therefore designates as 'mimetic' or 'imitative' discourse to distinguish it from the former, which he calls 'simple' narration. Although Socrates recognizes that both forms of narration are inevitable, he also leaves no doubt as to their fundamental dissymmetry, for imitation in general and imitative narrative in particular are fraught with dangers: 'Did you never observe how imitations, beginning in early youth and continuing far into life, at length grow into habits and become a second nature, affecting body, voice, and mind?' (*REP*, III, 395). The good and just man therefore will use it sparingly: 'He will adopt a mode of narration such as we have illustrated out of Homer, that is to say, his style will be both imitative and narrative; but

there will be very little of the former, and a great deal of the latter' (*REP*, III, 396). By contrast,

> there is another sort of character who will narrate anything
> [...] not as a joke but in right good earnest [...] He will attempt
> to represent the roll of thunder, the noise of wind and hail, or
> the creaking of wheels and pulleys, and the various sounds of
> flutes, pipes, trumpets, and all sorts of instruments: he will
> bark like a dog, bleat like a sheep, or crow like a cock; his entire
> art will consist in imitation of voice and gesture, and there will
> be very little narration. (*REP*, III, 397)

As this characterization makes clear, left to its own devices
mimetic discourse tends to consume, or at least to disrupt, narration itself. It becomes theatrical, a language of 'voice and gesture', with 'very little narration'.

And indeed, when, towards the end of *The Republic*, Socrates
finally concludes that, in the absence of a more adequate
defense than has hitherto been mounted, the imitative art of
the poets must be excluded from the State, his condemnation of
poetic mimesis turns on its subversive *theatricality*, which
leaves it incapable of rendering models worthy of emulation:

> And does not [...] the rebellious principle [...] furnish a great
> variety of materials for imitation? Whereas the wise and calm
> temperament, being always nearly equable, is not easy to imi-
> tate or to appreciate when imitated, especially at a public festi-
> val when a promiscuous crowd is assembled in a theater. For
> the feeling represented is one to which they are strangers.
> (*REP*, X, 604) [2]

---

2   Shortly thereafter, the corrosive effects of comedy and laughter are identified with the theatre: 'There are jests which you would be ashamed to

This reference to the dangers of the 'public festival' and its 'theater' is all the more telling when we recall that it is precisely festivals that set, and indeed *frame*, the scene of *The Republic* itself. The text begins with Socrates narrating the events of the previous day, when he had gone to Piraeus to see 'in what manner they would celebrate the festival [in honor of Bendis, the Thracian Artemis], which was a new thing' (*REP*, I, 327). After the festivities, as he is about to return home, 'to the city', he and his companion, Glaucon, run into some friends, who convince them to spend the night in Piraeus. The argument that carries the day is precisely the reminder that another

> festival will be celebrated at night, which you certainly ought to see. Let us rise soon after supper and see this festival; there will be a gathering of young men, and we will have a good talk. Stay then, and do not be perverse. (*REP*, I, 328)

The Republic consists in the discussions which ensue, not however, as suggested, *after* the festival but rather *between* festivals. In view of this curious position, it is not entirely surprising that its own style is not completely free of mimetic elements. For instance, it concludes with the telling of another story. 'Not one of the tales which Odysseus tells to the hero Alcinous, yet this too is a tale of a hero, Er, the son of Armenius', who, after having been slain in battle, returns to the land of the living twelve days later to tell 'what he had seen in the other world' (*REP*, X, 614). 'The story', Socrates tells Glaucon, 'would take too long to tell' (*REP*, III, 615). Given this length and complexity, I will not attempt to retell Socrates' account of the tale, except to reit-

---

2   (*cont.*) make yourself, and yet on the comic stage, or indeed in private, when you hear them, you are greatly amused [...] and having stimulated the risible faculty at the theater, you are betrayed unconsciously to yourself into playing the comic poet at home'. (*REP*, X, 606)

erate the moral of the story: 'He said that for every wrong which they had done to any one they suffered tenfold' but also that they could still 'choose' their 'genius', which would then be their 'destiny' in lives to come. From this story Socrates is thus able to discern one clear lesson at least: in anticipation of the retribution and the choice to come, one should 'leave every other kind of knowledge and seek and follow one thing only', namely, 'to learn and discern between good and evil, and so to choose always and everywhere the better life as he has the opportunity' (*REP*, X, 618).

The question that arises here concerns precisely the opportuneness of this opportunity. For its condition of possibility, it seems, is inseparable from the very storytelling that Socrates has taught his listeners to mistrust: 'And thus, Glaucon, the tale has been saved and has not perished, and will save us if we are obedient to the word spoken...' (*REP*, X, 621). And yet, to obey the spoken word of the story is only possible if one can discern its meaning and message reliably. In this case, they seem to consist in the necessity of acquiring the capacity of critical discernment itself. The need of such discernment, however, does not suffice to establish its possibility. And this is particularly so when such need is articulated as part of a narrative in which it is not always easy to tell who is speaking.

The story of Er, it is true, would appear to merit the confidence that Socrates places in it. Like *The Republic*, whose narrative it concludes, it begins with a clear attribution of discourse to a speaker. The latter is, at first, clearly distinguished from the narrator. But as the story wears on, this distinction recedes and is easily forgotten. What, however, is worse—at least from the point of view of Socrates—is the simple, or not so simple, fact that the story that concludes with the tale of Er in no way itself observes this distinction. For who is the true 'author' of *The Republic*: Socrates, who narrates it, or Plato, who signs it? The strictures that Socrates directs against the dissimulations of 'mimetic' narrative apply to the very narrative discourse that frames such strictures. How different is the narrative style of *The Republic* from that of the mimetic poets? Does the author of this text ever speak 'in his own person'? Does he 'never lead us to suppose that he is any one else'? (*REP*, III, 393). Who is really speaking: Socrates or Plato? Who is ultimately responsible? Who can be called to account? Can we ever know for certain? The 'imitative poet implants an evil constitution', Socrates remarks, inasmuch as he 'indulges the irrational nature which has no discernment [...] but thinks the same thing at one time great and at another small'; he is therefore 'a manufacturer of images and is very far removed from the truth' (*REP*, X, 605). But is *The Republic* itself any closer?

> [Socrates] But I suppose you would argue that such a style is unsuitable to our State, in which human nature is not twofold or manifold, for one man plays one part only?
>
> [Glaucon] Yes, quite unsuitable. (*REP*, III, 397)

A style of discourse in which mimesis cannot be restricted to 'simple', straightforward, non-mimetic narrative is one in which the unity of meaning, the unity of person—and with them, the unity of the State—can no longer be taken for granted. Such unity ceases to be certain once the relation between language and its subject—both as subject matter and as author—is no longer transparent. Unity, however, is not only 'the greatest good' of States (*REP*, V, 462). It also defines the being of the Idea, the only true object of philosophical knowledge, as distinct from opinion, which has as its object the multiplicity of sensible appearances.

It is precisely this unity that mimesis in general and mimetic forms of narrative discourse in particular call into question. Small wonder, then, that the practitioners of such discourses, be they pantomimes (*REP*, III, 398) or poets, are to be excluded from the State, albeit with honors. For 'the law will not allow them' (*REP*, III, 398). This judgment is unequivocal, without appeal, if, that is, we can take *The Republic* at its word. That, however, is, as we have seen, anything but certain. For the very same arguments that proscribe mimetic discourse also practice it.

The 'ancient quarrel between philosophy and poetry' thereby receives its classical sendoff in a text that arrives at a verdict only to suspend it, at least by implication.

II

Some two thousand years later, the 'ancient quarrel' is still far from settled. In a celebrated note to *Kritik der reinen Vernunft* [*Critique of Pure Reason*], Kant argues against the then spreading tendency to

> use the word *aesthetics* to designate what others call the critique of taste. Underlying this use there is the fallacious hope [...] of being able to bring the critical evaluation of the beautiful under rational principles and of elevating their rules to a science. This effort, however, is futile. The rules or criteria conceived derive above all from empirical sources and can therefore never serve as determinate *a priori* laws that our judgment of taste would follow [...] This is why it is advisable to allow this designation [...] to perish and to reserve it for that doctrine which is a true science...[3]

---

3 Immanuel Kant, *Kritik der reinen Vernunft*, §1, B35-36. [My translation—SW]

That Kant came to modify this position some years after, *Kritik der Urteilskraft* [*Critique of Judgment*] eloquently demonstrates. In the later text, his use of the word 'aesthetic' is no longer limited to its etymological meaning, signifying the 'true science' of sense-perception, as in the 'transcendental aesthetics' of the First Critique. In the interim, Kant has accepted the use of the word to designate the study of the Beautiful and the Sublime, or rather, of *judgments* concerning them. And yet, on one essential point his understanding of the word has by no means entirely changed: on the question of the rationality or scientificity that can be attributed to such 'aesthetic judgments'. It is precisely the extent to which aesthetic judgments of taste *resist* conceptual analysis while at the same time laying claim, like all judgments, to universal validity that they furnish the privileged object for a *Critique of Judgment* concerned with the question of whether the process of judging has its own, autonomous, *a priori* rules or whether it is merely a function of preexisting cognition. In other words, is the process of judging, which is defined as the bringing of a particular phenomenon under a general principle and which involves the acquisition of knowledge by bringing the unknown under the known, governed by its own principles? Is the activity by which laws are discovered itself lawful?

> This perplexity about a principle [...] presents itself mainly in those judgments that we call aesthetical, which concern the beautiful and the sublime of nature or of art. And nevertheless, the critical investigation of a principle of judgment in these is the most important part of a critique of this faculty. For although they do not by themselves contribute to the knowledge of things, yet they belong to the cognitive faculty alone...[4]

---

4   Kant, *Kritik der Urteilskraft*, Preface, 169 [My translation, here as elsewhere—SW]. Future references are given in the body of the text using the abbreviation *KU*.

What makes aesthetic judgment a more appropriate object for a transcendental critique of judgment than, let us say, experimental hypothesis or conjecture is precisely the 'predicament' or 'embarrassment' (*Verlegenheit*) to which Kant refers: such judgments demand assent as though they were based not simply on subjective feelings of pleasure or pain but on objective concepts; and yet at the same time they stubbornly and structurally, one might say, *resist* such conceptualization. Aesthetic judgments are inseparably bound up with *singular* appearances and events; and hence they can never, 'by themselves, contribute to the knowledge of things'. Notwithstanding, by virtue of their claim to universality 'they belong to the cognitive faculty alone'. It is with this singular claim to universality that Kant grapples in his analytic of aesthetic judgment.

What then, according to Kant, is the general situation in which something like 'aesthetic judgment' operates? That situation is characterized by what might be called—although this is my term, not Kant's—*radical ignorance*. Kant distinguishes two fundamentally distinct kinds of judgment. The first is the more familiar kind: a particular phenomenon or event is perceived and is identified as an instance of a more general concept, rule or category. In other words, we have no difficulty in finding a predicate to attach to a subject. Judgment thereby is said to determine the individual phenomenon, which it *subsumes* under a more general notion. Such judgment Kant therefore designates as *determining*, as opposed to another, more difficult sort of judging, in which 'only the particular is given, for which the universal has to be found'. In this case 'the judgment is merely *reflective*' (*KU*, Introduction, §IV, 179). Which is to say that, instead of determining something objective about the individual that is being judged, judgment 'turns back' upon itself in a certain manner, which Kant describes in the following way. In the absence of an accessible universal—law,

principle, concept—that might establish the objective significance of the matter at hand, judgment does precisely what it
does in cases of determining judgment. It considers unknown
phenomena

> in accordance with such a unity as they would have if an
> understanding (although not our understanding) had fur-
> nished them to our cognitive faculties so as to make possible a
> system of experience according to particular laws of nature.
> (*KU*, Introduction, §IV, 180)

Faced with the bewildering multiplicity of natural phenomena
which, by dint of their very number and heterogeneity, are 'left
undetermined by the laws given, *a priori*, by the pure understanding' (*KU*, Introduction, §IV, 179), judgment *projects*, as it
were, *the memory* of its previous acts of determination upon the
singular objects and events that elude its grasp. As Kant puts it,
judgment regards nature *as though* it were purposive, as
though it were the product of an 'understanding', which, however, cannot be 'our understanding', since the latter is precisely
incapable of bringing the phenomena at hand under the aegis of
a general principle, law or concept. In nevertheless considering
such events *as though* they were purposive—that is, as though
they were the effect of a general intention—judgment, Kant
insists, does not make an assumption about the objective character of what it is judging but only about the way in which it
must proceed if nature in its singularity and heterogeneity is
ever to be understood. Judgment qua reflective can thus be said
to *mime* or to *mimic* cognitive judgment qua determinative.

But such mimicry is anything but pure play. It is determined by the desire to make sense of the world by treating its
singularities *as though* they were *universals*, as though they
were the product of an understanding like our own. The other

is treated *as though* it derived from the same. And yet, the 'as though' here establishes a relationship not of *equivalence* or of *identity* but of self-mimicry: judgment imitates itself judging cognitively, objectively. In judging objects 'as though' they were purposive, reflective judgment does not judge those objects at all but rather itself, or rather, the *discrepancy* between its own intent to subsume and a singular event that eludes or resists such subsumption. Temporally, the 'as though' of reflective judgment recalls past judgments and *represents* them as present; its element is that of *representation* that is presented as such, namely, as *representing*. The 'as though' is the mark of a representation that does not claim to present the object; such presentation is deferred indefinitely. It is this deferral that opens the space and time of aesthetic judgment.

But aesthetic judgment is still a form of judgment; it is not simply hallucination. And so, even if it is not concerned with the object as such, it must be directed at and determined by a singular other that nonetheless possesses universality. The name that Kant assigns to that other, which is neither the object nor the purely subjective hallucination, is *form*. The entire analytic of aesthetic judgment depends upon this notion of form. And yet, as Kant proceeds to invoke it in the course of the Analytic of the Beautiful, it becomes increasingly apparent that what he calls *form* is incessantly in the process of *deforming* and *transforming* itself into something quite different from what the term traditionally implies. If form can be said to arise when a multiplicity of sensations are 'connected' to one another, thus resulting in a perceptual, but not conceptual, unity, such a *perceptum* can not be attributed to the object itself but rather only to how that object *appears at a certain time and place*.[5] Thus,

---

5   On one of the rare occasions in the Third Critique when Kant attempts to define form, he does so as follows: 'The Formal [element] in the representation of a thing, that is, the agreement of the manifold with a unity (it being

Kant describes form as either 'figure' (*Gestalt*) or 'play' (*Spiel*).
The distinctive trait of form as *figure* is precisely the *trait* itself,
or what Kant calls *Zeichnung*, translated as *delineation*. This
translation, although it by no means renders the most familiar
meaning of the word, is quite felicitous, for at least two reasons.
On the one hand, it calls attention to the linearity of the trait
which defines *form*: since the perceptual unity to which *form*
refers cannot be based on either the conceptual or the material
structure of the object, what form amounts to is something like
a *silhouette*, that is, the minimal trait required to individualize a
perception and to distinguish it from its surroundings. If one
subtracts matter and concept from the object of aesthetic judgment, what is left is that minimal spatial-temporal unity
required to distinguish a *Gestalt* from an *Ungestalt*, a figure
from a monstrous aggregate of elements. Form, then, is precisely that which *delineates shape* and in so doing distinguishes it
from the shapeless. The essence of form thus appears to be the
delineating contour. *On the other hand*, the singularity of the
event addressed by aesthetic judgment, as Kant describes it,
tends to *de*-lineate the contour, that is, to undo the line of
demarcation it is called upon to establish. Such undoing is pre-
scribed by the *aconceptual and singular universality* that, according to Kant, defines aesthetic judgment.[6] For such judgment
must respond to a unique appearance in a way that is both uni-

---

5   (*cont.*) undetermined what this ought to be), gives to cognition no objective
    purposiveness whatever'. (*KU*, §15, 227)

6   'In respect of logical quantity, all judgments of taste are *singular* judg-
    ments. For because I must refer the object immediately to my feeling of
    pleasure and pain, and that not by means of concepts, they cannot have
    the quantity of objective generally valid judgments'. To demonstrate that
    and how such singularity should nevertheless also be compatible with a
    judgment that 'carries with it an *aesthetic quantity* of universality' (*KU*, §8,
    215) constitutes the problematic task of the *Critique of Judgment*.

versally constraining and yet also resists conceptualization as well as formalization. Thus, although Kant describes form as 'figure', the latter, he goes on to insist, must not be confused with any sort of geometrical shape, for this would deprive it of precisely its singularity and render it reproducible in the manner of a concept: 'Hardly anyone will say that a man must have taste in order that he should find more satisfaction in a circle than in a scrawled outline (*einem kritzligen Umrisse*)' (*KU*, §22, 241). Yet it is no accident that Kant mentions the 'scrawled outline' here, since *it* is the monstrous shadow cast by his own attempt to work out a notion of form that would be adequate to the stubborn singularity of aesthetic judgment. The 'scrawled outline' *is* the *Ungestalt* that shadows, and even overshadows, the Kantian attempt to elaborate *form*. We will have occasion to return to this 'scrawl' shortly.

Kant's insistence on the singular universality of aesthetic judgment places a heavy burden on the notion of form as contour, or, as he also calls it, *outline*: in German *Umriß* or *Abriß* (*KU*, §14, 225). Charged with the task of circumscribing and demarcating form as figure (*Gestalt*), the outline unravels into a 'scrawl'. For the question remains: in virtue of what principle does such a line succeed in delineating and demarcating the interiority of a figure and in distinguishing it from its surroundings? The tendency of this singular line leads Kant to compare such figures with 'delineations *à la grecque*, lattice-work for borders or wall papers, [which] mean nothing in themselves; they represent nothing—no object under a definite concept—and are free beauties'(*KU*, §16, 229). But how 'free' can such 'beauties' be without their becoming indistinguishable from simple aggregates of lines and colors on the one hand or from mere 'aspects of things' on the other, both of which have no unity except that of the individual beholder, and hence which lack all universality? This is why, at the very end of the

Analytic of the Beautiful, Kant finds himself obliged precisely to
insist on the distinction between such perspectivism and his
notion of *form*:

> Still, beautiful objects are to be distinguished from beautiful
> views of objects [...] the sight of the changing shapes of a chim-
> ney fire or of a rippling brook, neither of which are beauties,
> although they have a charm for the imagination because they
> support its free play. (*KU*, 'General Comment on the First
> Division', 243-244)

Such 'free play' of the imagination Kant describes as *Dichten*,
'poeticizing', which he distinguishes from 'apprehending', by
which the imagination 'picks up' (*auffaßt*) a form that is not
merely its own creation or projection. But if such a warning is
necessary at all, it is because just such a confusion haunts the
Kantian notion of form throughout: the effort to *purify* it from
every vestige of conceptual or material determination tends at
the same time to undercut the minimal unity required to distinguish form from mere projection.

This is precisely the problem that leads Derrida to the question of the *parergon* in his reading of the *Critique of Judgment*,
published in an essay of the same name in *The Truth in Painting*.
If, as I have argued, the essential function of *form* in Kant's
analysis resides in its power to demarcate the object of aesthetic
judgment from its surroundings and thereby to define its internal unity in a manner that does not depend upon its conceptual
content or its material substance, then the frame emerges as
the enabling limit of the work. What allows the work quite literally to *take place*, that is, to localize itself and thereby to
acquire a distinct shape, is something that does not properly
'belong' to the work as an internal component but 'only exter-
nally as an adjunct (*Zutat*)', as a *parergon*, an '*hors-d'oeuvre*'

(Derrida), which, however, emerges as the essential condition and enabling limit of the *oeuvre* itself.

As one might expect, Kant is not entirely happy with such an implication. For if the frame turns out to be an indispensable condition of aesthetic form, its own status as aesthetic object is highly ambiguous. Is the frame itself part of the aesthetic judgment, is it an aesthetic object, or is it something else, for instance, a mere material ornament? Kant seems to decide the question univocally:

> But if the ornament does not itself consist in beautiful form, and if it is used as a golden frame is used, merely to recommend the painting by its charm, it is then called *finery* (*Schmuck*) and detracts from genuine beauty. (*KU*, §14, 226)

But this decision only displaces the problem that the 'frame' in a certain sense is called upon to resolve: for if the frame is what determines form as such and in general, how can form be invoked to determine the 'aesthetic' pertinence of the frame? Must there not be precisely a certain *non-aesthetic* quality of the frame, a certain *materiality*, for instance, in order for the frame to function precisely as that *other* capable of telling us just where form *stops*, and hence also where it *starts*? Otherwise, we would be confronted with a *regressus ad infinitum*: the frame would determine the outer limit of the form only insofar as it itself were part of it; and yet just this participation would require another frame, an outer edge, in order for it to be determined as form.

It would not be an exaggeration to assert that much of the rethinking of aesthetics that has emerged since Kierkegaard and Nietzsche and which has not ceased to gather momentum in the past half century—the names of Benjamin, Heidegger, Derrida and de Man can serve here as indices—has been in response to the unresolved aporia first articulated in the Kantian effort to elaborate a notion of an autonomous aesthetic form capable of articulating singularity with a certain generality or generativity. Since the notion of the modern academic 'discipline' in general and in particular those disciplines that are traditionally concerned with questions of aesthetic form (literary and film studies, art history, etc.) owe much of their institutional legitimacy to the post-Kantian notion of a relatively autonomous 'field' of inquiry, much more is at stake in this problem of form than merely 'theoretical' or 'aesthetic' questions. The structure and status of modern disciplines, as well as the cognitive model upon which the academic division of labor depends, are and remain neo-Kantian, even if most of the practitioners of those disciplines have never read even a word of Kant, much less of the neo-Kantians. This explains, at least in part, the passions and sense of urgency generated by recent debates on what would seem to be relatively recondite and local problems of what is called 'critical theory'. What is at stake in these discussions is also, and not least of all, the future of the university. Large questions frame the question of the 'frame'.

Such considerations may help to indicate why the tendency of the concept of form in the Third Critique to unravel—or, as Derrida might put it, of its *frame* to become unhinged—does not involve merely *peripheral* issues. It manifests itself, it is true, as a phenomenon of the periphery, of the outer edge; but its implications quite literally 'fold it back'—reflexively—into the very heart of what is called 'form'. In short, the delineating contour—what Kant in German calls the *Abriß*—does not merely lose its borderline function by spreading itself thin. Rather, it spreads itself *thick*, into the opacity of a materiality that does not 'fit in' with the essential immateriality of the aesthetic form it is called upon to delineate. Kant's word, as I

have suggested, is highly overdetermined (although much of
this tends to get lost in the English translations). If one con-
sults a modern German dictionary, one will find *Abriß* defined
as follows:

> 1. Demolition, tearing down, for instance of a house (*der Abriß
> eines Hauses*). 2. Part of something that is to be torn down (for
> instance, an admission ticket). 3. Obsolete: a silhouette or out-
> line (*Umrißzeichnung*). 4. A brief presentation, an overview,
> summary, a short textbook or compendium.[7]

Inasmuch as the *Abriß* can be said to be the essence of an
autonomous form, at least in its Kantian interpretation, it is
not merely active at the outer edge of the figure but within it
as well. Indeed, it can be said to *constitute* the innermost
essence of any form that is defined independently of its 'contents'. This is why Kant in his argumentation is drawn to
examples that tend to undercut the very notion of form he is
trying to elaborate, examples such as those already quoted:
'delineations *à la grecque*, lattice-work for borders or wall
papers', which 'represent nothing—no object under a definite
concept—and are free beauties' (*KU*, §16, 229). But if a representation 'represents nothing', if it does not signify any object,
how is it to be distinguished from a non-representation, from
the very 'scrawled outline' that imposes itself on Kant, albeit
as the negation of form? Since Kant must provide an account
of beautiful form which demonstrates how its essential singularity resists being regularized, repeated and retained, his
notion of form must constantly be haunted by the shadowy

---

7   *Deutsches Universal-Wörterbuch*, 1983. One of Freud's last texts, translated
in English as *Outline of Psychoanalysis*, is called in German *Abriß der
Psychoanalyse*.

tangle of inextricable traits.[8] We are not very far here from
those unlaced shoelaces that will so occupy Derrida in his discussion of Van Gogh's painting of shoes in 'Restitutions'.

But instead of pursuing this particular thread, I want to follow another of those *Züge* that make up the scrawled traits into
which the *Umriß* and the *Abriß* tend to dissolve. The root of
these two words—*Riß*—returns in Heidegger's discussion of
'The Origin of the Work of Art'. The *Riß*, translated as
'rift/design', indicates the conflictual dynamics that structures
the work. Playing on the derivation of the noun *Riß* from the
verb *reißen*, Heidegger mobilizes a series of colloquial German
phrases to suggest that the 'rift' must be conceived not so much
as a 'gaping hole (*das Aufreißen einer bloßen Kluft*)' but as the
trace of a struggle in which 'the conflicting parties' are inseparably bound up with one another. In tearing apart, the rift 'draws
together' (literally: 'tears together', *reißt zusammen*) the diverg-
ing forces. Thus, the rift manifests itself not so much as a 'mere
chasm' but rather as something material—Heidegger calls it
here the 'earth'—which, in its very opacity, 'juts into the open
(*ins Offene ragt*)'.[9] This *Riß*—which, Heidegger reminds us, is
etymologically related to the Old English *writ*, which also meant
letter or *document*—emerges, quite literally, not simply *from* the
earth but rather *as* that earth which, in drawing forth, simultaneously withdraws. The consequence that Heidegger elicits
from this should by now not come entirely as a surprise:

8 'Free delineations (*Zeichnungen*), outlines (*Züge*) intertwined with one
another without design (*ohne Absicht*), under the name of lattice-work,
signify nothing, depend upon no determinate concept and yet still please'.
(*KU*, §4, 207)

9 Heidegger, *Der Ursprung des Kunstwerkes*, 1967, 70-71 [My translation,
here as elsewhere—SW]. In English as 'The Origin of the Work of Art',
Poetry, Language, Thought, 1975, 63. Future references are given in the
body of the text using the abbreviations *UK* for the German text and 'OWA'
for the English text.

> The strife that is brought into the rift and thus set back into the
> earth and thereby fixed in place is figure, shape, *Gestalt*. [...]
> What is here called figure, *Gestalt*, is always to be thought in
> relation to *that* placing (*Stellen*) and emplacement (*Gestell*) in
> which the work consists (*west*), insofar as it sets itself up and
> forth (*sich auf- und herstellt*). (*UK*, 71-72/'OWA', 64)

The Kantian notion of form as figure, as *Gestalt*, returns but
this time as the repository of the trait that is no longer defined
as the outer edge but as that which enables the figure qua art
work to *take place*. *Taking place* is not the manner in which the
work simply occurs but rather the mode in which it *is*. The
work *consists—west*—in a certain *taking-[of]-place*. The problem
of the frame, of framing as form, has now opened upon that of
the relation of a certain figurality (*Gestalt*) to the *Gestell*, a word
translated by Hofstadter as *framework* but which I prefer to render as 'emplacement' in order to call attention to the 'place'
(*–stell*) that is its root.

It is surely not entirely fortuitous that the unhinging of form
as frame opens the space of an inextricably convoluted tangle of
traits which, for all of its irreducible spatiality, never quite gets
its act sufficiently together to form a visualizable, identifiable
object. Heidegger has an easier time explaining what the *Riß* is
not than what it is and this for the simple reason that it is *not*
whatever we are accustomed to visualizing or representing as
the form of an object, even a negative one, such as a chasm, a
hole, a *Kluft*. Indeed, to determine the composition of the 'rift' or
the 'writ' as a *figure* in the sense of a *Gestalt* is to suggest that fig-
uration is as much at home in verbal language, or as little, as in
the medium of visual images. In this respect, the English word
that translates *Gestalt*, namely, 'figure', seems apt. For 'figure'
refers both to visual shape and to verbal art, and in the latter,
more particularly to tropes: the deflecting of words from their

more familiar meanings. In this sense, Heidegger's writing carries figurality to a degree previously unheard of in modern
philosophical discourse. We have just witnessed an instance of
such figurality in the diverse uses of the word *Riß* and of its various verbal composites. What Heidegger observes about the
'truth' that reveals itself in the work applies equally to the figurality of his own discourse (which is, after all, the medium in
which that truth discloses itself):

> The truth that discloses itself in the work can never be proved
> or derived from what went before. What went before is refuted
> in its exclusive reality through the work. What art founds can
> therefore never be compensated and made up for by what is
> already present and available. Founding is an overflow, an
> excess, a bestowing. (*UK*, 86/'OWA', 75)

We see that we are still very much caught in the wake of
Kant's Third Critique and its account of 'reflective judgment'.
The 'available' store of knowledge and of generalities is precisely confounded by a certain *excess* of figure or of naming. What
Heidegger refers to as 'the power of nomination', which is
incompatible with the 'already present', including the already
named, can already be found at work in Kant's discussion of
'the aesthetic idea', which, he argues, constitutes the singular
endowment of 'spirit' and 'genius'. An aesthetic idea, as Kant
describes it, consists in

> a representation of the imagination which occasions much
> thought, without, however, any definite thought, that is, any
> *concept*, being capable of being adequate to it. It consequently
> cannot be completely compassed and made intelligible by
> language. (*KU*, §49, 314)

The reason why this kind of representation cannot be grasped by any single concept, Kant elaborates, is that it

> is bound up with such a multiplicity of partial representations [...] that for it no expression that designates a determinate concept can be found; such a representation therefore allows much ineffable thought, the feeling of which animates the cognitive faculty, and to language, as mere letter, adds spirit. (*KU*, §49, 316)

The only problem with this text is that the English translation drastically misrepresents the peculiar linguistic status of the aesthetic idea. For if the aesthetic idea is indeed irreducible to 'a determinate concept' and is hence incompatible with conceptualization, or even with semantics, it is nevertheless not simply the other of *language*, as the word 'ineffable' might seem to imply. Far from being that which cannot be uttered, it is in the nature of aesthetical ideas to be uttered all the time, as Kant's numerous examples drawn from poetry make abundantly clear. What Kant writes, in the passage quoted, but also shortly hereafter, is not that aesthetical ideas are 'ineffable' but rather that they are *unnamable* (in German *unnennbar*).[10] This is not to say that aesthetic ideas, as the effect of form in the process of becoming unhinged, cannot make use of names or of nouns but rather that such ideas will never be able to be named *properly*. Aesthetic ideas are by necessity 'overnamed', to cite a term of Walter Benjamin's, and as such they are also *undernamed*. But they are certainly not *ineffable*.

In short, the 'ancient quarrel' between 'philosophy and

---

10 '...*der also zu einem Begriff viel Unnennbares hinzudenken läßt*' (*KU*, §49, 316). Shortly thereafter Kant reiterates this thought, using the same word: 'The latter talent is actually what is called spirit. For to express *the*

poetry', or at least between a certain conception of philosophy
and of poetry, is, if anything, exacerbated by the unraveling of
form in the texts of Kant and Heidegger. For if 'aesthetic ideas'
can no longer be rendered by a univocal and proper name, how
will they ever permit anyone to know with any certainty just
who is speaking or writing? And if it can never be established
beyond the shadow of a doubt just *what* is being said, how can
anyone be held definitively accountable? How will it be possible
to attribute or restore a statement to its legitimate owner if the
statement does not stand still long enough to be unequivocally
identified? And are not such questions pertinent for visual representation as well as for verbal discourse? With the emerging
awareness that neither *name* nor *form* can be relied upon to
provide a reliable point of reference, the status of the *object* itself
is no longer certain.

III

These questions are symptomatic of real concerns. Since, however, there is no possibility of their being fully explored within
the limits of this essay—and since it must also be acknowledged
that the very notion of a 'full exploration' has been called into
question by our discussion of form, frame and name—it may be
helpful instead to conclude by retelling the story of a related
concern, in which some of the strands that have begun to
unravel in our previous discussion converge to form a suggestive knot. The story begins with an enigmatic word which soon
reveals itself to be the cause of a deep, and indeed almost

---

10 (*cont.*) *unnamable* in a state of mind through a particular representation [...]
    requires a faculty of seizing the quickly passing play of imagination and
    unifying it in a concept [...] that can be communicated without any con-
    straint of *rules*' (*KU*, §49, 317). [My italics—SW]

painful, concern on the part of the narrator:

> Some say the word *Odradek* stems from the Slavic, and they
> seek on this basis to retrace the formation of the word. Others
> again think it stems from the German, the Slavic having only
> influenced it. The uncertainty of both interpretations, howev-
> er, justifies the conclusion that neither is correct, especially
> since neither permits one to find the meaning of the word.[11]

The passage, of course, is the beginning of Kafka's short text
translated in English as 'The Cares of a Family Man' and which,
more literally, might be rendered as 'The Concern of a House
Father': *'Die Sorge eines Hausvaters'*. That concern is introduced
slowly, discreetly, so much so, indeed, that it is easy to overlook, at least at first. All that catches our attention in the beginning is a strange word, of uncertain origin, and whose meaning remains enigmatic despite the most persistent etymological
efforts. This inconclusive investigation therefore is soon
replaced by a more promising description, not of the word but
of the thing itself. *Odradek*, whatever its meaning may be, thereby reveals itself to be not merely a word but a name or a noun.
The thing attached to that name or noun, however, turns out
to be almost as enigmatic as the word it supplants:

> At first glance it looks like a flat star-like spool of thread, and
> indeed it does seem to be covered with thread...

But here again, the first view of the thing is no more reliable

---

11 Franz Kafka, *Sämtliche Erzählungen*, 1981, 157 [My translation, here as elsewhere—SW]. In English in *The Metamorphosis, The Penal Colony and Other Stories*,
trans. Edwin Muir, 1988, 160.

than the previous efforts to explain its name by discovering its
origins. The 'flat star-like spool' is neither entirely flat nor
entirely star-like: 'Out of its midst protrudes a small wooden
crossbar' to which 'is joined at a right angle yet another'. Nor is
the thread on the spool simply thread. Rather, it consists of
worn-out bits and pieces of thread, tangled up and twisted
('*aneinander geknotete, aber auch ineinander verfitzte Zwirnstücke
von verschiedenster Art und Farbe*'). The threads are thus neither
discrete threads, nor something entirely different from thread.
They are threads in the process of becoming *threadbare*. But
what do they thereby bare? Their kind and color are as varied
as possible, and yet in their very multiplicity the threads are
inextricably tangled up with one another. This tangle of *traits*
makes the figure extremely difficult to delineate. The progression of the description does not make things any easier. By
means of one of the crossbars and the point of its star 'the
whole can stand upright, as though on two legs'. Anything
that can 'stand' or be stood upright, 'as though on two legs',
obviously can lay claim to a more complex mode of being than
that of a mere spool of thread:

> One would be tempted to believe that this assemblage (*Gebilde*)
> had previously had some sort of purposive form (*irgendeine
> zweckmäßige Form*) and now has been broken...

There is, however, no sign of any such breakage: 'The whole
appears senseless, it is true, but in its way complete (*abgeschlossen*)'.
We have before us, in short, the perfect Kantian aesthetic
object: purposive form without purpose, structure without
meaning. This is especially manifest in the name, *Odradek*,
which can therefore lay claim to be considered an appropriate
translation of the word 'beautiful' as defined by Kant. *Odradek*,
like the aesthetic judgment of taste, tells us nothing about the

object but only points to its formal, if intangible, unity qua representation. And, as the House Father remarks: 'Nothing more can be said about it'.[12] Why? Because, once again, like the pseudo-object (or occasion) of an aesthetic judgment—which perhaps would be conceived more appropriately as an *event* than as an *object*—Odradek turns out to be always *on the move*. 'Nothing more can be said about it, since Odradek is extraordinarily mobile and impossible to catch'. Very much like aesthetic judgment, the singularity of which no verbal utterance can ever hope to catch up with.

And suddenly, Odradek takes off, usually for those zones situated on the fringe of the inhabited areas of the house: the attic, the stairway, corridors, the hallway. At this point in the House Father's account, where Odradek appears on the verge of getting out of hand, *it* receives a masculine gender and becomes a *he*. And when the House Father comes upon him, 'leaning against the banister down below', the desire to engage him in conversation is irresistible. Given its tiny size, the House Father starts with simple questions, as though he were speaking to a child: 'What's your name?'.

'Odradek', he says. 'And where do you live?' 'No fixed residence', he says and laughs; but it is only the kind of laughter one laughs without lungs. It sounds rather like the rustling of fallen leaves. This generally ends the conversation. Sometimes you don't get even these answers; he often stays mute for a long time, like the wood he seems to be.

---

12 The Muir translation replaces the reference to language—'nothing more can be said about it (*Näheres läßt sich übrigens darüber nicht sagen)*'—with a visual connotation: 'Closer scrutiny is impossible'. (160)

The effort to engage Odradek in conversation is rewarded first
by his name and then by a laugh that is strangely aphonic:
without voice, and indeed, without lungs. The laugh, one is
tempted to say, is on the voice itself and on the life it embodies.
In any case, on the House Father. All that is left is a sound
'rather like the rustling of fallen leaves'. The breath escapes
from the body not as the expression of a living soul but as the
premonition of approaching death. Or so, at least, it would
seem. For we are in the realm of the 'as if': nothing speaks for
itself, everything is only 'like' something else.

Which perhaps is why the questions henceforth are no
longer addressed to Odradek, neither to the thing nor to the
name, even if they concern him perhaps more than ever before.
They concern him at the same time that they turn away from
him and back upon the speaker himself, the narrator, who,
stymied in the present and the past, begins to reflect on the
future:

> In vain I ask myself what will happen to him. Can he die, after
> all? Everything that dies has previously had some kind of goal,
> some kind of activity from which it has worn itself out; that
> does not apply to Odradek. Does this mean that one day he will
> still roll down the stairs in front of the feet of my children and
> my children's children, clucking and trailing threads behind
> him (*mit nachschleifenden Zwirnsfaden die Treppe hinun-
> terkollern*)? He doesn't seem to harm anyone; but the idea that
> he might outlive me, to boot, is almost painful.

Odradek's curious laugh recalls Socrates' admonition against
laughter, as well as his strictures against mimicry:

> He will attempt to represent the roll of thunder, the noise of
> wind and hail, or the creaking of wheels and pulleys [...] his

entire art will consist in imitation of voice and gesture, and there will be very little narration.

Socrates' warning resounds—or, should one say, *rattles on*—in Odradek's voiceless laugh, with which he responds to the question of the House Father, who seeks to put him in his proper place: 'Where do you live?'. Nowhere and everywhere, replies the laugh, with the rustle of fallen leaves. How does one arrest a laugh? Where is the place of fallen leaves and their rustling in the just State?

The story of Odradek may be over; but the yarn, as it were, wears on. Like a pair of threadbare laces coming undone. The worries of the House Father are far from finished.

Objectivity and its Others

In order to explore the question of 'Objectivity and its Others',[1] I will take two texts as my guides: two texts which are as different in form and content, in purpose and provenance, as one could imagine. The first text is one we all share in common, even if many of us may never have opened the particular book in which it is contained. I am referring to *Webster's New Collegiate Dictionary*, originally published in 1916; the edition that I will be using, however, dates from 1961. The second text, which is less part of our shared experience, is by Martin Heidegger and is entitled, in English, 'Overcoming Metaphysics'. Written over a period of ten years, from 1936 to 1946, it was first published in 1954. As far apart as these two texts undoubtedly are, where the question of 'Objectivity and its Others' is concerned, they turn out to stand in a quite instructive relation to one another.

---

1   The title of this talk was chosen in response to a lecture series organized in 1990 at the University of Kentucky, Lexington, which was to address the topic of 'Objectivity and its Other'. In a brief preamble, which is omitted here, I stated my preference for addressing the question of alterity in the plural rather than the singular.

I

Let me begin with *Webster's New Collegiate Dictionary*. Since it defines 'objectivity' simply as the 'state, quality, or relation of being objective', I ask you to bear with me as I quote the entry for 'objective' in its entirety, since to abbreviate it would be to run the risk of treating objectivity unobjectively, as well as of truncating the complexity of the object with which we are concerned. Here, then, is the entry:

> ob-jec'tive adj. 1. Of or pertaining to an object, esp. to the object, or end; as, to reach our *objective* point. 2. Exhibiting or characterized by emphasis upon or the tendency to view events, phenomena, ideas, etc., as external and apart from self-consciousness; not subjective; hence, detached, impersonal, unprejudiced; as an *objective* discussion; *objective* criteria. 3. *Gram.* Pertaining to or designating the case of the object of a verb or preposition. 4. *Med.* Perceptible to persons other than the patient;—of symptoms. 5. *Perspective.* Belonging or relating to the object to be delineated; as, an *objective* line, plane, or point. 6.a. *Philos.* Contained in, or having the nature or status of, an object, or something cognized or cognizable; as, to render an abstraction *objective.* b. Existing independent of mind, pertaining to an object as it is in itself or as distinguished from consciousness or the subject; as, to deny the *objective* reality of things. Cf. SUBJECTIVE—*Syn.* See FAIR, MATERIAL [...]²

I interrupt this definition here so as to underscore just how much it has already told us about 'objectivity and its others'. The first 'other' of objectivity proposed by the definition is, of

---

course, the 'object' itself: there can be no objectivity that is not 'of or pertaining to an object'. But what is an object? The initial point made by the definition is suggestive above all in the example it gives: 'pertaining to an object, esp. to the object, or end; as, to reach our *objective* point'. An object, it would seem, is closely related to an 'end'. What, however, is an *end*? It is something that ends, that terminates, that stops. But such responses merely displace the question: what does the object end? In the example just cited, the object qua objective is a 'point' that ends a striving by allowing someone 'to reach' something: 'to reach our *objective* point'. An object is thus construed as something that can be aimed at and even reached; inversely, it seems legitimate to ask whether anything can be 'reached' that is not an object or an objective. An object qua objective both opens and *ends* the space of a *reach*. To sum up the implications of this initial definition: if the object is manifestly the other of objectivity, the other of the object entails in turn reaching toward an *objective*.

The second point in the definition differs from the first in a number of ways. First of all, whereas the initial definition determines the other of 'objective' positively as the object, the second designates that other negatively as the subject, from which it must be demarcated. 'Objective' is thus designated as that which is 'not subjective', as the negative other of subjectivity. Subjectivity in turn is determined above all as *self-consciousness*. Thus, objectivity is described as 'the tendency to view events, phenomena, ideas, etc., as external and apart from self-consciousness'. These definitions are, of course, quite general, but they already suffice to suggest that the notion of objectivity, as commonly understood, is not without its internal tensions and ambiguities. In the first place, the very phrase that seeks to define objectivity be demarcating it from subjectivity qua self-consciousness couches its own definition in terms that are

strongly suggestive of a certain subjectivity: objectivity is
described as 'the tendency to view events, phenomena, ideas,
etc., as external and apart from self-consciousness'. But can
such a 'tendency to view' be entirely 'external and apart from
self-consciousness', or at least from a subject? It would appear
that the very definition that seeks to determine objectivity in
terms of its independence from a subject defines it as a stance of
subjectivity: as a 'tendency to view'. The fact that the effort to
demarcate objectivity from subjectivity qua self-consciousness
is compelled to resort to notions of 'tendency' and 'perspective'
calls into question the radical distinction between objective and
subjective to which it appeals. The examples cited in this definition indicate what may be at stake in the insistence upon the
non-subjective nature of objectivity: 'as an *objective* discussion'
and '*objective* criteria'. An objective discussion would thus presumably be one in which the plurality of divergent and conflicting—viz. *subjective*—points of view can be resolved, or at least
measured and managed, by the authority of the objective criteria. Disputes are associated with subjectivity, arbitration and
authority with the objective.

Summing up: the others implied by this second definition
stand in a negative as well as a positive relationship to *object*.
Negatively, we find subjectivity as self-consciousness but also
as conflict. Positively, we find the negation of these negatives,
the resolution of partial self-interest through the intervention
of that which is distinguished from them: the objective. But the
effort to demarcate objectivity from subjectivity undercuts itself
when it defines the former in terms of a 'tendency to view'. The
ensuing dictionary definitions underscore the difficulties in
attempting to separate the two. The third definition cites 'the
objective case' as an instance where the word designates 'the
case of the object of a verb or preposition', thus implicitly linking that case to the notion of a grammatical *subject*. The allu-

sion to the 'verb' and to the 'preposition' suggests that there are two different aspects of that link: the object can be tied to the subject either through an action or process (the verb) or through its position (the preposition). This third definition thereby adds two further elements to the determination of objectivity: *process* and *position*.

The fourth and fifth definitions, referring to the medical and perspectival uses of the word, both formulate its meaning in terms of perception, negatively in the case of that which is 'perceptible to persons other than the patient' and positively in the case of an *'objective* line, plane, or point' which are held to belong or relate 'to the object to be delineated'. But a subjective reference recurs in both of these two definitions. First, in the case of perspective, the determination of the object as that which is 'to be delineated' raises the question of the agent: delineated by *whom?* Second, in the medical example, the implication of a subject is made explicit when the phrase cited refers to 'persons other than the patient' as those to whom the latter's 'symptoms' are 'perceptible'. In this example, the other of objectivity turns out to be the active non-patient medical observer and clinician, who sees what the patient cannot: the objective meaning of the subject's symptoms.

But all of these others converge in the sixth and final definition of the word, citing its use in philosophy, where, once again, the other of the objective is identified initially as the 'object'. This time, however, the object is described as that which contains or determines what may be called objective. This initial and rather tautological definition—objective is that which is 'contained' in an object—is then fleshed out, as it were, by being given a second and significant dimension. Objective is now said to refer not merely to an object, construed as a kind of container, but to 'something cognized or cognizable; as, to render an abstraction *objective'*. In this definition, the objective is equated with the known or the knowable and is thereby construed as a function of knowledge. This had already been implied in the preceding definitions; but in being made explicit here, it reveals itself to be highly problematic. For if knowledge is related to rendering 'an abstraction *objective*', it is difficult to conceive such 'rendering' without presupposing some sort of subjective agency. Does it make sense to speak of an 'abstraction', however 'objective' it may be rendered, independently of the activity of a subject?

Perhaps this is why the second half of the definition of the 'philosophical' use of the word given in *Webster's* returns to what I have described as *negative demarcation*, describing objective as 'existing independent of mind, pertaining to an object as it is in itself or as distinguished from consciousness or the subject'. That, however, this declaration of independence of objectivity from the subjective, the mental, the partial, etc., is not unequivocal is once again confirmed by the example given: 'as, to deny the *objective* reality of things. Cf. SUBJECTIVE'. And so, at the end of this definition, we find ourselves referred by way of the denial of 'the *objective* reality of things' back to the 'subjective'. Whatever else it might entail, the Other of Objectivity seems definitively, or at least definitionally, to involve the Subjective.

This impression is strengthened by the final section of the dictionary definition, which deals with the word 'objective' not as adjective but as noun. This final definition makes explicit what was implicit in the initial definition of object as a 'point' that was to be reached. *Objective* as noun is defined as 'an aim or end of action; point to be hit, reached, etc.'. An object is that which orients the direction of an action; it gives movement a determinate end. But an objective in this sense is not just the exclusive property of an object; it once again entails a reference to those performing the action. For instance—and the next example will be mine for a change, not *Webster's*—as in the phrase, 'The objective of recent United States' action in the Persian Gulf was to restore the sovereignty of Kuwait'. Or, if you prefer: 'The objective of recent United States' action in the Persian Gulf was to defend and expand its hegemony over that part of the world'. In both phrases (and in terms of the argument at hand, the difference between them can be regarded as immaterial) the word 'objective' itself functions as the other of objectivity, if by the latter term is meant something separated once and for all from 'subjective' forces and factors. But such separation reveals itself to be problematic. For an 'objective', as that focusing upon an object which gives direction to a movement or to a striving or as that 'point to be hit, reached, etc.', only arrests and focuses movement by in some way encountering and excluding others, it would seem: other possibilities. Perhaps this is why it is not entirely fortuitous if the chain of words we have been examining—objectivity, object, objective—also includes another element, which at the same time brings to light a very different dimension of this semantic group, namely, the word 'objection'. This in turn is related to the word *object* not as a noun but as a verb. *To object* is literally to cast something in front of, before, over-against something or someone else, thus producing an encounter and a shock that can be more or less violent, a collision that can be more or less conflictual. I will therefore conclude this discussion of the dictionary definition of 'objective' with the following suspicion or speculation: perhaps the firm fix-point that the object, as other of the subject, seems called upon to provide can fix into place only by virtue of encountering or opposing something else, some other or others, and that it is only through such fending-off of others, as it were, that what we call 'objectivity' can be associated with arbitration or stability. That this stability and arbitration is not necessarily devoid of tensions and tendencies is what our brief encounter with *Webster's New Collegiate Dictionary* has brought to light.

II

Curiously enough, questions of *stability* and *tension* are very much at the heart of the second of the two texts that I want to discuss here: Heidegger's *'Die Überwindung der Metaphysik'*.[3] Under this title are gathered a series of meditations, 28 in all, which, despite their fragmentary and extremely condensed character, attempt nothing less ambitious than to sketch out a relation between the history of Western philosophy, which Heidegger construes and designates as 'metaphysics', and the political tendencies that were working themselves out during the fateful decade in which the text was written (1936-1946). The title, Heidegger begins by acknowledging, is somewhat misleading, since 'metaphysics' is neither an 'opinion' that might be 'abolished' nor 'a doctrine' that is 'no longer believed' (*'ÜM'*, 64/'OM', 85). Rather, the term, he argues, designates an historical 'destination' (*Geschick*) in which the irreducible distinction between Being and beings—that is, between *being* used as a verb and *being* used as a noun—has been progressively effaced and forgotten while the conception of being qua *entity* has come to dominate the way in which *Being as such* is construed. This historical destiny Heidegger traces back to the origins of Western philosophy itself, to the thought of the Presocratics and its ensuing systematization and codification at the hands of Plato and Aristotle. Although 'metaphysics' thus is as old as Western philosophy itself, Heidegger's attention in this text is far more specific. It has to do with the consummation and conclusion (*Verendung*) of metaphysics, which,

---

3   *Vorträge und Aufsätze*, 1967. In English as 'Overcoming Metaphysics', *The End of Philosophy*, 1973. Future references are given in the body of the text using the abbreviations *'ÜM'* for the German text and 'OM' for the English text. [My translations—SW]

according to Heidegger, paradoxically, far from simply coming
to an end, in the sense of being over and done with, has consolidated and established its 'unconditional domination' all the
more extensively. If Heidegger describes this domination as
'unconditional' (*unbedingt*), it is because the effacement of the
difference between Being and being—or what one could
describe (although Heidegger does not do so) as the *hypostasis
of being*—leaves little room for the dimension of alterity and in
this sense is both uncompromising and unconditional. The
question of Being qua verb, which can be thought of both as
the *other* of beings qua noun and as their *condition*, is thus rendered increasingly inaccessible, and with it, the 'truth' of
beings as well.

Thus, the consummation and conclusion of metaphysics
entail the 'going-under' of the truth of beings insofar as this
truth entails a heterogeneity, a difference and an other that is
effaced and forgotten in the hypostasis of being as *entity*.
Heidegger writes, 'The consequences of this event (*Ereignisses*)
are the occurrences (*Begebenheiten*) of world history in this century' ('*ÜM*', 65/'*OM*', 86). The overall process of 'the submerg-
ing of the truth of beings' is described in general terms by
Heidegger as involving both 'the collapse of the world shaped
by metaphysics' and as 'the desolation of the earth', which also
'stems from metaphysics' ('*ÜM*', 64/'*OM*', 86). This then sets
the scene in which Heidegger will attempt both to sketch out
the apocalyptic dangers attendant upon the ending of metaphysics and to briefly sketch a possible perspective in which
they might be 'overcome'.

What might all of this have to do with the question of objectivity and its others? Quite simply this: the distinctively modern
form in which metaphysics consolidates and consummates its
unconditional domination brings with it, according to
Heidegger, the hypostasis of beings precisely as *objects*. If meta-

physics completes itself in part through the 'collapse' of the very 'world' it helped to shape, it is because that world has come to be construed as what Heidegger calls the 'truthless form of the real (*des Wirklichen*)' and of objects ('*ÜM*', 63/'OM', 85). The question, of course, which now must be addressed is: what is an object and in what way is it, or does it become, 'truthless'?

Heidegger's response to this question passes by way of a reflection on the historical emergence of modern philosophy with Descartes. Descartes, it may be recalled, sought to distinguish 'the search for truth' from the 'opinions' upon which one is customarily forced to rely in conducting most of one's affairs. As opposed to the uncertainty of such customary activity, he decided to reject

> as absolutely false everything in which I could imagine the slightest doubt, in order to see if there was not something left over after that, something in my belief that would be entirely indubitable.[4]

What precisely is Descartes doing in this celebrated passage? First of all, in generalizing the possibility of doubting, he is, by implication and by inversion, defining the object of his search as the negative of doubt: as the 'indubitable' or the doubtless. Truth, he is saying, should be beyond all doubt: it should be certain. Second, since truth is here construed in terms of the correspondence of thought with that which is being thought, the question of truth as indubitable certitude involves the relation of thinking and being. That relationship is not quite as simple to determine as one might believe. For the 'being' of the

---

4   René Descartes, '*Discours de la méthode*', *Oeuvres et Lettres de Descartes*, 1953, 147. [My translation—SW]

cogito is not one of material reality. Rather, it is the being of thinking itself; or more precisely, it is the being of a relationship of self-consciousness to itself. This is why Heidegger will gloss Descartes' celebrated position in the following way: *Ego cogito* is *cogito: me cogitare.* In English, *I think* is *I think: myself thinking.* In the light of the *cogito*, then, being is indubitable—and that means, acknowledged—only as the reflective relation of thinking to itself.

Up to this point, our brief review of Descartes' notion of the *cogito* and of Heidegger's response to it has nothing very distinctively Heideggerian about it. The emphasis upon reflexivity as constitutive of modern philosophical consciousness, and indeed, perhaps of modernity itself, is familiar and widespread. All that could be concluded from this is what is well known anyway: that the Cartesian *cogito ergo sum* initiates a quintessentially modern form of thinking by determining it as subjective idealism. 'In order to think, one must be', Descartes argues; but the 'being' to which he thereby refers is truly accessible only in and as self-consciousness, as thought thinking itself. It is precisely in continuing on beyond this familiar point, however, that Heidegger's interpretation of the *cogito* begins to forge its own way; and it does so first of all by demonstrating how a certain notion of the object and of objectivity is very much at work in the Cartesian *cogito*:

> The *ego cogito* is for Descartes that which in all *cogitationes* is already represented and produced (*vor- und hergestellt*), that which is present, unquestionable, which is indubitable and which has already taken its stand in knowing, as what is authentically known for certain, that which stands firm in advance of everything, namely, as that which places everything in relation to *itself* and thus 'against' everything else. ('*ÜM*', 66/'OM', 87)

What Heidegger is attempting to do here and in the passages
that follow is to elicit the implications of the famous *cogito*, a
notion whose very familiarity may well serve to hide the fact
that its significance is anything but self-evident. A major difficulty in discussing Heidegger's arguments here proceeds from
an aspect of German, and in particular of philosophical
German, which tends to get lost in English. I am thinking of the
spatial connotations of certain metaphors which are both central philosophical terms in German and also household words. I
am referring in particular to the words formed from the verb
stehen, to stand, from *stellen*, to place, and *setzen*, to set; but
there are many others as well. When we speak in English of
'objectivity' and of 'object', for instance, we rarely think of the
spatial aspect of those terms. We require a particular intellectual effort to recall that the word *object* is composed of words
meaning 'to throw against or before'. Although the word *object*
is also used in German, the more common, less technical word
to which Heidegger recurs in his discussion of the *cogito* is
Gegenstand, literally, standing-against. Whereas the etymology
of the English word *object* stresses the 'throw' or 'cast', the
German suggests that the point of that throw, at least in the
perspective of Descartes, is to take a *stand against* doubt and
thereby to establish a certain stability: the stability of certitude
itself. What provides this stability, Heidegger observes, is not so
much the contents of what is thought as thinking itself, inasmuch as it seeks to enter into a reflective relation with itself—
the *cogito: me cogitare*. In this sense, thinking accedes to truth
as certitude by recognizing itself over-against itself; and it does
this by recalling, as it were, that, however dubious the contents
of its representations may be, what is beyond all doubt is the
fact that representation itself is taking place. In German, the
word for 'representation', *vorstellen*, means, literally, placing-
before. Thus, Heidegger's account of the *cogito* can be summed

up as follows: for and with Descartes, thinking takes a stand
against doubt by placing itself—that is, its activity of placing-
before, of re-pre-senting—before itself. 'The original object',
Heidegger concludes, 'is objectivity itself'; but 'the original
objectivity is the "I think" in the sense of "I perceive"'.

From this a number of consequences can be drawn. First of
all, the essence of the object, in this context at least, is not simply objectivity but the process of *objectification*. Second, objectification involves a movement of setting-forth which also entails
taking-a-stand. Thirdly, what is at work and at stake in this
process of setting-forth and taking-a-stand is nothing other
than the subject as such, both in the familiar figurative sense of
self-consciousness and in the less familiar, more literal sense of
that which is 'thrown under' everything else, that is, which
under-lies everything that can be thought and said about reality. It is only in taking itself as its own object—as its own other,
one might add—that the *cogito* becomes the model of truth and
of certitude. By thus identifying the reflective recognition of
thinking by itself as the sole medium of truth, Descartes implicitly installs self-consciousness as the founding principle of all
reality, including 'objective' reality. From this Heidegger concludes: 'In the order of the transcendental genesis of the object,
the first object of ontological representation is the subject'
('*ÜM*', 66/'OM', 87-88).

What does this initial result of Heidegger's investigation tell
us about the question of Objectivity and its Others? First of all, it
confirms many of the points that emerged in our discussion of
the dictionary definitions: the other of objectivity is the object,
the other of the object is the subject, the other of the subject is
self-consciousness; self-consciousness in turn has something to
do with reaching an end, attaining an objective; at the same
time, in order for such an objective to be reachable, it must object in the sense of offering resistance to others, perhaps even

excluding them, in order that it maintain anything like a stable and attainable position. By maintaining that position the objective can function as a criterion upon which judgment can be based. In this sense, judgment, knowledge and truth also emerge as others of objectivity. But implicit in our discussion of the dictionary definitions of the word was the fact that this latter set of others, associated with the adjudicative, epistemological function of objectivity, was tendentially at least at odds with the other qua subjectivity. Indeed, one might argue that each of these two sets of others conditions the other. The fact that objectivity implies subjectivity as its primary other makes it all the more necessary that objectivity also imply an other of this other: cognition, judgment, truth.

It is precisely this tension between the two others that Heidegger discerns in Descartes, who seeks to determine an object that would be free of the 'doubt' that arises from the dependency of all objects on subjective thought-processes. Descartes attempts to resolve this problem in a way that, for Heidegger, turns out to be symptomatic of, and in this case decisive for, the development of modern metaphysics. Descartes identifies the truth object—that is to say, the only thing of which we can be certain—with the *process of objectification itself*, which Heidegger in turn interprets as an attempt of the subject to set or bring things before itself, to fix them in place and then to declare that place to be the 'proper' place of the thing by determining the latter as *object*. Once they have been determined as objects, the truth of things is never intrinsic to them but is rather a function of their ability to be brought forward and fixed in place (in German, *vorgestellt*, *hergestellt* and *festgestellt*). And this in turn is tantamount to saying that the truth of objectivity is thereby determined as its capacity *to fix and to secure the subject*.

The question then becomes: how must this subject, which

turns out to be the privileged other of objectivity, be conceived? For Heidegger, the Cartesian privileging of the notion of *certitude* indicates two things: first, that truth is now determined in terms of the reflective relation of the subject of representation to its representational activity; and second, that what is involved in this privileging of certitude is the project of *self-securing*. This attempt to secure the self depends upon the effort to fix things in place, which Heidegger interprets as their objectification.

The problem, however, is that this objective can never be entirely reached, since the only reliable object turns out to be the *process of objectification as such* and not any product it can determine. What counts in this perspective is the *bringing-to-the-fore* and *setting-into-place*, the representing and producing, not what is represented or produced. Or rather, what is represented and produced counts only insofar as it supplies 'raw material' for this process of objectification, representation and production.

This is why Heidegger is able to retrace the trajectory of modern metaphysics as extending from Descartes' determination of truth as certitude to Nietzsche's notion of the Will to Power. What is at work in the Cartesian theory of the reflexive *cogito*, Heidegger argues, turns out to be nothing other than the will to reduce the other to the self. Since, however, the essence of the self consists precisely in the process of bringing-to-the-fore and setting-into-place, which is to say, in the project of *securing*, the ultimate manifestation of the will to power can only be the *Will to Will*, for will entails the effort to set things into place. In other words, the 'power' that constitutes the objective of the will cannot be understood as being anything other than *the will itself: willing itself*. What power in this sense does is precisely to treat all alterity as raw material to be given form and set into place, which is to say, it strives to transform *things* into *objects* and objects into *objectives*. It is this process itself, rather than any determinate aspect of it, that constitutes the movement of the will willing itself.

From this discussion of the Will to Will as the ultimate manifestation of subjectivity, Heidegger adduces a number of implications relevant to the political situation in which he was writing and which, *mutatis mutandis*, remain quite pertinent today as well. I am thinking here in particular of the phenomenon of the Leader, whether one associates it with the German word *Führer* or with its ostensibly more anodyne English equivalent, *leadership*. What is of particular interest is the connection Heidegger establishes between the 'necessity of "leadership"' and the 'calculated planning to secure entities in their entirety' ('*ÜM*', 85/'OM', 105). Leadership and planning are elevated to universal and planetary principles of social organization, Heidegger argues, as 'necessary consequences' of a history that has seen 'entities go the way of errance (*Irrnis*)'. One might translate this as follows: with the loss of the difference and alterity of being, determinate beings are condemned to a concept of identity that is largely solipsistic and narcissistic, and hence empty. Planning and leadership are the inevitable but ultimately futile and destructive responses to this emptiness.

But the desperate dilemma of modernity emerges even more significantly in another area which constitutes what is undoubtedly for Heidegger the ultimate metaphysical other of objectivity: the question of *technics*. Heidegger's word is *Technik*, which I prefer to translate by the rather inhabitual 'technics' rather than as the more familiar 'technology', since in German the word can also mean 'technique' and since, in any case, Heidegger uses it in a way that is anything but simply familiar. Hence, the awkwardness of the word 'technics' in English gives it an advantage in this context over the all too common term, 'technology'. Like the Cartesian emphasis upon certitude, tech-

nics, according to Heidegger, is both 'the highest form of ratio-
nal consciousness' and at the same time profoundly associated
with a certain form of insensitivity (*Besinnungslosigkeit*), which
is described 'as the incapacity, organized so as to be opaque to
itself, of entering into a relation with what is both questionable
and worthy of being questioned' (*'ÜM'*, 79/'OM', 99). To be
certain is thus to exclude all alternatives insofar as they cannot
be brought before and set into place over against the subject.
The controlling essence of technics, as Heidegger describes it,
resides precisely in this ability to dislodge and to *re-place*, which
is to say, in its power of *emplacement*. As we have already seen,
the power to place is very different from any particular place or
any particular object; and this is why one of the primary mani-
festations of technics, as Heidegger interprets it, is the production and stocking of *energy* (and of its 'raw materials'). For it is
disposable, available energy that allows the process of emplacement to operate. What is distinctive in Heidegger's determination of modern technics as emplacement (*Gestell*)[5] is that it situates technics in relation to the unfolding of subjectivity as the
securing of self and ultimately as the Will not just to Power but
to Will. In short, modern technics thus emerges as the complementary and complicit other and even as the condition of the
unconditional and ultimately nihilistic voluntarism that,
according to Heidegger, marks the culmination and consummation of modern metaphysics.

If we keep in mind the extremely dynamic aspect of modern
technics as emplacement—although the word suggests that it
is also characterized by a certain stasis—and if we remember
that technics pursues its projects of self-securing as the Will to
Will by what Heidegger literally calls the 'placing of orders'—

---

5   Concerning this translation of *Gestell* by *emplacement*, see Weber,
    'Upsetting the Setup' and 'Television: Set and Screen', in this volume.

Bestellbarkeit—then we can begin to see why the very notion of 'objectivity' has perhaps begun to sound somewhat superannuated today. For that aspect of 'objectivity' that objects to or resists the subjective project of self-securing is progressively reduced as the object is increasingly treated as merely the raw material of objectives to be striven for and reached.

A simple and yet telling instance of this triumph of technics, in its more controlling aspects at least, can be seen in the privilege assigned to the private automobile over mass transportation in the United States. Mass transport subordinates the Will to Will to a certain organization of space, to a pre-arrangement of place and of time—to networks, trajectories and schedules—that cannot simply be rearranged at will. By contrast, the lure of the private automobile is associated with the greater 'freedom' it promises with regard to such predetermined circuits. It holds out the hope of escaping from established tracks and routes, the promise of being able to displace oneself at will: of being truly *auto-mobile*. That this hoped-for mobility of the self, which perhaps is in turn driven by the striving to secure oneself, as well as by the correlative fear of not being able to reach a position of complete security, is increasingly revealing itself to be something of a nightmare, as much a constraint as a means of liberation, can be regarded as symptomatic of the more general difficulties engendered by technics in its ambivalent effort to control the others of objectivity.

Is the ultimate objective of technics a certitude and a security that is unwilling to leave any place to incalculability and to chance? I will leave the last word, for now at least, to Heidegger:

> The fact that technological projects and measures succeed in yielding inventions and innovations which replace each other at breakneck speed in no way proves that even the conquests

of technics can make the impossible possible.[...] Nature and spirit [have become] objects of self-consciousness; the latter's unconditional domination forces both in advance into a uniformity from which metaphysically there is no escape. It is one thing merely to use the earth and quite another to receive its blessings and to be at home with the law of this receiving [...] by watching over the mystery of being and the inviolability of the possible. ('*ÜM*', 91/'OM', 109)

Upsetting the Setup:

Remarks on Heidegger's 'Questing After Technics'*

Is poststructuralist theory in North America beginning to catch up with its past? The 'past' I am alluding to can be described, at the risk of drastic simplification, as the problematizing of 'representation': in art and literature, in criticism and aesthetics, in theories of language, knowledge and history, in political and social thought. The problematic of representation has for some twenty years imposed itself through the writings of Derrida and Foucault, Lacan and Barthes, Deleuze and Lyotard. Their writings in turn promoted the rereading of a certain number of predecessors: Saussure, Freud, Nietzsche, Mallarmé, but also Plato, Kant, Hegel, Marx, etc. Such a list can, of course, be only indicative.

But the most glaring and symptomatic omission is clearly that of Martin Heidegger. Not that there have been no important texts written in North America seeking to reread Heidegger in relation to poststructuralist problematics: this is obviously not the case. What has happened, however, is that

---

* This essay is a revised version of 'Upsetting the Set Up: Remarks on Heidegger's Questing After Technics', *MLN*, vol. 104, no. 5, December 1989.

something of a cleavage has developed between the extensive rereading of Heidegger being conducted largely in the philosophical domain and what might be described as his literary-theoretical reception. Although there are signs that the situation even here is slowly beginning to change, it can hardly be denied that the concern with Heidegger in the area of 'critical theory' has been in no recognizable proportion to what one might have expected, given the importance explicitly attributed to Heidegger by Derrida, from his earliest writings on.[1] And the influence of Heidegger on Paul de Man is hardly any less pronounced, for despite the latter's critique of Heidegger's Hölderlin essays, de Man's work never ceased to define itself through an unremitting *Auseinandersetzung*, or struggle, with the German thinker.

And since there can be no doubt as to the role played by Heidegger in problematizing representational thought, the lack of attention so far devoted to his work by critical theorists is symptomatic of a resistance, one which is not very difficult to explain, but which can nevertheless prove quite instructive to analyze. To engage the work of Heidegger necessitates an approach to the problem of representation quite different from that to which we have become accustomed. To put it succinctly: to read Heidegger seriously is to cease treating representation as though it were simply one 'theme' among others or even an exclusively 'theoretical' issue. Rather, the problem of representational thought imposes itself in an intensely practical way, calling into question conventional styles of academic writing, scholarly or critical. The bizarre terms and turns of phrase that mark Heidegger's German and prevent it from being translated straightforwardly into English (or into any other language I know of) have the salutary effect of com-

---

1   See the early writings on Husserl, *Of Grammatology*, etc.

pelling the reader to reassess the status and significance of established and familiar forms of discourse. For those readers not sufficiently fluent in German, access to Heidegger's texts must necessarily be by way of existing translations. It should be noted that these translations are often the work of devoted followers, who have invested considerable time and effort in them. The following remarks are therefore not to be considered as a critique of such translations but rather as a reminder of certain problems they nevertheless pose and which tend to blunt the *Auseinandersetzung* with established discourse that constitutes, I will argue, an indispensable component of Heidegger's distinctive way of thinking.

To translate Heidegger requires a knowledge which, in the English-speaking world at least, is rarely accessible to those who have not had some professional philosophical training. It is not entirely surprising therefore that even a cursory reading of the English translations reveals them to be informed by what might be described as the goal of 'conceptual rendition', that is, of rendering the conceptual content of individual terms and turns of phrase in the most rigorous, coherent and consistent manner possible. Along this way towards univocal terminology, however, what often gets lost is precisely the twist in the turn of phrase. The loss of such twists and turns results not simply in semantic impoverishment (which, after all, to some degree is the destiny of all translation). Rather, what is lost in translation, often without a trace, is a certain practice of language, in which colloquial, idiomatic phrases play a decisive role. The twists and turns taken by the most familiar, most banal, most household terms in Heidegger's writing yield an effect of uncanniness that in turn constitutes a powerful incitement to rethink things often taken for granted, such as the privilege generally assigned to technical terminology over everyday language in philosophical discourse. To efface such

uncanniness—by which the familiar is made strange, doubling
itself, advancing and withdrawing at once—is to weaken con-
siderably the force of this incitement. For it derives its impact
from the shock of recognizing that the duplicities of ordinary
language are not imposed upon it from without but rather are
part of its innermost makeup. Only when the stability of the
most familiar phrases and concepts can no longer be taken for
granted, only when they reveal themselves to be possessed by
unsuspected significations that no conceptual univocity can
reliably predict or fully account for, only then does the reader
sense fully the necessity of calling into question the conceptual
matrix of modern representational thought: that of subject and
object. For to call it into question, one must already be on the
way elsewhere.

It is the incitement to venture along this way, and the force
with which it imposes itself, that most translations of
Heidegger, in English at least, tend to blunt. In varying degrees,
to be sure. There is an enormous difference between the all-too-
facile paraphrasing of Ralph Manheim and the far more
scrupulous translations of David Farrell Krell.[2] And yet in both
cases the relation to 'ordinary language' that gives Heidegger's
German its uncanny power does not always appear in English
with sufficient force. This is a problem that admits of no simple
solution. The play of Heidegger's language is extremely difficult
to translate, and indeed impossible, if by translation is meant
straightforward reproduction. But it is a problem that is liable
to acquire increased importance as the necessity of a thinking
confrontation with Heidegger's work becomes increasingly
manifest. This is the case today. Not merely because of the
recent media event provoked in France by Victor Farias' nefari-

2   Martin Heidegger, *An Introduction to Metaphysics*, trans. Ralph Manheim,
    1959; *Nietzsche*, vol. I: *The Will to Power as Art*, trans. David Farrell Krell, 1979.

ous collection of anecdotes, *Heidegger and Nazism*. Of far more
lasting significance are studies such as those published by
Derrida (*De l'esprit*, 1987), Philippe Lacoue-Labarthe (*La fiction
du politique*, 1987) and Jean-Luc Nancy (*L'expérience de la
liberté*, 1988). They form part of a long-standing and on-going
effort of deconstructive thinking to delimit the authority of representational thought by exploring its consequences in areas
that have hitherto been particularly resistant to such questioning, areas designated by the traditional, but increasingly problematic, titles: 'history', 'politics' and 'ethics'. If such essential
names are less and less able to be taken for granted, it is not
least of all due to the work of Heidegger and to the questions
opened (or reopened) by his writings. Not merely because the
necessity of rethinking history, sociality and politics is clearly
inscribed in Heidegger's project. But also and perhaps above all,
because his work emerges as a privileged place from which the
question of place itself is put into play. The name that
Heidegger assigns to this play, in which the question of determination joins that of institutionalization, is *technics*.

Lacoue-Labarthe has recalled the pivotal position occupied by
the notion of *technè* in the development of Heidegger's thought. It
is in the discourse on *technè*, he asserts, that Heidegger seeks to
think the essence of the political.[3] *Technè* is always associated by
Heidegger with another Greek word, *epistèmè*, knowledge. It is,
however, a particular kind of knowing:

> When now man, in the midst of of beings (*physis*) to which he is
> exposed (*ausgesetzt*), seeks to gain a stand (*einen Stand zu gewin-
> nen*) and to establish himself, when in the process of mastering
> beings he proceeds in such and such a way, then this proceed-
> ing against beings is supported and guided by a knowledge of

---

3   Philippe Lacoue-Labarthe, *Heidegger, Art and Politics*, 1990, 53.

beings. This *knowledge* is called *technè*.[4]

Thus, the knowledge that is technics is not addressed at making or producing particular things but rather at 'the unlocking of beings as such'. In this sense, *technè* is a form of *poièsis* that in turn is closely related to art. The text in which the determination of *technè* as *poièsis* is most fully elaborated is *'Die Frage nach der Technik'*.[5]

If I refer to this essay by its German title, it is because it confronts us with one of those problems in translation to which I have just alluded. In fact, there is probably no better approach to this text, in English at least, than by way of the patient exploration of precisely such problems. Let us begin, then, with the title. At the outset it presents the English reader with at least two difficulties. First, there is the term that designates the subject matter of the essay and which is, as I have noted, commonly translated as 'technology': *Technik*.[6] But with regard to the German, the English word seems both too narrow and too theoretical: too narrow in excluding the meanings *technique, craft, skill* and at the same time too theoretical in suggesting that the knowledge involved is a form of applied science. This conception of *Technik* Heidegger's analysis explicitly denies. Science, he argues, depends both in its principle and in its practice upon *Technik* rather than the other way round, as is generally thought. For this reason I prefer to translate the title with the less theoretical, but also less habitual, English word 'technics'.

---

4   Martin Heidegger, *Nietzsche*, Bd. I, 1961, 96-97 [My translation—SW]. English as *Nietzsche*, vol. I, 81.

5   Heidegger, *'Die Frage nach der Technik'*, *Vorträge und Aufsätze*, 1967. Future references are given in the body of the text using the abbreviation *'FT'*.

6   See Heidegger, 'The Question Concerning Technology', *The Question Concerning Technology and Other Essays*, 1977. Future references are given in the body of the text using the abbreviation 'QCT'.

The second difficulty of translation is perhaps more reveal-ing, because more familiar and specific. It involves the German preposition used in the title, *nach*, which is rendered in the English text as 'concerning'. Now everyone who has read *Being and Time* knows just how Heideggerian the notion of concern or care (*Sorge*) is. The only problem is that *Sorge* has very little to do with the term used in this particular title. *Nach*, as any first year student of German soon learns, has two primary mean-ings, each of which is quite straightforward when considered separately but which make a rather odd couple when forced to cohabit as here in a single word. These two meanings are 'toward' and 'after'. They coexist uneasily, not merely because the one is spatial and the other (predominantly) temporal but because they seem to move in different, if not divergent, direc-tions: the one moving toward, the other following after. In at least one instance, this former sense will be explicitly and emphatically inscribed in the essay itself, when Heidegger uses the word '*nachstellen*'—to pursue or hunt down—to describe the relation of modern technics to 'nature'. But both meanings will play a significant role in Heidegger's train of thought as it moves towards the question of technics, but only by going (and coming) after it in a certain way. Heidegger's approach to tech-nics is thus situated in a certain *aftermath*. It goes after technics in order to show how, in a certain sense, technics itself follows something else, for instance, that which is called today 'nature' (and which the Greeks called *physis*). Or also, how technics in its modern form comes after another kind of technics more closely associated with the meaning the term has, or had, in ancient Greek.

The structure of Heidegger's essay itself reflects this after-math. Of its three sections, the first is centered around a discus-sion of technics in general and its meaning for the Greeks; the second retraces the emergence of its particularly modern form;

and the third attempts to indicate its possible destiny or destination as it affects the future of the 'quest'. Given the importance of this spatial-historical aspect of the term for the structure of technics 'itself', I suggest that the equivocal title be
translated as 'Questing After Technics'. For '*Frage*', question,
here as elsewhere in Heidegger's writing designates something
very different from a mere striving after an answer, in the sense
of cognition or information. Rather, it involves a movement
very similar to that of *technè* itself: an opening of oneself to
something else in what is described as a 'free relationship' to
that which is considered worthy of being questioned.

Toward what, however, does the questing as opening
move? The question brings us to a second major difficulty in
translation, involving another all-too-ordinary German word,
one which would seem to have its English equivalent ready at
hand. This German word is used by Heidegger to describe just
what it is, precisely, that he is questing after. Not technics as
such but its *Wesen*, that is, its 'essence'. But is it essence that
Heidegger is really after? The all-too-available English word
tends to close off rather than open up the question. Technics,
Heidegger will argue later in the text, compels us to rethink the
meaning of *Wesen* and no longer to construe it in the sense
either of 'genre or of *essentia*' ('*FT*', 30). The etymology of the
German word points in another direction: 'It is from the verb
[*wesen*] that the noun (*das Wesen*) is derived'. As a verb, *wesen*
signifies 'to hold sway', to 'stay in play' (*im Spiel bleiben*) ('*FT*',
30), to 'go on'. I therefore propose to translate *Wesen*, in this
particular context, as *goings-on*.

The goings-on of technics are on-going, not just in the sense
of being long-standing, staying in play, lasting, but in the more
dynamic one of moving away from the idea of a pure and simple self-identity of technology. What goes on in and as technics,
its *Wesen*, is not itself technical. With this apparently trivial

assertion Heidegger's argument is on its way. If 'essence' tends to imply a general concept or idea under which the phenomenon in its particularity may be subsumed, the goings-on of technics as Heidegger describes them exceed all such categorization. As something that *goes on*, technics moves *away* from itself in being what it is.[7] By determining the goings-on of technics as radically different from technics itself, Heidegger leads his readers in a quest after something that is not simply equivalent to technology, although it is that without which technology would not be.

Wesen, as Heidegger uses the word here and elsewhere, involves the *movens* of a phenomenon, its 'cause', not in the sense of a mechanical antecedent that would generate a certain effect but rather in that sense of *indebtedness* Heidegger attributes to the Greek word translated by 'cause': *aitía*. The Greek word, he asserts, designates a relationship of 'being-due-to' (*Verschuldetsein*). This in turn involves not merely a privative or negative relation: to be 'due to' is to appear, to be 'brought into play (*ins Spiel kommen*) thanks to' something else ('*FT*', 8-9).

Through this movement of being 'due', something is 'brought forth' (*hervorgebracht*), that is, brought from a kind of concealment out into the open. It is this process of *bringing-out* or bringing-forth that Heidegger associates with *poièsis*, usually translated as 'making' or 'producing'. Through his reinterpretation of *poièsis* as *Hervorbringung*, Heidegger frees the

---

7   Heidegger follows a strategy similar to that employed in *Sein und Zeit* [*Being and Time*]: categories traditionally used to establish equivalence, such as 'as such', 'as a whole', are used instead to dislocate identity, de-limiting what they appear to totalize. The entity (*das Seiende*) 'as such' or 'as a whole' becomes a sign or signifier of something radically different: of *Being*. See, for instance, §§46-53, 'The Possible Being-whole of Being-there-and-then (*Dasein*) and Being-to-Death'.

notion from a dependency upon either an object (the product) or a subject (a producer). Instead, *poièsis* now can be considered less an act than a change of place or of situation, a move 'from a state of concealment out into the open (*aus der Verborgenheit in die Unverborgenheit*)' ('FT', 11). This movement, which the Greeks named *aletheia*, has as its modern translation *truth*. The word here assumes a meaning very different from that of mere 'correctness', from the adequation of thought, considered as representation, to the object represented (*adequatio intellectus et rei*). The word that Heidegger employs to describe the move from concealment to unconcealment, from *Verborgenheit* to *Unverborgenheit*, is *Entbergung*. Since the goings-on of technics are determined by Heidegger to be a way of *Entbergung*, the understanding of this word is decisive, but also extremely difficult, as the English translators of the essay observe in a long and instructive note. 'Because of the exigencies of translation', they write, '*entbergen* must usually be translated with "revealing"'. But this is less than half of the story:

> *Entbergen* and *Entbergung* are formed from the verb *bergen* and the verbal prefix *ent-*. *Bergen* means to rescue, to recover, to secure, to harbour, to conceal. *Ent-* is used in German verbs to connote [...] a change from an existing situation. It can mean 'forth' or 'out' or can connote change that is the negating of a former condition. *Entbergen* connotes an opening out from protective concealing, a harbouring forth. [...] None of the English words used—'reveal', 'conceal', 'unconceal'—evinces with any adequacy the meaning resident in *bergen* itself; yet the reader should be constantly aware [of] the full range of connotation present in *bergen*... ('FT', 11)

The question is thus clearly posed by the translators but hardly

addressed by them. How is the reader to 'be constantly aware of
the full range of connotations' if these connotations are so disparate and if this disparity to boot is effaced by the ostensible
positivity and reassuring univocity of the word finally used:
'revealing'?[8] What is the relation between revealing and 'harbouring forth', for instance? The former generally connotes a
movement of unveiling or disclosure, by which something hidden or latent becomes manifest. It suggests a priority of the
inward, which is revealed in its truth through the stripping
away of the outward facade that has veiled it. 'Harbouring
forth', on the other hand, is a movement from the inside out, as
it were, in which self-identity is subordinated to and determined as a change of place. Moreover, there is a curious contradiction in the phrase, one which makes it the most suggestive of those given by the translators. To *harbour* something—a
grudge, for instance—is to protect and cherish it, to keep it
secure. But to harbour *forth* is to venture into a certain insecurity, precisely by leaving the harbour, which is a shelter (etymologically, a military shelter, from the Icelandic, *herbergt*). In
the translators' note, this aspect of leaving shelter becomes a
mere condition of what they describe as 'Heidegger's central
tenet', namely, that 'it is only as protected and preserved—and
that means as enclosed and secure—that anything is set free to
endure, to continue as that which it is' ('QCT', 11, Note 10).
But the ambiguity of the word renders any such effort to subsume it under a putative 'central tenet' itself extremely tenuous. What is 'revealed' by the word, as the translators them-

---

8   'Univocity' (*Eindeutigkeit*) and 'contradiction-free unity of judgment' are
    described by Heidegger as the goal of scientific (i.e. cognitive) thinking,
    which in turn 'emerges ever more univocally as a decisive function and
    form of the goings-on of modern technics', in particular of its drive to 'place
    into safety' (*Sicherstellung*). See Heidegger, *Der Satz vom Grund*, 1957, 201.
    English as *The Principle of Reason*, 1991, 123.

selves indicate, entails not so much a process of 'protection and preservation', much less one of 'enclosure and securing', but almost the contrary: a loss of shelter, an abandonment, a disclosure. Were 'protection and preservation' the primary goal, it is difficult to see why anything should ever 'harbour forth', that is, leave home, to begin with. For such a movement to be able to take place, the home must already be somewhat insecure. A shelter, by definition, can never be entirely air-tight. As the military etymology suggests, where there is a shelter, a harbour, a safe place, it is always in response to or in anticipation of a danger, a threat.

This aspect of the word becomes strikingly apparent when we consider the colloquial meaning of the German term that serves Heidegger here as root: *Bergung*. It signifies not merely 'shelter' or even 'rescue' but also the *salvaging* of what remains after an accident or a catastrophe. In short, *Bergung* is never an absolute point of departure. It comes after (*nach*) something else. I therefore propose to translate *Entbergung* as *unsecuring*, which, whatever else it may do, at least preserves the unsettling sense of the initial, initiating outbreak by which something gets under way.

At the same time, this translation suggests something that is by no means obvious in Heidegger's analysis (although it is implied there, albeit not without contradiction). If the goings-on of technics are part of a larger movement of *Entbergung*, understood as the ineluctable, irreducible path of unsecuring, then the unsettling effects of technics cannot be considered to be an exclusive aspect of its peculiarly modern form. Rather, the danger associated with *modern* technics is—as Heidegger explicitly asserts—a consequence of the goings-on of technics as such and in general as a movement of unsecuring. The danger is there from the startling start, and technics must be conceived both as a response to this danger and also as its perpetuation. As unsecuring, technics starts out from a place that is determined by that which it seeks to exclude. Insecurity is its enabling limit, although it is a limit that must be effaced in order for the place to be secured. What Heidegger's analysis of the goings-on of technics as unsecuring discloses is above all the necessity of this dissimulation, which in his argument assumes the form of the twofold distinction through which these goings-on are articulated: first, that which distinguishes technics in general from its Greek other, *physis*; and second, that which distinguishes modern from premodern technics. Let us take a closer look at these two determining distinctions:

1. *Technè* und *physis* are both forms of *poièsis*, i.e. of *bringing-forth*, but with a decisive difference. What goes on as *physis* possesses its outbreak (*Aufbruch*), its setting-forth, 'in itself (*hen heauto*)', whereas what is brought-forth as *technè* has its opening-up 'in another (*en alloi*), in the craftsman or artist' ('*FT*', 10-11). This difference allows Heidegger to assert that '*physis* is indeed *poièsis* in the highest sense' ('*FT*', 10), 'highest' because of the immanence of its opening. *Physis* is thus presumably a higher form of *poièsis* than is *technè*, which lacks this self-enclosed immanence. On the other hand—and with Heidegger things are never simple—that which is thus described as intrinsic to *physis* immediately breaks up that interiority. Accordingly, the innermost principle of 'nature' is its impulse to open itself to the exterior, to alterity. Thus, it begins to look as though the 'truth' of *physis* is nothing other than *technè*, which, by virtue of its very heteronomy, emerges as more natural than nature itself.

2. Heidegger, to be sure, says nothing of the kind, not explicitly at least. But the examples he uses in drawing the second, and this time, *intratechnical* distinction—between traditional and modern technics—argue for some such interpretation. The example of traditional technics is drawn from the

sphere of preindustrial agriculture, that is, from a form of culti-
vation through which technics cooperates to bring forth 'open-
ings' initiated more or less spontaneously but which require
external intervention in order to come forth fully. Heidegger
exemplifies this distinction by pointing to the semantic evolu-
tion of a single German word: *bestellen*. In the technics that pre-
vails in traditional, preindustrial agriculture, the peasant
'*bestellt*' the field, whereby '*bestellen*'—tilling, working—still
means cherishing and taking care of (*hegen und pflegen*). The
peasant's work does not challenge nature, does not goad and
drive it forth and thus transform it into a mere source of 'energy, which as such can be extracted and stored' ('*FT*', 14). But
in the era of industrialization, nature is no longer *bestellt*—
worked and cultivated. It is *gestellt*, literally, 'placed', but in the
very particular and somewhat ominous sense of being cornered, entrapped, maneuvered into a place from which there is
no escape. With this change of place (which also involves a
change of pace, an acceleration), the word *bestellen* assumes its
more familiar, contemporary meaning, that of 'placing an
order' or 'ordering a place' (but also that of ordering someone
to appear at a certain time and place). Nature is *placed on order*.
The ostensibly spontaneous or at least self-contained order of
places that for Heidegger characterizes nature in regard to traditional technics is shattered and *replaced* by a different kind of
'order': the placing-of-orders that tends to dislocate and level all
preestablished orders of places:

> The hydroelectric plant is not constructed in the current of the
> Rhine as was the old wooden bridge that joined bank with bank
> for hundreds of years. Rather, the river is obstructed (*verbaut*),
> dammed up in the power plant (*Kraftwerk*). The river is what it
> is now, as river, because of the goings-on of the power plant.
> ('*FT*', 15-16)

Traditionally a way of bringing-forth, technics has now become a driving- or goading-forth: ex-ploiting, ex-tracting, ex-pelling, in-citing. *Hervorbringung* has changed into *Herausforderung*, a goading, exacting challenge to go out, but which at the same time is also a *Herausförderung*, not just an *exacting* but also an *extracting* of that which henceforth counts only as raw material.

The shift in the movement of unsecuring is marked by a change in direction. Instead of being brought 'up front'—her-*vor*-gebracht means, literally, brought hither to the fore—the goings-on of technics become demanding, exacting, outward-bound (*her-aus-fordernd*). In this sense, the centrifugal thrust of modern technics can be regarded as continuing the goings-on of premodern technics, or indeed of technics as such, which, from the outset, we recall, were heterogeneous, other-directed. The demanding extractions of technics are 'setup (*abgestellt*) in advance to promote something else (*anderes zu fördern*)' ('FT', 15). But that something else is no indeterminate *other*. Rather, it is subject to a stringent economy of the *same* which operates according to the criterion of *commensurability* and accordingly strives to achieve 'the greatest possible use at the smallest expense' ('FT', 15). But this economy is not that of the capitalist maximization of profit, which it admittedly resembles (and which Heidegger would doubtless contend it includes but also surpasses). It is merely the pretext for 'regulating and securing' (*Steuerung und Sicherung*), and these in turn, Heidegger argues, constitute 'the major traits' of the exacting goings-on of modern technics. Since, however, such goings-on remain a form or way of *Entbergung*, of 'unsecuring', the specifically modern aspect of technics, the obsession with securing, with placing into safety, can be seen as a response to the unchanged unsecuring in which technics as such continues to take part. The

translation of *Entbergung* as *unsecuring* thus foregrounds
what I take to be the decisive question that emerges from
Heidegger's quest: how a movement of unsecuring comes to
evoke as response its diammetrical opposite—the frantic
effort to establish control and security. The effort is all the
more 'frantic' or 'furious' (*rasend*) because it is constantly
goaded on by the unsecuring tendency of technics as such.
That such goings-on, involving the effort to control and
secure, should at the same time still be a way of unsecuring—*Entbergung*—is what must be accounted for.

The turn, as I have already mentioned, is indicated by the
shift in the meaning of the word *bestellen*. The root of this word
is, of course, *stellen*: to set, to place, to set in place. If spatial categories are indispensable in Heidegger's problematizing of ontological difference from *Being and Time* on—the most obvious
instance being that of *Dasein*, but this is only one of many—
what emerges with increasing clarity in his discussion of technics is the importance not just of space but of *place*. Heidegger's
examples set the tone. The bridge spanning the river, joining
one bank to the other, suggests an orderly arrangement of
places. Technics takes its place as that which assembles the disparate in a fixed and stable order. The bridge, Heidegger
asserts, is 'constructed into the Rhine', unlike the hydroelectric
plant, by which the river is obstructed (*verbaut*).

Ever since Aristotle's *Physics*, 'place' has been defined in
terms of immanence, stability and containment, as 'the innermost motionless boundary of what contains'.[9] In the goings-on
of modern technics, by contrast, this 'innermost boundary' is
forced, driven out of its motionless state. It begins to move. To
be sure, this was already true of ancient technics, which was a
way of unsecuring, of unsheltering, of displacing. In its modern

---

9   Aristotle, *Physics*, 1984, IV, 4, 212a.

version, however, the principle of containment no longer serves as the self-evident prerequisite of order. Instead, place as container breaks up and in so doing discloses the problematic consequences of an ordering that can no longer be taken for granted. This is why I translate *Bestellen* in Heidegger's text not simply as 'ordering' (as in the English translation of the essay) but as the *placing* of orders. For what is at stake in the goings-on of technics is not simply an order, in the sense of a disembodied command or demand, no mere *Forderung*, but an *Herausforderung*, a driving-forth out of which a different kind of topography emerges. To name this distinctive topography of modern technics Heidegger uses the word *Gestell*, which in 'ordinary usage...means some sort of apparatus, e.g. a book-case' ('FT', 20), but which can also signify 'skeleton'. In the English translation, the word is rendered as 'enframing'. Although this takes the collecting, assembling function of the *Gestell* into account, it effaces the tension between verb and noun that resounds in the German and that points to the strange, indeed uncanny, mixture of movement and stasis that distinguishes the goings-on of modern technics and upon which Heidegger places considerable emphasis.

This tension resounds in the word proposed by Lacoue-Labarthe to render *Gestell*: *installation*. I would like to suggest another possibility, one that has the virtue of pointing towards the lexical 'root' of *Gestell*, *stell*: *emplacement*. If I prefer this word to 'installation', it is because it signifies not so much the setting-up of an apparatus as the set-up *tout court*, 'the assigning or appointing of a definite place'.[10] What is at stake is not the placing of something but the staking out of place as such. This is why the military connotation that emplacement shares with installation is in this context anything but irrelevant. A

---

10 *Webster's Unabridged Dictionary*, 1954.

place that has to be staked out is one that cannot stand on its own. It must be defended, even if this defense entails the mounting of further attacks.

The notion of emplacement, then, collects and assembles the various ways in which everything, human beings included, is 'cornered' (*gestellt*) and set in place. But since the places thus setup are the result of emplacement, they can never simply be taken for granted. Places must continually be established, orders continually placed. As emplacement, the goings-on of modern technics thus display a markedly ambivalent character: they arrest, bring to a halt, by setting in place; but this placement itself gives way to other settings, to the incessant re-placing of orders through which new places are set up and upset. The name that Heidegger assigns to the result of this incessant, long-standing placing of orders is *Bestand*, generally translated as 'standing reserve', and which I would render as 'standing stock'. Under the pressure of the standing order, objects lose their distinguishing traits and become stock-in-trade against which orders are placed. It is in the relation of two stances—the *opposing* stance of the object (*Gegen-stand*) and the standing stock of the *Bestand*—that the duplicitous destination of technics begins to emerge.

For it must not be forgotten that the goings-on of modern technics, emplacement, remain above all a way of unsecuring (and of disclosing). Emplacement, understood not only as a static state of affairs but as a dynamic process, can serve not just to close down but at the same time to open up. This *possibility* crystallizes in the peculiar relation of technics to the objectifying, representational thought that Heidegger associates with the subjectivism and voluntarism of modern metaphysics. In a lecture on Rilke, delivered in 1946 ('Poets—to what end?') [*'Wozu Dichter?'*], Heidegger asserts that

the fact that man becomes a subject and the world an object
is a consequence of the institutionalizing of technics, not
vice-versa.[11]

If the institutionalization of the subject/object relation—the
matrix of representational thinking—is a result of the emplacement that goes on in and as modern technology, then those
very same goings-on undermine the objectivity upon which the
matrix depends. By determining reality as standing stock, representational thinking treats objects as calculable data, as
information to be taken into account or accounted for. Thus,
whether in economic practice or modern art, objects are deob-
jectified by becoming increasingly subject to the calculations of
a subjective will struggling to realize its representations and
thereby to place itself in security (*sich sicherzustellen*).

    But—and that is the irony, or duplicity, of the goings-on of
technics as emplacement—there are no secure places.
Emplacement itself remains tributary of that movement of
unsecuring that it ostensibly seeks to escape or to ignore. And it
is here that the dangerous destiny of technics emerges: the possibility of forgetting entirely the dependence of emplacement
upon the *displacement* of a poetical 'bringing-forth' that breaks
ground and opens up ways:

> What is dangerous is not technics. There is no demonism of
> technics; but there is, on the contrary, the secret of its goings-
> on. As a send-off of unsecuring, the goings-on of technics are
> the danger. ('FT', 28)

The danger is not technics but its secretive goings-on, and

---

11 Heidegger, *Holzwege*, 1963, 268. Literally: 'a result of the goings-on of
    technics institutionalizing themselves, not its cause'.

they are secretive inasmuch as they inevitably tend to efface
their own heterogeneity. They set in place, but the fixity of such
place-setting turns into a placing of orders that can never stop.
The more technics seeks *to place* the subject into safety, the less
safe its *places* become. The more it seeks to place its orders, the
less orderly are its emplacements. The more representational
thinking and acting strive to present their subject matter, the
less the subject matters, the more it idealizes itself as pure will,
as the Will to Will.

One need not look very far today to find confirmation of this
spiral. Rarely has the complicity between technocracy and voluntarism been as manifest as it is today. All the more pertinent
therefore is Heidegger's concluding discussion of the enabling
limits of emplacement. These limits derive, paradoxically, from
the fact that, as emplacement, technics cannot stop. It goes on.
Indeed, as mentioned earlier, Heidegger contends that it is precisely technics which challenges us to rethink 'what is usually
understood as "*Wesen*" (essence), to think it in another way'
('*FT*', 30). In what way? As something that is on-going (*währt*)
and that grants (*gewährt*). What it grants is destination, the
Geschick, the send-off that opens the way of unsecuring. With
regard to modern technics, this can only mean that as emplacement, places and placing can no longer be taken *for* granted.
Rather, they must be taken *as* granted, that is, as the consequence of a granting that cannot be reduced to or derived from
a subject. At most, subjectivity responds to this granting,
which, in giving, opens up a way that can never be entirely
secured. It is a grant that can never be matched. For this reason, the challenge grant of technics exhorts, goads forth, sets
on its way. And since it is a way of emplacement, it goes
nowhere, neither forward nor backward, nor even sideways,
but simply *on*, on-going from place to place, always in place,
never in place.

This perhaps is why, in questing after technics, Heidegger finally finds himself led elsewhere, in another direction, toward that *poièsis*, that bringing-forth, which recalls the goading-forth of technics and yet is sufficiently different from it to permit an *Auseinandersetzung* with its goings-on. In this confrontation, unsecuring and securing converge in a happening (*Ereignis*) that is all the more singular for never fully taking place. Because of this uncanny, duplicitous, ambivalent singularity, the questing after technics never arrives at the stable acquisition of knowledge. Or at least it cannot be measured in terms of cognition.

The alternative to the calculations of technical rationality, to its inability to abide (with) limits, is not, however, simple irrationality. It is rather a certain sensitivity, a certain *coming to...* But to what? From where? At the least to a mode of thought that can never be reduced to emplacement or comprehended in its terms. In this sense, the goings-on of technics find their truth in the displacements that mark the encounter with poetry and with art in general. But can we take such an encounter for granted, especially if it is no longer contained or restrained by the canonical emplacements of aesthetics and criticism, by forms that are unraveling? Does not the set-up of modern technics disrupt and upset these other settings—those of poetry, art and aesthetics—as well?

Mass Mediauras, or: Art, Aura and Media in the Work of Walter Benjamin

I

Do you get the picture?

Perhaps it will become somewhat clearer if we recall some dates. 1936: Walter Benjamin publishes, in a French translation, his essay on the 'Work of Art in the Age of its Technical Reproducibility'. 1937: Benjamin begins work on a Baudelaire book that is to be a 'miniature model' of his projected study of 'Paris, Capital of the 19th Century'—the famous 'Arcades' project (*Passagenwerk*). 1938: An initial text on Baudelaire and Paris is completed but encounters strong criticisms from Adorno, who finds the treatment of Baudelaire too economistic. 1939: Benjamin completes a second study of the French poet, 'On Some Motifs in Baudelaire', and sends it off to New York shortly before the Wehrmacht marches into Poland...

In 1938, some 600 km. east of Paris, on the other side of the border, Professor Martin Heidegger is invited by a local Society for Medical and Scientific Research to participate in a lecture series devoted to the topic, 'Foundations of the Modern View of the World': *'Begründung des Weltbildes der Neuzeit'*. My translation, although idiomatic, is not quite accurate. The topic is not

exactly the modern 'view' of the world but rather, more literally, the modern 'image' or 'picture' of the world. At any rate, out
of this invitation emerges first a lecture, and much later—after
the war—a published essay bearing the title, 'The Age of the
World-Picture': *Die Zeit des Weltbildes*. To insist on a literal
translation here seems important enough, given the fact that in
the essay Heidegger emphatically distinguishes between world-
view, or *Weltanschauung*—a word that at the time played an
important role in Nazi political discourse—and world-picture:
'Once the world has become an image, the human position
grasps itself as a *Weltanschauung*'.[1]

Why, however, complicate the picture with this detour via
Freiburg, a detour that Benjamin himself could not make? If, as
has long been argued, most recently by Rolf Tiedemann, editor
of Benjamin's work and one of those most familiar with it, 'the
concept of the image (*Bildes*)' is 'central' for all of Benjamin's
work relating to the 'Arcades' project; and if, beyond that, a
certain pictoriality or figurality ('*Bildlichkeit*') distinguishes
Benjamin's own style of writing and of thinking from the very
first, then any attempt such as Heidegger's to situate the question of the *Bild* at the problematic centre of modernity can
hardly be indifferent to Benjamin's project. For if it is clear that
the Arcades Project was concerned with a specific and delimited historical period and geographical region—Paris as 'Capital'
of the 19th century—it is no less evident that Benjamin's concern with this period is in turn part of an even more comprehensive effort to rethink modernity. Benjamin's analysis of the
French 19th century builds quite extensively therefore on his

---

1   Heidegger, *'Die Zeit des Weltbildes'*, *Holzwege*, 1963, 86 [My translation,
    here as elsewhere—SW]. In English as 'The Age of the World Picture', *The
    Question Concerning Technology and Other Essays*, 1977, 133-134. Future
    references are given in the body of the text using the abbreviations 'ZW' for
    the German text and 'AWP' for the English text.

study of the German Baroque and in particular on the theory of allegory. In the context of this attempt, it is striking that for both thinkers, however different they are, pictoriality, *Bildlichkeit*, acquires a pivotal significance.[2]

Let me begin, then, by attempting to recall certain salient aspects of Heidegger's approach to the question of the world-picture. Seizing upon the phrase that names the subject of the lecture series in which he was participating, Heidegger argues that what characterizes modernity since the Renaissance—in German the *Neuzeit*—is not the fact that it substitutes one world-view for another but rather that it defines itself through the attempt to 'conquer the world as image (*die Eroberung der Welt als Bild*)' ('ZW', 87/'AWP', 134). To determine the world as having the structure of a picture or image is thus to embark upon a project of conquest in which the heterogeneity of beings is accepted only insofar as it can be objectified and represented, *vorgestellt*, a word in regard to which Heidegger urges his audience to 'seek out the originary naming power (*Nennkraft*)'. This *Nennkraft* consists in a double, or dual, movement: that of setting things *out in front* of oneself (*vor sich hin*) and at the same time bringing things *toward oneself* (*und zu sich her Stellen*) ('ZW', 85/'AWP', 132). Entities are brought closer to the subject and yet at the same time kept at a safe distance from it. This 'back and forth', to and fro movement ('ZW', 85/'AWP', 132) is, however, Heidegger stresses, subordinated to the overriding aim of putting things in their place. This movement of *Stellen*, by fixing things in place, thereby confirms the place of the sub-

---

2   In juxtaposing the approaches of Heidegger and Benjamin, another remark of Tiedemann's will find ample confirmation: 'Benjamin always assigned an incomparably greater significance to pictoriality than is usual in philosophy; his own language speaks at length in, and even more out of, images'. Rolf Tiedemann, in *Walter Benjamin 1892-1940*, ed. Rolf Tiedemann *et al.*, *Marbacher Magazin* 55, 1990, 260.

ject which, through the power to represent, becomes the 'reference point of beings as such' ('ZW', 81/'AWP', 128). When such a movement is understood as encompassing the totality of beings as such, the 'world' itself has become a 'picture' whose ultimate function is to establish and confirm the centrality of man as the being capable of depiction. The 'Age', or more literally, the 'Time' (*Zeit*) of the World-Picture thus turns out to be that of the presentation, the *Vorstellung*, the bringing-forth-and-setting-before (the subject) of all things.

Those familiar with Heidegger's later writings on technics will recognize in this analysis of the world-picture as a process of placing, of *stellen*, the anticipation of what will later be understood as the essence of modern technology: that total availability of being *placed* and *displaced at will* designated by Heidegger as '*Bestellbarkeit*', the susceptibility of *being-placed-on-order*.[3] If, however, in this perspective, things are allowed to *take place* only insofar as they can be *put in place*, this entails a radical change in the traditional manner of conceiving the relation and constitution of place and space. Already in his 1938 lecture, Heidegger mentions as instances of this transformation through modern technology the 'destruction of great distances through the airplane' and, correlatively, the ability of the media, in particular radio, to render the remote instantaneously present through the flick of a switch ('ZW', 87/'AWP', 135). In this abolition of distance and of difference he sees particularly conspicuous and symptomatic effects of the determination of the world-as-picture and the correlative determination of the human as the founding, constitutive subject.

Heidegger's 1938 talk, addressed as it was to a non-specialized public—and, of course, to a quite particular public in the Freiburg of 1938—seeks to make available to a larger audience

---

3   See Weber, 'Upsetting the Setup', in this volume.

the critical interpretation of technology which he was at the time engaged in elaborating. As a result, however, the essay, even in its published version, enriched by a series of supplements, remains at a relatively schematic level. It raises far more questions than it can explore, much less answer. It is precisely the unanswered space of these questions that will lead us back to Benjamin. One of these questions concerns the schematic itself. For the two structural characteristics that Heidegger attributes to the world-as-picture, the pictorialization of the world, are, first of all, its pretensions to universality and totality, which Heidegger will also refer to as the 'planetary' ambitions, and indeed reality, of technology; and second, its tendency to be schematic or systematic: 'Where the world becomes a picture, the system becomes predominant, and not only in thinking' ('ZW', 93/'AWP', 141). The systematicity of this system, according to Heidegger, consists not in the mere bringing-together of diverse elements but rather in the representational structure (*Gefüge*) to which they are expected to conform. However, this 'structure', as we have seen, is anything but simply static. It consists in a highly ambivalent oscillation of bringing-forth (*her-stellen*) and setting-before (*vor-stellen*), with the aim of securing the foundations of the subject *at* and *as* the center of things.

The dynamics of this process of *vorstellen* must be kept in mind if one is to understand one of the most obtrusive characteristics of modern technics cited by Heidegger: the tendency to move with ever greater velocity and, perhaps even more significantly, with ever greater acceleration. If the growing preponderance of speed in determining movement undermines the basis of traditional spatial relations, the question remains to be addressed of just how pictures, *Bilder*, can contribute to this race for speed and acceleration, particularly when it is driven by the more or less hidden agenda of securing the place of the human subject.

In short, Heidegger's interpretation of the subject-securing function of the world-picture raises the question of what might be called the kinetic or 'cinematic' structure of that picture, a question that, of course, leads us directly back—or is it forward?—to Benjamin.

This detour via 'The Time of the World-Picture' allows us to approach Benjamin's work in what might be called the 'shadow' of Heidegger's writings. This shadow is named explicitly in the essay I have been discussing as that which does not quite fit into the world as picture. Once the human has been determined as subject and the world as picture, Heidegger remarks, an 'invisible shadow is cast over all things', a shadow which prevents them from ever being put fully into their proper places, that is, being fully depicted. This shadow is not simply external to the world as picture; it is an inseparable part of it. The world as picture reveals itself—which is to say conceals itself—as shadow. But *shadow* here does not name 'simply the lack of light', or even less 'its negation'. It designates that which escapes and eludes the calculating plans of total representation, of which it at the same time is the condition of possibility: 'In truth the shadow bears overt and yet impenetrable witness to the concealed glow' ('ZW', 104/'AWP', 154). Concerning the 'truth' of this shadow and the 'glow' to which it 'bears impenetrable witness', Heidegger can say only that it 'points toward something else, the knowledge of which is denied us today' ('ZW', 88/'AWP', 136). But, he warns, 'man will not even experience and meditate on this refusal so long as he busies himself merely with the negation of his age'. Rather than exhausting itself in negation, real thought today, Heidegger concludes, must open itself to a certain 'in-between' (*Zwischen*). The thinker who, more than any other—with the possible exception of Heidegger himself—explored the relation of the 'age' with that interstitial zone was

Walter Benjamin. And while we will see that he too followed the
lead of a certain shadow, the direction in which it led him was as
far removed from the path of Heidegger as Paris is from
Freiburg. As far...and as close.

II

From 'The Time of the World-Picture' to 'The Work of Art in
the Time of its Technical Reproducibility' the leap is a large
one, but it takes place in the space of a shadow. Despite its obvious awkwardness, I use the word 'Time' here, rather than the
more idiomatic 'Age', to translate 'Zeit' in both texts, because
what is involved in both is precisely a question of *time* and of an
alteration in its relation to space. In each text the question to be
explored is presented at first in narrative, historical terms, as a
gradual emergence which, while reaching back to the origins
of Western culture, assumes distinctive form in the modern
period. For Heidegger, the decisive turn is identified with
Descartes, who, he emphasizes, stands in a tradition that he
continues but also transforms. For Benjamin, the decisive turn
takes place in the middle of the 19th century, when, with the
increasing mechanization of reproductive techniques, the traditional distinction between production and reproduction
begins to break down. The index of this steadily accelerating
breakdown Benjamin finds in the progressive elimination of
what he calls the 'aura' of art works. 'The process', Benjamin
remarks, 'is symptomatic' for its

> significance points far beyond the realm of art. The technique
> of reproduction, to formulate generally, detaches that which is
> reproduced from the realm of tradition (*löst das Reproduzierte
> aus dem Bereich der Tradition ab*). In multiplying reproduction
> [of the art work], it substitutes a plurality of copies for a unique

existence. And in permitting the reproduction to meet the beholder or listener [*dem Aufnehmenden*: the receiver, but also—significantly—the *recorder*, as a photographer, camera-man, recording engineer, etc.—SW] in their particular situation, it actualizes that which is reproduced. These two processes lead to a tremendous shattering of tradition which is the obverse of the contemporary crisis and renewal of mankind. Both processes are intimately connected with contemporary mass movements. Their most powerful agent is film.[4]

This quotation follows by and large the published translation by Harry Zohn. Although Zohn's translation of this passage is essentially 'correct', attention to the literalness of Benjamin's German opens up perspectives that tend to disappear in the more fluid, idiomatic style favored by Zohn (and by most of Benjamin's translators). What does not change in a more literal rendition of the passage is the fact that the withering of the 'aura' of art works as a result of their technical reproducibility constitutes a phenomenon, event or process—none of these words is entirely appropriate—whose implications far exceed the aesthetic sphere in which such 'events' are generally situated. The decline of the aura constitutes a 'tremendous shattering of tradition', an historical shock that plunges humanity into a crisis even while holding out the possibility of its 'renewal'. What also appears clearly in the English translation is that this critical possibility is associated on the one hand with 'contemporary mass movements' and on the other with 'film'.

---

4   Walter Benjamin, '*Das Kunstwerk im Zeitalter seiner technischen Reproduzierbarkeit*', *Gesammelte Schriften*, I/2, 1980, 477-478 [My translation, here as elsewhere—SW]. In English as 'The Work of Art in the Age of Mechanical Reproduction', *Illuminations*, 1968, 221. Future references are given in the body of the text using the abbreviations '*KW*' for the German text and '*WA*' for the English text. Also, further reference to Benjamin's *Gesammelte Schriften* uses the abbreviation *GS*.

What, however, is far less legible in the published English translation than in Benjamin's German is the way this association is rooted in the structure of technological reproduction itself. In Zohn's translation, the latter process is described in terms of 'plurality': 'By making many reproductions it substitutes a plurality of copies for a unique existence'. But a more literal rendering of the text would read: 'By multiplying the reproduction [of the art work, the technique of reproduction] replaces its unique occurrence with one that is massive or mass-like—*massenweise* (*setzt sie an die Stelle seines einmaligen Vorkommens sein massenweises*)'. The work of art, which throughout the tradition was conceived in terms of a single and unique 'here and now', takes place, takes its place qua reproduction, not simply as a *plurality*, that is, as a mere collection of individual occurrences, but rather as a *mass*. When Benjamin therefore goes on to draw a connection between this process and 'the mass movements of our day', he is merely continuing a line of thought that has its roots in the *massive, mass-like* character of 'reproduction'. However this 'mass' is to be construed, its emergence is therefore closely tied to the structure and operation of the reproductive technique itself.

But what are we to make of this 'mass'? Nothing could seem more dated than this heavy-handed notion of 'mass', which reeks of the collectivist discourses of the Thirties. And yet, the word returns sufficiently in this and other late texts of Benjamin to suggest that he, for his part, did not consider it to be as inert as it might seem today. Let us therefore take a closer look at the way Benjamin uses this word.

We can begin by noting that, in the passage quoted, Benjamin does not speak simply of the 'mass' or 'masses' but of 'mass movements'. This practice turns out to be consistent with his use of the word elsewhere. For whatever else is meant by 'mass' in his writings, it entails a dynamic element that demands attention. Mass movements are the result, or rather, the corollary, of that movement of *detachment*, *ablösen*, that marks the decline of aura. For aura relates to mass not just as uniqueness does to multiplicity but also in spatial terms, as a fixed location does to one that is caught up in an incessant and complex movement. This is why aura is intimately related to the idea of a *setting*, or even a *case*.[5] The shift from the uniqueness of the original work of art to 'copies' which from the very start are made to be reproduced and exhibited (*ausgestellt*) involves not just the substitution of one kind of work for another but rather a modification in the way works of art quite literally *take place*. To be considered an original, or capable of originality, works of art must, as Benjamin puts it, be 'embedded' in the tradition, which is to say, they must have their unique and uniquely inimitable *site* in respect to which their uniqueness is constituted.

But what does it mean to be thus embedded in a tradition, and what guarantees, as it were, the unicity of place in which the work of art can, as original, take place? In order to elucidate this question, Benjamin resorts to the following image, or rather, scene:

> On a summer afternoon, resting, to follow a chain of mountains on the horizon or a branch casting its shadow on the person resting—that is what it means to breathe in the aura of these mountains, of this branch. ('*KW*', 479/'*WA*', 222-223)

You begin to get the picture now, surely, for it recalls in cer-

---

5   In one of his earliest notations on the subject of aura, Benjamin writes of the aura as 'an ornamental surrounding (*Umzirkung*) in which the thing of being lies embedded (*eingesenkt*) as in a case (*Futteral*)'. *Über Haschisch*, 1972, 107. Cited in Werner Fuld, *Walter Benjamin: Zwischen den Stühlen*, 1981, 268.

tain essential respects that discussed by Heidegger in 'The
Time of the World-Picture': the world *brought forth* and *set
before* the subject, whose place thus seems secured by the
object of its representation. What holds the aura of originality
in place, as it were, is the subject as its point of reference, just
as, conversely and reciprocally, the subject is ensconced,
'embedded', held in place and at rest, by the scene that it both
observes and also 'breathes in' (this phrase is omitted in the
English translation). The only difference between the world of
this picture and Heidegger's world-picture is that Benjamin's
subject is depicted as being 'in the picture' and that being *in*
it, it cannot quite *get* the picture in its entirety (despite the
fact that in German 'getting the picture' is expressed as being
'in' it: *im Bilde sein,* an expression that Heidegger cites). The
'aura' that Benjamin here attempts to depict is therefore not
simply equivalent to the world-picture itself; it is somewhat
separate from it. Precisely that separation will define the difference in Benjamin's approach to the picture and
Heidegger's. This suggests why, in regard to Benjamin's use
of imagery here and elsewhere, it might be more fitting to
speak of *setting a scene* than of painting a picture. But it is not
only the subject that is 'in' Benjamin's scene or scenario.
There is also that 'shadow' that falls over the resting subject
and which is therefore not simply 'invisible' in terms of the
world-picture, as Heidegger suggests, but rather which has
become quite visible, providing we are prepared to *read* it as
marking the space within which the relation of subject to
object takes place. Distance and separation are therefore
explicitly inscribed in the scene, or even the scenario, of the
aura, and that from its very inception.

    In this sense, the 'decline' or 'fall'—*der Verfall*—of the aura
would not be something that simply befalls it, as it were, from
without. The aura would from the start be marked by an irre-

ducible element of *taking-leave*,[6] of departure, of separation.
Were this to be the case, however, then the narrative, sequen-
tial, 'historical' aspect of the aura, expressed in a movement of
decline and fall, might well turn out to be part and parcel of its
mode of being. So understood, aura would name the unde-
pictable *de-piction* of distancing and separation.

But if aura, also designated by Benjamin as the 'unique
appearance of a distance, however close it may be', is inseparable from a certain separation, this can also help to explain
something that Benjamin himself at times seems to have had
difficulties coming to terms with: the fact that the aura, despite
all of its withering away, dilapidation and decline, never fully
disappears. Far from it, since it returns with a vengeance, one
might say, in those forms of representation that would, according to Benjamin's account, seem most hostile to it: film, for
instance, and we can now add, television as well. The aura
would be able to return in the age of technical reproducibility
because, as the appearance or apparition of an irreducible separation, it was never uniquely itself but always constituted in a
process of *self-detachment*: detachment *from* the self as demarca-

---

6   In §18 of *Being and Time*, Heidegger describes the purposive, referential status
    of 'equipment' [*Zeug*] as constituted by a similar movement of leave-taking.
    Rather than simply serving some instrumental purpose, the equipmental
    entity is described as taking leave of itself. The 'destiny' of such stuff is to be
    involved in something beyond its control. It thereby must be left alone to
    follow its bent, take its own turn, *bewenden lassen*. The noun which
    Heidegger uses to describe what results from this being-left-alone
    [*Bewandtnis*] seems not unrelated to the dimension of *leave-taking* that
    emerges as an irreducible, originary constituent of aura as Benjamin con-
    ceives it. The paradoxical relation of proximity and distance that marks
    Benjamin's notion of aura finds its correlative in the English translation of
    the Heideggerian *Bewandtnis: involvement*. *Involvement in leave-taking* is per-
    haps the common source of the aura that emanates no less from the texts
    of Benjamin than from those of his great adversary, Heidegger. See
    Heidegger, *Being and Time*, 1962, esp. 115ff.

tion *of* a self. The aura would then be something like an
enabling limit, the *emanation* of an object from which it
removes itself, a *frame* falling away from a picture and in its fall,
in its *Verfall*, becoming light: a *bright shadow*.

This process of falling or falling-away is associated by
Benjamin with the tendency of 'the masses' to reduce or overcome distance:

> To bring things spatially and humanly 'closer' (*näherzubringen*)
> is a no less passionate inclination of today's masses than is
> their tendency to overcome the uniqueness of every given
> [event] (*Gegebenheit*) through the reception (*Aufnahme*) of its
> reproduction. ('KW', 479/'WA', 223)

The 'passionate inclination of today's masses' is passionate not
simply because it is intensely felt but because it bears witness to
an aporia: to bring something 'closer' presupposes a point or
points of reference that are sufficiently fixed, sufficiently self-
identical, to allow for the distinction between closeness and far-
ness, proximity and distance. Where, however, what is
'brought closer' is itself already a reproduction—and as such,
separated from itself—the closer it comes, the more distant it
is.[7] This tendency is rooted not only in works that are, from the
very start, as it were, constituted as reproductions. It results no
less from the nature of those to whom such works are
addressed. Nothing indicates more clearly the fact that these
addressees are not merely a massed version of the traditional
contemplative subject than the word that Benjamin uses, with
great frequency, to describe the function of this mass. It is a

---

7   The ambivalence of this process, related to Heidegger's notion of *Ent-fer-
nung*, an 'un-faring' that does not exclude distance, is of particular pertinence to television, as I have tried to indicate elsewhere in this volume. See
'Television: Set and Screen'.

mass of *Aufnehmenden*, and its function with respect to the technical reproduction of art is that of the *Aufnahme*. But just what is meant here by *Aufnahme*? *Aufnehmenden*? What does it mean to try to bring works or images closer to an *Aufnehmenden*?

In the passage under consideration, I have translated *Aufnahme* as 'reception': the masses tend 'to overcome the uniqueness of every given through the reception of its reproduction (*durch die Aufnahme von deren Reproduktion*)' ('KW', 479/'WA', 223). Literally, *aufnehmen* is 'to take up' or 'apprehend'; and its most obvious meaning, in the context of Benjamin's remarks, is that of reception. But what is striking for the reader of Benjamin's German text is that the very same word is used to describe the process of reproduction itself, as it goes on in the film studio, for instance:

> For the first time human beings come to the point of having to work with their entire living being but without its aura. For aura is tied to its here and now. It cannot be depicted. (*Es gibt kein Abbild von ihr.*) The aura that surrounds Macbeth on the stage cannot be separated from that which for the living audience surrounds the actor who plays him. What is peculiar to the shots taken (*der Aufnahme*) in the studio is that they replace the audience with the camera (*Apparatur*). ('KW', 489/'WA', 229)

If Benjamin is obviously fascinated by the techniques of film production, it is because he is convinced that what happens on the set and what goes on afterwards both involve a similar, if not identical, process: that of recording, of reproductive inscription, of *aufnehmen*. In place of living subjects, be these conceived as producers, actors or receivers (audience), the techniques of reproduction set up an 'apparatus', a camera or instrument of reinscription (photographic, phonographic, cinematographic). Such an apparatus 'takes up' the 'given' and does three very strange things to it: first, it apprehends it the way a policeman apprehends a suspect, arresting what seems to be its spontaneous or intrinsic movement and submitting it to a series of operations that have nothing to do with its 'natural' inclinations; second, it opens the way for those elements to be dislocated and relocated, broken down into elements and recombined into ensembles that have little to do with their initial state; and finally, the finished product is placed into circulation, accompanied by the semblance of what has been radically undermined—publicity about the 'personalities' of stars, directors and producers. The cinematic cult of personality imparts the aura of individuality to a product which 'takes place' in many places at once, in multiple here-and-nows, and which therefore cannot be said to have any 'original' occurrence.

But here an obvious objection must be considered. If it is true that such simultaneous taking-place is unthinkable for the prototypical works of plastic art that Benjamin has in mind in introducing the notion of 'aura', it is far less obvious just how the 'reproducibility' of photographs or of film is different from that of a piece of music or a work of literature, in which the 'here-and-now' of the aura seems to be entirely compatible with the proliferation of its material embodiments (books, performances, scores, etc.). It is in reflecting upon the peculiar way in which what Benjamin calls the 'mass' 'takes up' what it seeks to 'bring closer' that the singular configuration of aura, image and mass movement in the Age of Reproducibility begins to emerge.

Benjamin gives us a suggestive hint of how the notion of mass is related to that of reproducibility when he elucidates the specific difference between the traditional painter and the reproductive cameraman—in German *Operateur*—by comparing the practice of the magician to that of the surgeon. Both seek to heal, but in very different ways:

> The magician maintains the natural distance between himself
> and the person being treated, or more precisely, he reduces it
> by laying his hand on the patient only a little and increases it
> by virtue of his authority considerably. The surgeon proceeds
> inversely: he reduces the distance to the patient considerably
> by penetrating into his interior and he increases it only a little
> through the careful movement of his hand among the organs.
> In a word: by contrast with the magician (who still survives in
> the general practitioner) the surgeon at the decisive moment
> abstains from taking his distance and confronting the patient
> face to face (*Mensch zu Mensch*); he penetrates him operatively
> (*operativ*). ('KW', 496/'WA', 233)

Benjamin's comparison of the therapeutic practice of cameraman and surgeon brings out, by contrast, the violence involved
in their respective 'penetration' and reminds us that, in English
at least, a film is said to be 'shot'. Like the projectile from a gun,
it 'penetrates deep into the fabric of the given', violating bodily
integrity and producing images which are very different from
those of the painter. The latter are 'total', whereas those of the
cameraman are 'torn apart'—*zerstückelt*—cut into pieces that
must then 'find their way together again in accordance with
new laws'. Those laws, which, for Benjamin, are above all
those of the cutting table, where the film is edited, pertain to
the massed public that 'takes up' (*aufnimmt*) no less than to the
film 'itself', which has already been 'taken up'—*aufgenom-
men*—'shot' in the studio (or on location). The fact that the
same German verb—*aufnehmen*—is used to designate cinematic production as well as reception suggests that both ends of the
process may share some very basic features. One of those features is designated by Benjamin with a German word that is dif-

ficult to translate but which perhaps holds the key to the transformations his essay is attempting to articulate. That word is
Zerstreuung.

In the English translation of Benjamin's text, this word is
generally translated as 'distraction' and occasionally as
'absentminded[ness]', as in the famous remark: 'The audience (of a film) is an examiner, but an absentminded one'
('*KW*', 505/'*WA*', 241). Once again, however, the literal
resources of the German word, and hence its connotations,
are far richer than the essentially privative terms 'distraction' and 'absentminded' might lead one to believe. The root
of the German word—the verb *streuen*—is cognate to the
English 'strew, strewn' and carries with it a strong spatial
overtone. Moreover, the word has its history, in Benjamin's
writings no less than in those of Heidegger; and it demonstrates that its significance can in no way be encompassed by
the concept of 'distraction', however important that notion
undoubtedly is. In his essay investigating the question of
'Sexual Difference, Ontological Difference' in certain texts of
Heidegger, Jacques Derrida has devoted several extremely
suggestive pages to Heidegger's use of the word *Zerstreuung*
and its variants both in *Being and Time* and in his lectures of
1928, from which it emerges that *Dasein*, far from simply losing itself, is constituted by/as being-scattered, as *Zerstreuung*
or *Zerstreutheit*. Although this is not the place to engage this
discussion in any detail, I will simply note that it establishes
a link between *Dasein's* physicality—or more exactly, its
'fleshliness', its *Leiblichkeit*—and its fragmented, dispersed
ways of being. This dispersed corporeality or fleshliness
Heidegger describes by using a neologism, *Mannigfaltigung*,
which can be rendered as 'manifolding', a term that comes
close to designating the kind of dispersion that Benjamin
considers to constitute an essential quality both of the film

itself and of the public, or 'mass'.[8]

But it is the history of the term in Benjamin's own writings that bears directly on the questions we are investigating. In his study of *The Origin of the German Mourning Play*, completed and published three years before *Being and Time*, Benjamin describes the mode of signification peculiar to the German Baroque mourning play—*allegory*—and in particular its relation to emblematics in the following terms:

> Allegory [...] in its most developed form brings with it a court (*einen Hof*); around the figural center, which is never missing from genuine allegories, in opposition to conceptual circumlocutions, a host of emblems is grouped. They seem arbitrarily arranged: *The Confused 'Court'*—title of a Spanish mourning play [by Lope de Vega—SW]—could be cited as the schema of allegory. 'Dispersion' (*Zerstreuung*) and 'Collection' (*Sammlung*) name the law of this court. Things are brought together according to their meaning; indifference to their being-there (*Dasein*) disperses them once again.[9]

When one remembers that the German word for 'court', *Hof*, that Benjamin uses here in order to describe the collecting and dispersing of emblems around their allegorical center can also, in contexts not so very different from this one, be translated as *aura*,[10] certain aspects of his later work emerge in a somewhat

---

8   See Heidegger, *Metaphysische Anfangsgründe der Logik im Ausgang vom Leibniz, Gesamtausgabe*, Bd. 26, §10 (*Das Transzendenzproblem und das Problem von Sein und Zeit*), 1990, 173ff; and Jacques Derrida, *'Différence sexuelle, différence ontologique'*, Psyche. Inventions de l'autre, 1987, esp. 405-414.

9   Benjamin, *Ursprung des deutschen Trauerspiels*, 1963, 210 [My translation—SW]. English as *The Origin of the German Tragic Drama*, 1977, 188.

10   The 'aura' or halo around the moon is called in German its *Hof*.

different light. First, the tendency toward dispersion that Benjamin discerns in the collective structures specific to the 19th century metropolis no longer appears to originate with the emergence of urban masses but rather to go back at least as far as the 17th century in Germany. Second, the dispersed, centrifugal structure of mass phenomena shows itself to be bound up with articulatory processes at work long before Baudelaire began to 'fence' with 'the ghostly crowd of words'.[11] Baudelaire's words are ghostly not simply because they represent or present something that is absent but because *as words* they have a tendency to *buckle* under the shocks to which they are exposed.[12] They are ghostly because, like the apparition of the *passante* in Baudelaire's poem, they only *come to be* in *passing away*: *'Un éclair...puis la nuit!'*. In the middle of the phrase, three dots or points punctuate and puncture the suspended allegorical centre of a certain *Hof*—court or street. What *is* comes to *pass* as *nothing*...but a certain aura. The *passante* emerges from the deafening din of the street as a *visual* figure set off against the inchoate *noise* of the amorphous crowd of pedestrians. But in thus setting itself *off* from its pedestrian surroundings, this emergence also sets itself *apart* and reveals thereby its affinity with everything pedestrian. It is the affinity of an *apparition*. The *passante appears* only to *disappear*, almost instantaneously. It is in the invisible but legible space of this quasi-instant that the poem takes place. Arresting the 'fugitive beauty', as in a photographic snapshot, the poem

---

11 Benjamin, *'Über einige Motive bei Baudelaire'*, GS, I/2, 618 [My translation, here as elsewhere—SW]. In English as 'On Some Motifs in Baudelaire', *Illuminations*, 165. Future references are given in the body of the text using the abbreviations *'ÜMB'* for the German text and 'OMB' for the English text.

12 'Rivière has pointed out the subterranean shocks that rock Baudelaire's poetry. It is as though a word were to collapse into itself'. (*'ÜMB'*, 617/'OMB', 164)

repeats the balancing act of the woman herself, *'balançant le feston et l'ourlet'*, as she passes by. Unlike the subject of Heidegger's world-picture or that of Benjamin's auratic scene, however, the poet does not merely 'breathe in' the scene—he imbibes it. And it is hardly insignificant if the spectacle he both absorbs and is absorbed in consists not so much in visible objects as in the source of vision itself—the woman's *eye*, which is also the eye of a storm[13]: *'Moi, je buvais, crispé comme un extravagant / Dans son oeil, ciel livide où germe l'ouragan'*.

The flash that intervenes—*'Un éclair...puis la nuit!'*—is suspended by the very same three points or dots that mark the passing of the *passante* and allow her Medusa-like gaze to hold out the promise of a resurrection: *'Dont le regard m'a fait soudainement renaître'*. Organized around its allegorical centre, those three dots, the poem suspends the shock by reinscribing it in a narrative sequence of death and rebirth. This suspension is itself *allegorical* in the sense given to the word not by Benjamin but by Paul de Man, for what it does is to temporalize and temporize the disruptive force of an encounter which comes as a *shock* precisely insofar as it *interrupts* temporal narrative and progression.[14] The shocking encounter with the abysmally ambivalent apparition of the passerby is sorted out, as it were, by the retrospective glance of the poet, which Benjamin aptly describes as 'love not so much at first sight as at last'. Such 'love...at *last* sight' imposes direction and meaning upon an

---

13 The poet here is in a position that closely resembles that of the Angelus Novus, whose stare is fixed upon the storm of history, piling up rubble behind (or is it in front?) of the angel that it blows backward (or is it forward?) into the future (or is it the past?). We begin to see why the reader of Benjamin begins to wonder whether history is coming or going, or whether the difference between the two is really so decisive...

14 '[A]llegory appears as a successive mode capable of engendering duration as the illusion of a continuity...'. De Man, 'The Rhetoric of Temporality', *Blindness and Insight*, 1983, 226.

apparition whose transfixing power, Benjamin insists, reposes *exclusively* upon a mass which as such is never depicted or named.[15] The 'mass' here, invisible and nameless, is precisely that ambivalent, divergent *movement* that carries the *passante* even as she appears to emerge *out* of it. The movement of the mass is ambivalent because it entails stasis no less than mobility, suspension no less than progression. It is a movement that is going nowhere, and yet it is never just marking time.

An instance of such a 'movement' can be seen in this reemergence of 'allegory' in the 19th century. The 17th century conception of what Benjamin called 'Natural History'—history as the permanent decline of a world that, in the wake of a positive theology, discovers itself to be *infinite in its finitude*—continues in the 19th century, except that the disintegration does not congeal in a focus upon the external and immobile body of the corpse as its privileged emblem, as in much German Baroque art and theatre, but extends into a fascination with something far more inchoate and amorphous: a mass. 'Baroque Allegory sees the corpse only from outside. Baudelaire sees it also from within', writes Benjamin in one of the notes published later as 'Central Park'.[16] The corpse 'seen from within', although Benjamin does not declare this explicitly, is yet another form of the 'mass': that mass of organs on which the surgeon—and the cameraman—'operate'. It is the transformation of the body from an organic form into an allegorical 'mass' that the apparition of the passerby both announces and conceals.

The law of dispersion and collection that governs the ambivalent movement of the allegorical mass can therefore be

---

15 'The mass is for Baudelaire so inward that in his texts one will seek its depiction in vain. Similarly one hardly ever encounters his most important objects in the form of descriptions'. (*'ÜMB'*, 621/'OMB', 167)

16 *GS*, I/2, 684. In English as 'Central Park', *New German Critique*, 34, Winter 1985, 51, Note 36.

designated by the term: *coming-to-pass*. The mass qua crowd appears as what it is in withdrawing before what seems to be an individual, feminine figure, that of the *passante*. But the ostensible individuality of this passerby is anything but individual: she comes to be only in passing by. And in so doing, she reveals herself to be the allegorical emblem of the mass, its coming-to-be in and as the other, in and as the singularity of an ephemeral apparition. The mass movement—the mass in/as movement—produces itself as this apparition, which provides an alternative to the formed and mobilized masses of the political movements of the Thirties, to which we—with Benjamin— will have occasion later to return.

But if the encounter of the poet with the passerby is an alternative to the collectivist spectacle of the mobilized mass, it also sets the stage for the mass movements to come. For what is inseparable from the fleeting encounter is the desire to mingle and to mix, to drink in and to be absorbed into the condition of all spectacle: the gaze of the other. This specular desire, however, does not lead to the fantasy of a direct and present union or reunion. Rather, it takes the fugitive passage of the *passante* as the point of departure for a reflection that, in explicitly stating its own fictionality, can still entertain the fantasy of a certain reciprocity: '*O toi que j'eusse aimée, ô toi que le savait*'. Desire invests and seeks to appropriate the other as the *sujet supposé savoir*, if not the *sujet supposé aimer*.[17] And the means designed to effect this impossible appropriation is

---

17 Although Benjamin does not address this question explicitly, a close reading of Baudelaire's poem reveals that the encounter between poet and passerby remains ambiguous: the poet is 'abruptly reborn' through 'the glance' of this 'fugitive beauty'. But 'reborn' is not the same as 'seen'. Whether or not the poet has been *seen*, however, remains rigorously unanswerable. The auratic quality of the *passante* depends upon this question remaining open: something has happened, an event has taken place, but what has been encountered is an alterity that resists all reciprocity, all exchange, all synthesis, all appropriation. The glance of the *passante*—the

the insertion of the chance encounter in a narrative. The elusive
spectacle is thus to be appropriated as a moment of *retrospection*.
The undecidable present of a coming-to-pass is recalled and reinscribed as the imperfect past of a 'Once upon a time'.[18] The *passante* would thus be put in her place—the past of a voluntary rec-
ollection—by this poetico-narrative reinscription, thus accom-
plishing the defensive function of shock, as Benjamin describes it:

> Perhaps the special achievement of shock-defense may be seen
> in its function of assigning to an incident a precise temporal
> place in consciousness at the cost of the integrity of its con-
> tents. (*'ÜMB'*, 615/*'OMB'*, 163)

What Benjamin refers to as 'shock', however, is invariably
ambivalent: it designates *both* the traumatic incursion *and* its
defensive warding off. Perhaps this is what is most shocking
about 'shock': the inseparability of danger and of the effort to
defend against it. Such ambivalence also characterizes the
techniques of reproducibility with which Benjamin is concerned, as his remark about photography suggests: 'The camera—*der Apparat*—imparts to the instant an as it were posthumous shock' (*'ÜMB'*, 630/*'OMB'*, 175). In German, the word
translated here as *instant* is *Augenblick*, that is, literally, *eye-look*.
And it is precisely in the space, or time, of an eye-look, or, as
the word is often mistakenly but suggestively translated in
English—in the 'blinking of an eye'—that the decisive transfor-

---

17 (*cont.*) 'eye' of the storm—thus prefigures the 'eye' of the camera, which
     records, inscribes and produces images without itself *seeing* or *looking* at
     anything in particular, or itself perhaps being seen.
18 Such narrativization is the temporal correlative to the prosopopoeia that
     both de Man and Benjamin place at the origin of lyric poetry. See
     Benjamin, *'ÜMB'*, 647/*'OMB'*, 200, Note 17, and de Man,
     'Anthropomorphism and Trope in the Lyric', *The Rhetoric of Romanticism*,
     1984, 122. See infra, 103ff.

mations take place in the relations of picture and world, of original and reproduction, of mass and movement, and last but not least, in Benjamin's own theory of the aura itself.

Or rather, theories. For the encounter of the poet with the *passante*, and through her, with the mass and its movements should remind us that Benjamin's *theory* of the aura is as little unique, as little independent of the laws of a certain reproduction, as is the process it purports to describe and to comprehend. For his theory of aura disintegrates, falls, *verfällt*, into at least two theories which repeat each other while yet saying very different things. In 'On Some Motifs in Baudelaire', Benjamin takes up the theory of the aura but in a context that is quite different from, if not unrelated to, his earlier account. Instead of designating the unapproachable distance of a unique 'here and now'— that of the work of art embedded, as it were, in the tradition— aura is now described by Benjamin in the following manner:

What in the daguerreotypes must have been felt to be inhuman, even lethal, was the (prolonged, by the way) staring into the camera (*Apparat*), since, after all, the camera takes a person's picture (*das Bild des Menschen aufnimmt*) without returning his glance (*ohne ihm dessen Blick zurückzugeben*). The glance, however, expects inherently to find a response wherever it gives itself. Wherever this expectation finds such a response, [...] it experiences aura to the fullest. 'Perceptibility', remarks Novalis, 'is a kind of attentiveness'. The perceptibility of which he thus speaks is none other than that of the aura. The experience of aura thus rests upon the transfer (*Übertragung*) of a form of reaction that is current in human society to the relation human beings have with the inanimate or with nature. The person who is looked at or who believes himself to be looked at looks up (*schlägt den Blick auf*). *To experience the aura of an appearance is to endow that appearance with the ability*

*to look up (den Blick aufzuschlagen). ('ÜMB', 646/'OMB', 187-
188) [My emphasis—SW]*

Baudelaire's poem, *'A une passante'*, articulates this 'experience'
of the 'aura', an experience which is, it turns out, more the
experience of a *desire* than of a unique and unapproachable reality. At the same time, the most powerful desire is that which
remains unfulfilled. Baudelaire succumbs most entirely to the
fascination of 'eyes that do not see': *'les yeux fixes/ Des Satyresses
ou des Nixes'* ('ÜMB', 649/'OMB', 190). If such eyes can hardly
be called 'human' any longer ('ÜMB', 649/'OMB', 190), they
are perhaps of the same family as the even more 'inanimate' eye
to which people relate increasingly in the age of technical reproducibility: the eye of the camera. What is peculiar to this eye,
however, is that it is always ready, always prepared (*apparare*),
to take in and take up everything without ever looking back.
The recording apparatus, whether visual or auditory, 'takes up'
everything but never looks back, never returns the glance. It
blinks but never *winks*. Instead, what it does is to arrest and separate and reproduce the 'here-and-now' again and again in a
proliferating series of images which go here and there, a mass of
pictures that cannot keep still even if they are instantaneous
'snapshots'. The German word for such 'still photos'—
Momentaufnahmen—indicates that what is ultimately arrested,
'taken up', broken down, spliced back together again and then
let loose...is the *moment* itself. The 'time' of reproducibility is that
of this 'posthumously shocked', immobilized, dispersed, recol-
lected and finally forgotten moment, ever *on the verge*, always
coming to pass.

But in a world on the verge, traversed and indeed constituted out of such circulating series of images, it is difficult to establish the kind of set and secure position that Benjamin initially
associates with the aura and Heidegger with the world-picture.

These are pictures that you do not *get*—you are *gotten* by them. To such pictures there can be a number of very different responses, and Benjamin describes several of them. Of these, I will here touch on only two.

First of all, there is the very real possibility that aura will be reproduced in and by the very media responsible for its 'decline'. For what is clear from Benjamin's discussion, even though he does not say it in so many words, and what has become increasingly evident ever since, is that *aura thrives in its decline* and that the reproductive media are particularly conducive to this thriving. In a remark that is prophetic beyond its presumed intention, Benjamin observes that 'radio and film transform not only the function of the professional actor but also that of those who, like politicians in power, present themselves before them' ('*KW*', 492/'WA', 247, Note 12). This remark suggests how and why the media would in fact go on to reduce the difference between the two categories, actor and politician, to the point of allowing the one to become the other. The Star and the Dictator had a similar function and origin. In both, the 'amorphous mass' could find a face and a voice that it might call its own, or if not its own, that it could at least recognize and use to secure its own position. A face with eyes that seemed to look back and a voice that seemed to address one directly.

This is what emerges at the end of the essay on the 'Work of Art' when Benjamin comes to utter what has doubtless become the most-cited phrase he ever wrote, even if—or perhaps *because*—it is one that means little separated from the arguments leading up to it. And the more this phrase is quoted, it seems, the less those arguments are read. The statement, that fascism entails 'the aestheticization of politics', does not in itself say very much about *how* that aestheticization is to be conceived. Let us therefore reread the arguments that precede it.

Benjamin introduces the Postscript to his essay by noting that 'the growing proletarianization' and the growing formation (*Formierung*) of the masses are 'two sides of one and the same occurrence'. But what, we must ask in the light of our previous discussion, does the 'formation' of masses entail if one of their distinguishing characteristics turns out to be precisely a certain amorphousness, a certain *dispersion*? 'Fascism', Benjamin responds, 'attempts to organize the growing proletarian masses without touching (*antasten*) those property relations that these masses attempt to do away with'. But if fascism is able to avoid 'touching' property relations, how is it able nevertheless to win the allegiance of the 'proletarian masses'? It accomplishes this feat, Benjamin suggests, by offering them something quite different: 'Fascism sees its salvation in giving these masses not their right but instead a means of expressing themselves'. Fascism offers the masses *self-expression*. In what does this self-expression consist? We must go to a footnote to find out. Here, in alluding to the weekly newsreel, Benjamin observes that

> mass reproduction (*Der massenweisen Reproduktion*) is aided especially by the reproduction of masses. In big parades and monster rallies, in mass sporting events and in war, all of which today are brought before the cameras [*der Aufnahmeapparatur zugeführt*: more literally, brought before the recording apparatus] *the mass looks itself in the face*. ('KW', 506/'WA', 251) [My italics—SW]

Fascism allows the mass to look itself in the face and thereby to find a gaze that ostensibly looks back. Fascism thus reinstates the aura of the world-picture by means of the very media that undermine it. By contrast, in his study of Baudelaire, Benjamin, as we have seen, insists on the fact that the urban mass, although it is omnipresent in Baudelaire's poetry, is never represented or depicted as such. It is, in short, never made the object of a picture, although its effects and workings are everywhere. The contrast with the fascist formation of the masses could hardly be more striking: through the use of the media, above all film, what is in its innermost structure dispersed and distracted is given a form and a shape, a voice and a face.[19] The reproductive apparatus that creates the mass as a dispersed and faceless phenomenon—or rather, as a movement that is not simply going anywhere—at the same time restores the semblance of a face to that amorphous mass. The same could be said for its voice as for its body. But since what is represented and depicted beneath the monumental forms and figures, voices and faces, remains tied to a movement of dispersion, *Zerstreuung* will always be very close to *Zerstörung* (destruction). In Marinetti's Futurist manifesto, war is exalted as that domain in which the movement of dispersion and destruction can be given a *figure* and represented as a *form*: 'The fiery orchards of the machine guns' and 'the dreamed-of metallization of the human body' conceal the ghastly mutilation of that body through the impact of that very metal. Such depictions are still very much with us today and indeed have given a new resonance to the notion of journalistic 'coverage'.[20]

It is this giving of voice and face that one of the most inci-

---

19 Benjamin was undoubtedly deeply influenced in his conception of the masses by the work of his good friend, Siegfried Kracauer, who also saw in the fascist approach to the masses an effort to produce the 'semblance' of their 'reintegration': 'The masses are compelled to look at themselves (mass rallies, mass parades, etc.). The mass is thus always present to itself and often in the aesthetically seductive form of an ornament or of an effective image'. Siegfried Kracauer, *Das Ornament der Massen*, 1962, cited in Peter Reichel, *Der schöne Schein des Dritten Reiches: Faszination und Gewalt des Faschismus*, 1991, 25.

20 I have sought to read certain traits of this 'coverage' in the reporting of the Gulf War on American television in 'The Media and the War', *Alphabet City*, Summer 1991, 22-26. Reprinted in *Emergences*, 3/4, Fall 1992, 16-26.

sive readers of Benjamin, Paul de Man, in a rather different and yet by no means unrelated context, identified as the rhetorical process of prosopopoeia.[21] If de Man saw this device as constitutive of much of what we call literature, Benjamin—and this brings me to the *second* response to the elusiveness of the world-picture that I promised to discuss—speculates that the auratic projection of the reciprocated glance constitutes one of the origins of poetry itself. Once again, this conjecture is hidden away in a footnote. In that note, Benjamin asserts that it is precisely the 'endowing' (*Belehnung*) of others—whether human, animal or inanimate—with the 'power of looking up (*den Blick aufzuschlagen*)' that is a major source (*Quellpunkt*) of poetry. And yet, as his study of Baudelaire makes clear, in the age of mass reproduction and on the threshold of the arrival of mass media, such a source grows increasingly problematic. What Baudelaire encounters—and indeed, what then gives him a certain intense pleasure—is the human equivalent of the apparatus: eyes that 'look up' but do not look back, or even look *at*. And with this glance that does not look back and yet sees, a very different kind of aura emerges: that of a singularity that is no longer unique, no longer the *other* of reproduction and repetition but their most intimate *effect*. What Benjamin calls the 'decline of aura' emerges here not as its simple elimination but as its alteration, which, however, turns out to repeat what aura always has been: *the singular leave-taking of the singular*, whose singularity is no longer that of an original moment but of its

---

21 De Man, 'Anthropomorphism and Trope in the Lyric', which can be read as, among other things, a silent, implicit dialogue with Benjamin's reading of Baudelaire, a dialogue, however, which avoids, at least in part, 'the endless prosopopoeia by which the dead are made to have a face and a voice which...allows us to apostrophize them in our turn' (122). In this text Benjamin is not named.

posthumous aftershock—'*Un éclair...puis la nuit!*'.[22]

But Benjamin did not need to wait for Baudelaire and 19th century Paris in order to discover this '*éclair*'. Fifteen years before, he had already concluded his reading of Goethe's *Elective Affinities* by singling out the 'falling star' above the heads of the ill-fated lovers as the allegorical emblem of the work. Or, as Benjamin called it at the time—he had not discovered allegory yet—'the mystery':

> Mystery in the dramatic is that moment in which the latter overshoots the realm of its own language towards a higher and unattainable one. It can therefore no longer be expressed in words but only through presentation (*Darstellung*); it is 'dramatic' in the strictest sense.[23]

---

22 In *La machine de vision*, 1988, Paul Virilio explores the implications of 'the sight without a look' (*vision sans regard*) that he finds at work in contemporary efforts to produce automated forms of vision: 'The electro-optical image is, for the computer, only a series of coded impulses of which we cannot even imagine the configuration since, precisely, in this "automation of perception", *the return-image is no longer guaranteed*' (153). For Virilio, the 'logic' that governs this new form of vision is 'paradoxical', privileging 'accident, surprise, at the expense of the durable substance of the message' (138). If many—although by no means all—of Virilio's arguments will be familiar to readers of Benjamin, the latter will not be surprised to find him conclude with a quotation from Baudelaire in which he appears to find a precocious interpretation of the contemporary transformation of vision through the digitalization of images: '*L'ivresse est un nombre*'. To this Virilio adds: '*De fait, l'optique numérique est bien une figure rationnelle de l'ivresse, de l'ivresse statistique [...] Comme si notre société s'enfonçait dans la nuit d'un aveuglement volontaire, sa volonté de puissance numérique achevant d'infecter l'horizon du voir comme du savoir*' (158). For an interpretation of 'number' and of the numeric in Baudelaire which implicitly casts light both on Virilio's notion of '*ivresse statistique*' and on Benjamin's conjoining of 'reproducibility' with 'shock', see de Man, 'Anthropomorphism and Trope...', 250ff.

23 Benjamin, '*Goethes Wahlverwandtschaften*', *GS*, I/1, 200-201.

Although Benjamin does not indicate just what this 'strictest sense' of the dramatic might be, its etymology suggests that it has to do with a *happening* or an *event*. Mystery happens dramatically when language overshoots its semantic-thematic function and takes place as an event. To the extent to which it eludes or exceeds signification, such an event can only be fugitive, fleeting, like a falling star or a flash. What this meteoric event leaves behind in its wake is what I would be tempted to call—if a neologism can be allowed—the *mediauric:* auratic flashes and shadows that are not just produced and reproduced by the media but which *are* themselves the media, since they come to pass in places that are literally inter-mediary, in the interstices of a process of reproduction and of recording— *Aufnahme*—that is above all a mass movement of collection and dispersion, of banding together and of disbanding. In this movement, different elements collide with and glance off one another. Any attempt to get one's bearings by looking for a look that looks back is doomed to leave the stage 'empty-handed', as Benjamin says of Baudelaire and as he had already said of the 17th century allegorist. All such attempts ultimately depart empty-handed, *gehen leer aus.*

And yet precisely in such an empty-handed exit something both very new and very old makes itself felt: the irreducibility of a certain separation, of a stage which is not simply the setting of a picture or the scene of a glance but at the same time a scenario of inscription. Not necessarily of images alone, for, as Benjamin reminds us:

> Words too can have their aura. Karl Kraus has described it thus: 'The closer you look at a word, the more distantly it looks back'. (*'ÜMB'*, 647/*'OMB'*, 200, Note 17)

What this *distant* 'looking back' of words announces is perhaps the advent of uncanny eyes that no longer look back at all, precisely in order to keep on seeing. In any case, this aura of words offers a very distinct alternative to the fascistic, aestheticizing use of aura. For what one 'sees' in the ever-more-distant word is not simply a reproduction of the same but something else, a distance that *takes up* and moves the beholder towards that which, though remote, is also closest-at-hand, in the sense of that 'optical' or 'tactical/tactile' (*taktisch*) unconscious that Benjamin discerned in the most familiar, habitual gestures. This distance embodies therefore the 'decline and fall of the aura', its 'shrinking' and 'withering away', but also its resurgence, which Benjamin did not live to explore but which his work, like perhaps none other before or since, prepares us to understand.

What is condemned in the age of technical reproducibility is not aura as such but the aura of art as a *work* of representation, a work that would have its fixed place, that would take its place in and as a world-picture. What remains is the *mediaura* of an apparatus whose glance takes up everything and gives nothing back, except perhaps in the blinking of an eye.

Television:
Set and Screen

The following remarks seek to explore a phenomenon that is so close to us, so ubiquitous and so powerful, that it has proved particularly resistant to thought. Not that there has not been an enormous amount of literature written on the subject of television, much of which is extremely illuminating. But in reading through such work, one is struck by the fact that as soon as empirical description is forsaken and analysis or interpretation attempted, the results are generally quite disappointing. They are disappointing not because what they have to say is wrong or irrelevant but because the attempted analysis rarely seems to take sufficiently into account the *distinctive specificity of the medium*. What we most often find are content-analyses, which could just as well apply to other media, for example, to film or to literature. And where an effort is made to go beyond content-analysis to a discussion of formal elements, the latter in turn are generally borrowed from more traditional aesthetic genres—for instance, narrative fiction—thus leaving the question of the specificity of the televisual medium itself unaddressed.[1]

---

1 I should mention a few of the more notable exceptions to this general tendency to ignore the question of the specificity of the medium: first, Stanley Cavell's 1982 essay, 'The Fact of Television', in *Video Culture: A Critical*

And yet, a simple *reaction* to this neglect or omission, one which would strive to articulate just what it is that makes television *different* and distinct from previous aesthetic media, almost inevitably finds itself confronted by another trap: that of ontologizing television.[2] The attempt to work out the *differential specificity* of the medium—to get at that which distinguishes it from other media—runs the risk of transforming, albeit unawares, a *differential determination* into a *positive* and *universal essence*. The apparently innocent fact that we use a singular noun, 'television', to designate an extremely complex and variegated phenomenon can all too easily encourage us to overlook the heterogeneity of the medium with which we are concerned.

This is why it seems advisable at the outset to emphasize that to attempt to uncover something of the specificity of television does not necessarily mean to suppose that the medium possesses an invariable and universally valid essence or structure. Rather, *specificity* here is used as a *differential category*: television is *different*, not just from *film*, as has often been observed and explored, but also from what we generally mean by the word *perception*. Television—despite its name—involves the transmission of sight *and sound*; and yet to take the *specificity* of it as a mode of transmission into account is to *distinguish* the way the sights and sounds it transmits are apprehended from the way sights and sounds have hitherto been perceived. Television entails artifice, technique and even technology; and

---

1   (*cont.*) *Investigation*, 1986; second, Jane Feuer's 'The Concept of Live Television: Ontology as Ideology', in *Regarding Television: Critical Approaches—An Anthology*, 1983; and more recently, Mary Ann Doane's 'Information, Crisis and Catastrophe', in *Logics of Television: Essays in Cultural Criticism*, 1990. Finally, an as yet unpublished essay by Deborah Esch, 'No Time Like the Present', reflects, to my knowledge for the first time, on the 'allegorical' structure of the medium.

2   The essay by Jane Feuer mentioned in the previous note deals with this tendency.

yet here, too, its specificity is constituted by the way its technique *differs* from what we have previously called 'art' and 'aesthetics'.[3]

But the *constitutive heterogeneity* of television does not stop at such external contrasts and demarcations. What is perhaps most difficult, but also most important, to keep in mind are the ways in which what we call *television*—a singular noun—also *and above all differs from itself*. Television differs from itself in a number of ways. In the first place, the singular noun covers a complex process that can be divided into at least three distinct, albeit closely interrelated, operations. For the sake of convenience, those operations can be described by using terms that antedate the advent of television and that therefore may not be entirely apt to designate what is at stake in this medium. Nevertheless, in order not to complicate the matter excessively here at the outset, let us say that television consists primarily of three operations: *production, transmission* and *reception*. However unified one may take the medium of television to be, it should not be forgotten that the singular noun hides these interrelated but also very different operations, each of which raises a set of very distinct questions and issues.

However, this is not the only way in which 'television' can be said to differ from itself and, in so doing, to raise questions about its internal unity and self-identity. Other aspects of the diversity of the medium are related to differences that can be called 'cultural', 'national', 'linguistic' and 'socioeconomic'. By contrast, few discussions of television take this diversity sufficiently into account or even allow for its consideration. Most are restricted to the television of a single nation and, within

---

3 The major shortcoming of Cavell's seminal essay, already mentioned, is that it does not sufficiently elaborate on this distinction. Television is defined in opposition to film but within a continuum of 'aesthetic' experience or perception, as Deborah Esch convincingly argues.

that country, are generally limited to a single language. This is difficult to avoid, but it is possible to study and compare televisions of different countries and languages. What is far more difficult today, however, is to appreciate the differential specificity of socioeconomic factors, simply because a radical socioeconomic alternative to a capitalist market system has become almost impossible to find. Nevertheless, within that overall and increasingly global system, there remain sufficient differences to provide a kind of internal criterion for comparison. For instance, television in the United States and television in Europe remain even today sufficiently diverse to make any attempt at generalization based on only one national television extremely hazardous. To be sure, there is an undeniable tendency of American television to impose its laws, features and programming upon the other televisions of the world; and it also seems likely that this tendency towards homogenization is not unrelated to the global dynamics of the televisual medium itself. But the differences are still there, and they must be taken into account if one hopes to articulate the distinctive specificity of the medium.[4]

Let me therefore clarify, at the outset, that my own discussion of television is based on the experience I have had of it in the United States, in France and in Germany. Although they are diminishing, the differences among the televisions of these three countries remain striking enough to caution against any hasty attempt at generalizing about 'the medium'. And yet, although I

---

4 An example: according to a recent policy decision, the First German Television Channel, *ARD*, has decided to no longer broadcast operas since their viewer ratings are too low. If this indicates that the difference between 'public' and 'private' television programming is steadily diminishing in Europe, it also calls attention to the fact that such differences still are important enough to warrant attention. In France, a law prohibits more than one interruption for advertising during the broadcast of a film, on private as well as on state-owned stations.

hope it does not come across as hasty, I will still attempt precisely to uncover certain underlying features that I take to be characteristic of the medium in its specificity. I will be speaking of television as it is found in the countries I mention, but I strongly suspect that many of these traits will obtain in the television of countries that I know nothing about. The fact remains that, however general the traits I describe may be, they are formulated on the basis of television *as it exists today* in three countries and therefore cannot pretend to exhaust *all* the possibilities of the medium. Nevertheless, if television today has assumed the forms it has, nothing would be more naive than to suppose that its development has been the result of purely *external* forces, be these determined historically, socially, economically, politically, culturally, linguistically or technologically. Rather, it seems far more likely that a profound *complicity* obtains between the *medium of television* and the *world* composed by those forces; and one of the aims of this investigation is to move toward an understanding of this complicity. It is an aim that at best can only be adumbrated within the limited scope of the present essay. For in approaching the question of television, we must take as little for granted as possible. Television is very close to us, it is increasingly widespread; but it is not, for all of its ubiquitousness, very well understood.

In order to allow the medium of television to unfold as a question, then, I will begin by taking a detour that may seem unnecessary to many of you. I will approach television by a reflection on the way we speak about it in English, but I will also upon occasion compare the ways television is named and articulated in certain other languages with which I am familiar, above all, French and German.

Let us start, then, with the word used in English to designate the medium with which we are concerned. *Television*—and the words are essentially equivalent in French and German—

means, of course, something like 'seeing at a distance'. What does 'seeing at a distance' entail? If we translate the Graeco-Latinate word into more familiar English roots, we come up with a curious, but suggestive, result—*farsightedness*. In English, this word has two interestingly divergent meanings, one general and more 'figurative', the other more specific and more literal. In the more general and perhaps more common use, the term signifies not so much a particular act of sense-perception as a *way of being*. Farsighted is something one *is*, not *does*. To *be farsighted* is to be ready for any eventuality. The spatial connotation suggested by *far* is transformed here into a primarily temporal one: to be *farsighted* is to anticipate what is likely to happen in the more or less distant future and to take appropriate actions in advance. Yet the second meaning of the word contrasts curiously with the first. Here the spatial dimension reasserts itself, but only at the cost of a strange trade-off, for 'seeing far' in its medical use does not, of course, simply mean seeing *better*. To be farsighted is to see things that are distant more clearly than those that are close at hand. It is the opposite of being nearsighted, and what it suggests is that the ability to see at a distance is heightened only at the expense of the ability to see what is closest. Both notions of 'farsightedness', then, include a defensive, compensatory connotation. Were this to be limited to an isolated linguistic instance, it would hardly be worth retaining. But as we shall see, the paradoxical combination of increased power with increased vulnerability is something that will confront us again and again as we proceed in our discussion of television.

Let us for the moment continue to pursue certain of its linguistic aspects. If the notion of 'distance' and, in general, considerations of space have received less attention in English-language discussions of television than has the dimension of time, it is perhaps in part because in English the prefix *tele-* has tended to be absorbed into the set of nouns that it modifies and thus to lose its semantic independence. In nouns such as *telepathy*, *telephone*, *telescope* and *telegraph*, the notion of 'distance' is preserved only as an *obstacle* to be *surmounted*, either by an intangible 'sixth sense' (telepathy) or, more frequently, by some sort of mechanical device or electronic apparatus (telescope, telephone, television). Moreover, the overcoming of distance in all of these cases is linked to the ability to transcend the spatial limitations usually associated with the body. This technological triumph over distance reaches something of a linguistic high-point in American English, where the prefix tele- disappears practically without a trace in the abbreviation *TV*. Whether or not the notion of distance remains closer to consciousness in languages such as British English or French, in which the prefix *tele-* is retained to designate the medium, is a question I will not try to answer here.

More important, in any case, is that 'distance' figures in the designation of the medium as an obstacle to be overcome, a fact that is made quite explicit in the French designation for 'remote control': *télécommande*. The question that emerges here is whether this 'accessory' does not name one of the deepest phantasms provoked by the medium itself. The fascination and power of television as medium would derive, in great part, from its promise of providing a *remote control*, commanding not just *at a distance* but *over distance as such*.

Such a promise, however, has long been associated with technology in general. Ever since Plato, one of the most decisive purposes in the development of art, artifice and technology has been interpreted to be that of overcoming the shortcomings of nature, human or otherwise. This relationship has also been the source of a continuing suspicion that the reliance upon technique and technology could well turn out to be a cure worse than the disease. To resort to 'artificial' means of overcoming 'natural' deficiencies would thus be to confirm, and perhaps to aggravate, a relationship of dependency. The modern attitude toward television continues this tradition of ambivalence toward technology in general.

If we restrict this account to the specific case of television, the limitation that is to be overcome is tied to the individual body. The body as such has always been defined by a certain spatial limitation. A body is thus understood as something that occupies a determinate extent of space and occupies it exclusively. From this it follows that a body, as traditionally construed, can be defined in part as that which occupies a place, and more precisely, which occupies one place at a time. This means both that a body cannot take place in *more* than one place at a time and that the place it 'takes' is held to be off-limits to all other bodies: two bodies cannot take or share the same place at the same time. (The case of the *parasite* may be cited here as the exception that proves the rule.)[5]

If television thus names 'seeing-at-a-distance', what it appears to overcome thereby is the body, or more precisely, the spatial limitations placed by the body upon seeing and hearing. But the same, it could be remembered, was done some 400 years earlier by the telescope. The comparison between the telescope, at least in its original, mechanical form, and television allows us to elaborate just what is peculiar to the particular 'farsightedness' of the latter. First of all, it is significant that we speak of 'the' telescope, using the definite article to designate a particular kind of apparatus or instrument, whereas we speak of 'television' in general, without any article at all. This usage suggests that while our relation to the telescope is above all that to a particular kind of instrument, our relation to television confounds both apparatus and the medium in general. A second distinction, proceeding from the first, is that in contrast to the telescope, television does not merely allow the viewer to

---

5   In French, radio or television interference—'static'—is called *parasite*.

'see at a distance' things that otherwise would be invisible. It *transports vision as such* and *sets* it immediately *before* the viewer. It entails not merely a heightening of the naturally limited powers of sight with respect to certain distant *objects*; it involves a transmission or transposition of vision itself. The televisual spectator can see things from places—and hence, from perspectives and points of view (and it is not trivial that these are often more than one)—where his or her body is not (and often never can be) situated.

Television can thus be considered the most detached type of vision and audition—and we should never forget that, despite its name, it entails both seeing *and hearing*—insofar as it makes vision available to its viewers independently of the limitations of their physical situation. In this sense, television *overcomes* distance and separation; but it can do so only because it also *becomes* separation. Like radio, which in a certain manner it incorporates,[6] television is perhaps first and foremost a method of *transmission*[7]; and transmission, which is movement, involves separation.

One could say that this was already the case for film and photography, and indeed, for any form of inscription. But what distinguishes television from these other media is its power to combine such separation with the presentness associated with sense-

---

6   Without prejudicing the results of a more ample investigation than can be conducted here, it seems likely that the ambivalent character of the electronic media that we are elaborating with respect to television would be no less applicable to radio. By separating sound from sight, radio delocalizes and disembodies the relation to the world even more than does television. This *deprives* sound of its visual accompaniment, thereby impoverishing its 'reality', while at the same time *heightening* its power and scope by liberating it from the constraints of a visually determinate situation.

7   I wish to thank Professor Klaus Hofmann, of the University of Frankfurt, who read an earlier version of this paper, for having insisted on the importance of this elementary but essential aspect of television.

perception. What television transmits is not so much *images*, as is almost always argued. It does not transmit *representations* but rather *the semblance of presentation as such,* understood as the power not just to see and to hear but *to place before us.* Television thus serves as a surrogate for the body in that it allows for a certain sense-perception to take place; but it does this in a way that no body can, for its perception takes place in more than one place at a time. Television takes place in taking the place of the body and at the same time in transforming both place and body. For, by definition, television takes place in *at least three places at once*: 1. In the place (or places) where the image and sound are 'recorded'; 2. In the place (or places) where those images and sounds are *received*; and 3. In the place (or places) *in between,* through which those images and sounds are transmitted.

The unity of television as a medium of presentation thus involves a *simultaneity* that is highly ambivalent. It overcomes spatial distance but only by *splitting the unity of place* and with it the unity of everything that defines its identity with respect to place: events, bodies, subjects.[8] The unity of place is split

---

8 Stanley Cavell, in the essay mentioned (see note 1), uses the category of *simultaneity* to determine 'the material basis of television'. But his account of television 'as a current of simultaneous event reception' and his determination of 'monitoring' as the mode of perception peculiar to the medium leave little place for the ambivalent structure of television qua medium. Where ambivalence appears in his account, it is as a psychological after-effect, one which derives essentially from the *reality* the medium is felt to *represent*—'the growing uninhabitability of the world'—rather than from *the reality of the mode of representation itself* ('The Fact of Television', 217). The same observation holds for Cavell's discussion of 'monitoring', which describes it as a reaction to an inhospitable reality existing independently of television rather than as a function of the way in which the medium tends to redefine the relation to and the structure of 'reality'. If this is so, then the 'fact' of television, as Cavell conceives it, must be distinguished from Heidegger's notion of 'facticity', which designates the 'thrownness' of being-there-and-then—*Dasein*—precisely insofar as it *resists* causal explanation.

because the 'act' of viewing television does not 'take place' simply *in front* of the television set, as it might were it simply to
involve the viewing of *images*. But, as I have already suggested,
what one looks at in watching television is not first and foremost images. As the name of the medium says very precisely,
one looks at *a certain kind of vision*. And that vision is taking
place not simply on the screen but simultaneously—or rather,
quasi-simultaneously, since there is always a time-lag—somewhere *else*.

Perhaps this is one reason why one does not usually speak,
in English, of 'seeing' television but rather of 'watching' it. To
'see something' suggests a more or less direct contact of perceiver and perceived; and this in turn implies the givenness of
an object to be *seen*: a *perceptum*. We do on the other hand
speak of '*looking at* a television *program*'. To 'look at' entails a
far more mediate, more distanced relationship. As the 'at'
makes clear, we are dealing with an indirect object. But the
verb that is most specific to television is not 'looking at' but
rather 'watching'. For we still speak of 'looking at a painting' or
a 'photograph'; but we would rarely dream of *watching* them.
(Interestingly, we also do not speak of 'watching' a film.)
Rather, we *watch* events whose outcome is in doubt, like sporting events. To *watch* carries with it the connotation of a scrutiny that suggests more and less than mere *seeing* or *looking at*.
To watch is very close to *watching out for* or *looking out for*, that
is, being sensorially alert for something that *may* happen. In
the case of television, the primary 'object' of our watching is
neither a particular image nor even a particular program: it is
the medium itself, which includes its institutions—above all,
stations and networks. We watch television—or CNN—just as
we listen to *the radio*. The specificity of both of these media,
radio and television, is that they confront their viewers and listeners primarily *as media*, and only secondarily as specific

instantiations, that is, *as programs*.

This indicates that where television is concerned, one of the most fundamental categories of traditional aesthetics no longer retains its decisive status: the category of the individualized *work*. Art is inseparable from the *work of art*: a delimited, self-contained, significant unit, localizable in space and time. The language in which we speak of the media of tele-transmission—radio and television—strongly suggests that with respect to these media such individuation is no longer a determining factor. This is one of the reasons why we do not speak of 'seeing' a 'work' of television but rather of watching television as such. The unity of the medium is no longer based upon the individuated unity of the work.

This also suggests a further reason why we 'watch' television. To 'watch' something that itself cannot simply be seen, because it is not composed primarily of *images*, is to *be on the alert*, to watch *out* for something that is precisely not perceptible or graspable as an image or a representation. To 'watch' is to look for something that is not immediately apparent. It implies an effort, a tension and a separation.

I have already outlined certain ways in which television sets a separation before us. And yet, again using as a guide the language in which we speak of this medium, we can also say that what television sets before us is first and foremost the television *set* itself. This set is defined by two factors: its situation and its screen.

Before we discuss either of these two determining factors, let us dwell for a moment on the word itself and what it implies. According to the *Oxford English Dictionary*, the use of the word *set* to describe a technical apparatus such as a radio or television receiver appeals to one of the traditional meanings of the term, namely, that of 'setting-together' or assembling. To be sure, the *OED* here seems to be referring to the assemblage of different parts that make up a complex apparatus. But not all such assemblages or apparatuses are designated as 'sets'. A further specification is thus required. Our previous discussion of the spatial dimension peculiar to television may help us further. As Mary Ann Doane, in one of the most thoughtful of recent essays on this medium, has observed, 'Television's greatest technological prowess is its ability to be there—both on the scene and in your living room',[9] to which one should add that this 'being-there and here' goes on *at the same time*, in that quasi-simultaneity to which I have referred. However, if television is both here *and* there *at the same time*, then, according to traditional notions of space, time and body, it can be *neither fully there nor entirely here*. What it sets before us, in and as the television *set*, is therefore split, or rather, it is a *split* or a *separation* that camouflages itself by taking the form of a visible *image*. That is the veritable significance of the term 'television *coverage*': it *covers* an invisible separation by giving it shape, contour and figure. The rendering visible of this coverage takes place before us, usually in our living room, not just *on* the screen but, even more, *as the screen*. What, however, is a screen generally, and what is peculiar to the television screen in particular?

A screen is first of all a surface upon which light and shadow can be projected. In film, this appears to take place in a relatively straightforward manner. Something that has already taken place is re-presented by being projected onto a screen. The temporal relation of past and present, the mimetic relation of a previously existent original and a subsequent copy, seems to remain essentially intact.[10] In television, however, as with

---

9 Mary Ann Doane, 'Information, Crisis and Catastrophe', 238.

10 Needless to say, the importance of the cutting-table in the construction of the film indicates how tenuous such an ostensible linearity in fact is. The 'post-production' process of 'editing' has long been recognized as an essential dimension of film-making.

radio before it, the hierarchy implied in this relationship is severely perturbed; and consequently, the logic and ontology that govern the traditional relationship of mimesis, reproduction and representation are unsettled. For what appears on the television screen is not a previously accomplished work but the quasi-simultaneity of *another vision* reproduced here and now. The minimal difference necessary to distinguish reproduced from reproduction, model from copy, repeated from repetition, is reduced, tendentially at least, to the imperceptible. One can no longer distinguish, visually or aurally, between that which is reproduced and its reproduction. Indeed, one cannot even discern *that* or *when* reproduction or repetition, in the manifest sense of recording or replaying, is taking place. We must be informed whether or not what we are seeing is 'live'. In short, we cannot distinguish through our senses alone between what we take to be simply 'alive' and what as reproduction, separated from its origin, is structurally posthumous. The television screen is the site of such an uncanny confusion and confounding. In the uncanniness of such confusion, what Derrida has called the irreducible 'iterability' of the mark[11]—that repeatability that both allows a trait to constitute its identity while splitting it at the same time—manifests itself in the only way open to it (since it is not of the order of manifestation), namely, as the *undecidable being of the televised images we see*.

Those images are undecidable not simply because they are separated from their previous context—and it is in this sense that I insist that what we see on the TV screen is not so much 'images' but *another kind of vision*, a vision of the other (to be understood as both an objective and subjective genitive). What we see on the screen is undecidably other for two reasons: first

---

11 Derrida, 'Limited Inc a b c...', *Limited Inc*, 1988, 53. See Weber, 'After Deconstruction', in this volume.

of all, because the power of vision that is transmitted is separated from its link to a situated individual body; and second,
because whatever we see is no longer clearly distinguishable
from the distant vision being transmitted. What we see, above
and beyond the content of the images, is someone or something
seeing. But that someone or something remains at an irreducible, indeterminable distance from the television viewer;
and this distance splits the 'sameness' of the instant of perception as well as the identity of the place in which such viewing
seems to occur. When we 'watch' television, we are watching
out for this split, for this instant and place turned inside out.

The television transmission does not therefore, as is generally supposed, simply *overcome* distance and separation. (This is
the illusion of a 'global village'.) It renders them invisible, paradoxically, by transposing them *into* the vision it transmits.
Transmitted vision and audition 'contain', as it were, distance
and separation while at the same time confounding the points
of reference that allow us to determine what is near and what is
far, what is connected and what is disconnected. For those
points of reference involve precisely the unequivocal determination of place and of bodily situation that the television transmission tends to undermine. This is why the television set turns
out to be something like a Trojan Horse introduced into the
heart of the domestic fortress that we call 'home'. In front of it
the family assembles as it once did before the Penates; but the
space defined by the television set is already fractured by the
undecidability of that which appears on the screen. Is it taking
place here, or there, or anywhere? The development of video,
and above all, of the digitalization of images, renders the question even less susceptible of an unequivocal answer.

In this sense, the television screen can be said to live up to
its name in at least three distinct, contradictory and yet interrelated senses. First, it serves as a *screen* which allows distant

vision to be *watched*. Second, it *screens*, in the sense of *selecting* or *filtering*, the vision that is watched. And finally, it serves as a screen in the sense of standing between the viewer and the viewed, since what is rendered visible covers the separation that distinguishes the *other vision* from that of the sight of the spectator sitting in front of the set.

Up to now, I have attempted to elaborate what I take to be certain of the distinctive traits specific to television as a medium. However, if the term 'uncanny' is at all appropriate to the undecidable effects I have tried to elaborate, then this would suggest that the specificity we are dealing with, although certainly 'new' in its particular configuration, is not simply *opposed* to the old but in a sense grows out of it. What I would like to argue is that the technological novelty of television must be understood both as the *consummation of a very old tradition* and at the same time as the *heightening of its internal ambivalences*. Perhaps the most comprehensive account we have of that tradition, insofar as it involves the process of thinking, is that of Heidegger. And interpreted in a Heideggerian perspective, television can be described as the culmination and consummation—the *Vollendung*—of the metaphysical tradition of representation. In German, the word that is translated as representation is *Vorstellung*. Curiously enough, however, in German it is primarily a spatial rather than temporal term. *Vorstellen* means, literally, to *place before*. It involves a determination of space and place such that a subject can take its place as the focal point of such 'placing-before'. To place before implies that there is a point that can be used to determine and distinguish *front* from *back*, 'before' from 'behind'. What is placed before, in and as the television set, is, as I have tried to emphasize, above all the very faculty itself of placing-before: the power of vision qua *Vorstellung*. In this placing-before, representation and presentation almost converge; but since the

simultaneity of television transmission remains a *quasi*-simul-
taneity, the faculty of pre-senting sight and sound—that is, of
bringing them *before* the *senses*—is itself re-pre-sented on and *as*
the screen of the television set. This set remains a *re-ceiver*,
which is to say, an apparatus that re-produces and re-peats.
What television does, then, is to 'materialize', in a relatively
immaterial manner, the irreducibility of that iterability, in the
mode of presentation we call 'vision' and 'audition'.

In this sense, the television set can be said to consummate
not just the metaphysical age of representation but, more
specifically, that which, according to Heidegger, is its charac-
teristically contemporaneous form: technology. The essence of
modern technology for Heidegger is what he calls the *Gestell*.
The word can be translated as 'framework', 'installation' or
even 'skeleton'. I prefer *emplacement*, in order to retain the reference to place and to placing which is paramount in
Heidegger's discussion of the phenomenon.[12] At the same time,
the peculiar *reality* of television explains why the translation by
'skeleton' is also not inappropriate. For the more technology
seeks to put things in their proper places, the less proper those
places turn out to be; the more displaceable everything
becomes and the more frenetic becomes the effort to reassert
the propriety of the place as such. If the word 'television' in
ordinary usage applies not just to the medium as a whole but,
more precisely, to its materialization as the receiving *set*, this
emphasizes just how determining the aspect of 'setting' and
'placing' is for a medium that deprives distance as well as proximity of their traditional stability and hence of their power to
orient. What is distant is set right before us, close up; and yet
what is thus brought close remains strangely *removed*, indeter-
minably *distant*. And what is traditionally proximate is *set*

---

12 See Weber, 'Upsetting the Setup', in this volume.

apart, set at a distance.

The reality of television thus no longer follows the traditional logic and criteria of reality. It is no longer a function of identity or of its derived form: opposition. Far and near are no
longer mutually exclusive but rather converge and overlap.
Such convergence brings a different aspect of reality to the
fore—the reality of *ambivalence*. For what is ostensibly 'set in
place' as the television set is also and above all *a movement of
displacement*, of *transmission*. What results strongly resembles
what Walter Benjamin, in his work on the German Baroque
theatre of the 17th century, described as the 'court' that
emanates from all allegory:

> Allegory [...] in its most developed form brings with it a court
> (*einen Hof*); around the figural center, which is never missing
> from genuine allegories, in opposition to conceptual circumlo-
> cutions, a host of emblems is grouped. They seem arbitrarily
> arranged: *The Confused 'Court'*—title of a Spanish mourning
> play [by Lope de Vega—SW]—could be cited as the schema of
> allegory. 'Dispersion' (*Zerstreuung*) and 'Collection' (*Sammlung*)
> name the law of this court. Things are brought together
> according to their meaning; indifference to their being-there
> (*Dasein*) disperses them once again. The disorder of the allegor-
> ical scenery stands in contrast to the gallant boudoir.[13]

Like the allegorical court, television brings the most remote
things together only to disperse them again, out of 'indifference
to their being-there', or rather, out of the undecidability of their
being-there (*Dasein*). To be sure, in contradistinction to the allegorical court, television—in the sense of its reception—is gen-

---

13 Benjamin, *Ursprung des deutschen Trauerspiels*, 1963, 210 [My translation—SW]. English as *The Origin of the German Tragic Drama*, 1977, 188.

erally situated in the private space of the home. But the uncanny undecidability of television—of the distant vision it transmits and renders visible—is probably as much a source of disorder today as the allegorical scenery was in the 17th century German principalities and duchies. Both then as now, the lack of a unifying, totalizing worldly instance—be it the Nation-State or the Universal Church—was keenly felt. What today in part claims to make up for that instance is television itself. The global network, CNN for instance, presents itself as a model for such totalization. But the all-encompassing unity that it proposes remains as ambivalent as the indefinitely repeated sets of television monitors that constitute its favorite backdrop. Thus, the question remains open as to how, out of indefinite repetition, anything like an integrated whole might emerge, or rather, whether such a whole is even thinkable any longer.

This, then, is one of the tendencies that renders television a set of the most ambiguous, most ambivalent kind: it sets only by unsettling. And yet, this unsettling tendency is also constantly being recuperated and reappropriated; and this allows television also to function as a bulwark of the established order. The more the medium tends to unsettle, the more powerfully it presents itself as the antidote to the disorder to which it contributes.

I want to conclude by briefly analyzing one such instance of recuperation. I have tried to describe how the primary setting of television, as a set, is the private space of the home. The major alternative to home viewing, in the United States at least, is the collective television watching usually situated in bars. The preferred program of such collective television watching is—once again, in the U.S.—almost exclusively the competitive sporting event. What does the viewing of a sporting event have to offer the television public? Precisely what television itself tends to undermine: the possibility of an unequivocal *deci-*

sion. In competitive sports, there is always a winner and a loser; and where there are more than one of each, there are unequivocal rankings to determine their *placement.* In professional competitive sports, which television does not merely transmit but also, through sponsoring, helps finance, the technological dream of planning and control is rendered visible. Whoever wins or loses, the outcome is clear and decisive. In watching such events, television viewers can forget, at least temporarily, just how ambivalent and undecidable the reality of their world has become, not least of all by virtue of television itself. In the world as we know it, seeing and hearing—understood as individual, self-contained acts of perception—are perhaps less than ever before reliable means of acceding to 'reality'.

Televised sports allows viewers to take comfort in the possibility of unequivocal decisions, of being able to distinguish winners and losers, as well as in the possibility of 'records' that are quantifiable and measurable. In so doing, televised sports reconfirms the individual body as focal point of a reality that television itself calls constantly into question. The body that appears in the televised sporting event is one that accepts its limitations only in order to surpass them, in an infinite progress of record-breaking and record-making performance. The shadows that such performances are meant to eclipse reappear on the margins, where, however, they often turn out to be quite determining for the field itself. For instance, the use of steroids to increase performance or the vulnerability of the superstar to AIDS serve as reminders of what the televisual sporting event—*media event* par excellence—simultaneously seeks to *cover*, to wit, the frailty and limitation of the individual body.

No wonder that the sporting event has emerged, in the United States at least, as one of the central discursive paradigms for representing reality, be it political, economic or social. Ever since the Vietnam War, conflicts of all kinds, even the most brutal and violent, have been described—and televised—as though they were sporting events. If this age turns out to be that of American television—a conjecture, not a hope—then the televisual sporting event will undoubtedly stand as its allegorical emblem, leaving everything as open and shut as the instant replay with which the medium demonstrates its control of the event, if not of its outcome.

After Deconstruction

Das Staunen darüber, daß die Dinge, die wir
erleben, im zwanzigsten Jahrhundert 'noch'
möglich sind, ist kein philosophisches. Es steht
nicht am Anfang einer Erkenntnis, es sei denn
der, daß die Vorstellung von Geschichte, aus der
es stammt, nicht zu halten ist.[1]
Walter Benjamin

If there is still the slightest doubt lurking in anyone's mind as to whether the individual subject might yet turn out to be master of his, her or its fate, then all such doubts should be definitively dispelled by the fact that this text is entitled 'After Deconstruction'. For this is not a title that would ever have occurred to me spontaneously, 'of my own free will'. And yet, I

---

1   'Astonishment that the things we are experiencing [today] are "still" possible in the 20th century is *not* philosophical astonishment. It does not stand at the beginning of any knowledge, except perhaps that of the untenable character of the conception of history from which [such astonishment] derives'. *'Über den Begriff der Geschichte', GS,* I/2, 697 [My translation—SW]. In English as 'Theses on the Philosophy of History', *Illuminations,* 257.

have every reason to be grateful for this 'gift' which came to me from Italy and for which I want to express my thanks to Professors Raimondi and Franci.[2] When one is surprised by a title or a subject or a topic that one would never have come upon unaided, the gift invites one to reflect upon the reasons why it would never have spontaneously imposed itself. And the more I reflected on my feelings about this title, the more it imposed itself on me, not spontaneously, but irresistibly nevertheless. Let me therefore begin by examining some of the reasons why this title, 'After Deconstruction', came as such a surprise to me and then turned out to be what I hope will prove to have been a productive *challenge*.

The main reason why I would never have thought of such a title 'on my own' is that it can easily be understood to suggest that deconstruction—whatever is understood by that much abused term, something we will have to go into a bit later on— is purely and simply *over*, that it is dead and gone, that it belongs to the *past* once and for all, and that we therefore now have to begin to think seriously about just what comes *after* its demise. I don't in the slightest think that anything like this was intended when the phrase was suggested to me, if only because I would be an unlikely person to choose if what one wanted was to commemorate the passing of deconstruction once and for all, so that we could all at long last return to business as usual, to the *status quo ante*.

If therefore the title 'After Deconstruction' is understood

---

2   This text was originally given as a lecture at the University of Bologna, held at the invitation of Professors Ezio Raimondi and Giovanna Franci. In a letter, Professor Franci suggested that I address some aspect of the contemporary critical scene 'after Deconstruction'—whence the title of the talk. Unfortunately, it was only after this text was written that I discovered her very discriminating discussion of this question, *'Oltra la decostruzione?'*, in *L'Ansia dell'Interpretazione: Saggi su hermeneutica, semiotica e decostruzione*, 1989, 281-313.

simply, and I believe simplistically, to mean that our business
as writers and readers, critics and scholars, can once again be
conducted without worrying too much about the questions
and problems raised over the past few decades—a little bit in
the manner of Stanley Fish telling his readers how he, and presumably they, should 'stop worrying and learn to love interpretation'—then this title would, in my judgment, not be very
productive. If scholars and critics would like to ignore deconstruction, they are, of course, free to do so. It is, however, one
thing to ignore deconstruction and quite another to claim to
situate oneself 'after' it. For one cannot hope to go 'beyond'
deconstruction if one has not first *encountered* it. And this, you
may have noticed, is easier said than done. It involves consid-
erably more than mere name-dropping, which unfortunately
seems increasingly to be taking the place of anything like a
genuine encounter, at least in certain quarters. This, then, is
the major reason that the title, 'After Deconstruction', took me
by surprise.

But, of course, Benjamin's remark, which serves as the
epigraph to this text, reminds us, albeit negatively, that surprise or astonishment can *also* serve as the beginning of
knowledge.[3] So the very fact that I was surprised by the title,
'After Deconstruction', encouraged me to look a little bit further. I realized that the title could also be understood as rais-

---

3   Benjamin's implicit allusion is presumably to the famous remark from
    Aristotle's *Metaphysics*: 'For it is owing to their wonder that men first
    began to philosophize'. *Metaphysics*, 982b. For an extensive discussion of
    the problem of astonishment and its relation to Western philosophy—a dis-
    cussion that precedes Benjamin's remark by only a few years, although it is
    conducted precisely in dubious proximity to the very 'things' to which
    Benjamin alludes—see Heidegger's Freiburg lectures of 1937-1938, enti-
    tled *Grundfragen der Philosophie* (*Basic Questions of Philosophy*), in which
    there is a prolonged analysis of the role of *Er-staunen, thaumazein,* in Greek
    thought. Heidegger, *Gesamtausgabe*, Bd. 45, esp. 157-180.

ing the question of the *aftermath* of deconstruction. This question would ask us to consider not the pure and simple disappearance of deconstruction but rather the *transformations* it has brought about, the *perspectives* it has opened up and the *tasks* it has placed on the agenda. *Aftermath* strikes me as a particularly apt word if one remembers that it derives, not as one might think, from the Greek *mathesis*, learning or knowledge, but from the Anglo-Saxon *meth*, meaning 'mowing'. If deconstruction initially emerged as a form of what Derrida called 'dissemination', then its aftermath would signify the 'second' or 'subsequent' mowing of what had initially been 'strewn' about.

However, 'aftermath' still seems to me misleading inasmuch as it suggests a clear-cut *split between* an *event* or *advent* of deconstruction, now definitively past, and its subsequent effects. This kind of pat distinction between 'before' and 'after' presupposes precisely that temporality of *presence* that Derrida, following and radicalizing Heidegger on this issue, from the very first sought to call into question. In this respect, any reflection upon deconstruction—upon its own history and upon its relation to the concept of history—cannot avoid raising the question of its *curious and singular mode of being*, which is to say, of the peculiar way in which deconstruction must be said to *take place*. Any discussion of deconstruction that does *not* address this question runs the risk of mistaking the singularity of what it seeks to name. And this specificity in turn redefines the way in which *naming* works. To speak of deconstruction therefore without taking this redefinition of the name—and of language—into account is to remain 'this side' of deconstruction. To sum up the problem: any attempt to move 'beyond' deconstruction runs the risk of never getting to it and therefore winding up back where one started, *before* deconstruction.[4]

Having gotten this far in my response to the title I had been offered, I came to the conclusion that the real challenge of the title was to describe the encounter with deconstruction in a way that would allow the question of its aftermath, 'After Deconstruction', to reveal its full force. For it is only after having determined as rigorously as possible just what the salient and distinguishing traits of deconstruction are that it is possible to address the question of its aftermath, or, one might also say, the question of its *wake*.

Why 'wake'? Let me try to explain why I feel it is perhaps most accurate to speak of the current critical scene, 'after deconstruction', particularly in regard to North America, in terms of a 'wake'—one which is at once the wake of criticism and that of deconstruction. The literary allusion here, of course, is to *Finnegans Wake*. That text, as you perhaps know, is an extremely important one for Derrida, who has written a short but significant essay on it,[5] one in which we find the following remark: '[E]very time I write, and even in the most academic pieces of work, Joyce's ghost is always coming on board' ('TWJ', 149). If Derrida acknowledges here that from the very beginning—which is to say, from his first published essay on Husserl's text, *The Origin of Geometry*—his work has been

---

4   It might seem to some inappropriately 'referential' to assert that the encounter with deconstruction depends upon not simply ignoring, or 'mistaking', the 'singularity of what' the word 'seeks to name'. But contrary to certain polemically strategic simplifications, a deconstruction never ignores referential or denotational meanings or intended meanings, for it is only by pursuing and following such intentions out to the furthest point possible that their limitations and aporias can be made legible. This is why Derridean deconstructive readings are never simply arbitrary, why they never can be used to justify saying *'n'importe quoi'* or to argue for simple indeterminacy. It is only by reading as precisely as possible that the limits of precision can be remarked and put into play.

5   'Two Words for Joyce', in *Post-Structuralist Joyce*, 1984, 145-158. Future references are given in the body of the text using the abbreviation 'TWJ'.

'haunted' by Joyce's 'ghost', then the particular way he
describes this haunting relationship plays directly on the
ambiguous, overdetermined word *wake*. First of all, you will
have noticed that Derrida writes that Joyce's ghost 'is always
coming on board'. On board what? On board a ship. What does
a ship do as it moves through the waters? It leaves behind a
trace, called in English: a *wake*. But not only ships leave wakes
behind them. Any powerful body in movement, an army for
instance, does the same. And in a longer passage on his relationship to Joyce that I am about to quote, you will notice that
Derrida links *Finnegans Wake* to a certain *mobilization*.

But I am getting ahead of myself. Let us go back to the word
'wake' as it is used in Joyce's title. It has *three* major meanings
there, at least. First of all, it refers to the Irish funeral ritual that
marks the death of a friend or loved one by organizing festivities in the presence of the corpse. Secondly—a meaning that is
inseparable, although distinct, from the first—the word suggests *awakening*: the deceased is not simply dead and gone but
awakens—as in the Irish ballad with the same name as Joyce's
'novel'—to join the festivities. This in turn refers to a third
meaning, implied perhaps in the more widespread custom of
having someone constantly 'watch out for' the corpse between
the time of death and that of burial, ostensibly to protect the
dead body from harm but perhaps also, as has often been sur-
mised,[6] to make certain that the deceased precisely does *not*
come back, 'wake' and return.

But the ambiguity of the phrase, the 'wake of deconstruction', is not limited to the different meanings of the individual
nouns it involves: wake, deconstruction. Rather, this ambiguity
seems to radiate out from the words to contaminate the very
grammar of the phrase they comprise. For the preposition, 'of',

---

6   By Freud, among others, in *Totem and Taboo*.

in the phrase does not merely establish a clear-cut relation of belonging or dependence. It can, and indeed should, be understood as constituting both an *objective* and a *subjective genitive*. The 'wake' that deconstruction can be said to have caused or provoked in its passing (objective genitive) would, in this reading, already have been at work in its very coming-to-be, in its advent or event. Deconstruction would therefore have to be understood—in the sense of the *genitivus subjectivus*—as a *wake*, as itself a wake, an *aftermath*, and not simply as something that, *having taken place once and for all*, leaves behind certain effects with which we have now to deal. To encounter deconstruction therefore would be to open oneself to the possibility that it did not ever take place *once and for all* but rather that, from the very beginning, it *came to pass as a wake*. Let me try to explain in what sense deconstruction *itself* could be considered, must be considered, as having come to pass as a *wake*, in all of the senses of that word just mentioned.

In the essay on *Finnegans Wake* to which I have just alluded, Derrida explains in what way his work was from the very first 'haunted' by 'Joyce's ghost':

Twenty years ago, in the *Introduction to 'The Origin of Geometry'*, at the very centre of the book, I compared the strategies of Husserl and of Joyce: two great models, two paradigms with respect to thought, but also with respect to a certain 'operation' of the relationship between language and history. Both try to grasp a pure historicity. To do this, Husserl proposes to render language as transparent as possible, univocal, limited to that which, by being transmittable or able to be placed in tradition, thereby constitutes the only condition of a possible historicity; [...] The other great paradigm would be the Joyce of *Finnegans Wake*. He repeats and mobilizes and babelizes the (asymptotic) totality of the equivocal, he makes

> this his theme and his operation [...] This generalized equivo-
> cality of writing does not translate one language into another
> on the basis of common nuclei of meaning [...] [as does
> Husserl—SW]; it talks several languages at once, parasiting
> them [...]. ('TWJ', 149)

'Husserl' and 'Joyce' here are, of course, proper names that
refer to two individual authors; but at the same time it is surely
not insignificant that the 'two great models' or 'paradigms'
they are said to represent coincide with the two general modes
of discourse with which Derrida's writing has been primarily
concerned: the 'philosophical' and the 'literary'. The philosophical discourse, here represented by Husserl, strives to determine
language as a *univocal*, transparent medium, which is to say, as
a medium that effaces itself before the thought it is held to
express or transmit. The other mode of discourse, here represented by Joyce, the *literary*, moves, as it were, in the opposite
direction, towards an accumulation of ambiguity and equivo-
cation, towards the 'babelization' of languages rather than
towards their unification. Far from tending to efface itself before
any meaning it might represent, the language of *Finnegans
Wake* is described by Derrida with three words that are of capital significance for his deconstructive mode of writing. Joyce's
use of language, Derrida asserts, '*repeats* and *mobilizes* and
babelizes the (asymptotic) totality of the equivocal' [My italics—
SW] to the point of engendering a certain form of linguistic *par-
asitism*. Let us dwell for a moment on these words and in particular on the one with which, perhaps significantly, the series
begins.

　　It would not be an exaggeration to see in the paradoxical
notion of *repetition* the origin—*Ursprung*—of deconstruction. I
use the German word here not simply because of its philosophical and speculative overtones—one thinks both of Benjamin's

Origin of the German Mourning Play (*Ursprung des deutschen Trauerspiels*) and of Heidegger's *Ursprung des Kunstwerks* (*Origin of the Work of Art*)—but because the German word contains within itself, quite literally, precisely what will turn out to be at stake in the process of repetition as origin of deconstruction. The word is composed of *Ur*, primordial, and *Sprung*, spring or leap. This is well known and has been amply commented upon. What is less familiar but no less important, however, is that the word *Sprung* in German can also mean *crack, fissure*. And this is precisely what is involved in the process of repetition: the irreducibility of a certain constitutive crack or break—the *Ur-Sprung*, the primordial crack. It is this crack that will come back to haunt us, as it haunts Derrida, among others, in the form of Joyce's ghost 'always coming on board'. A vessel with a crack in it does not have a very long life-expectancy, especially when that vessel is a ship. There is, you see, sufficient reason for Derrida to be concerned. We will return to this shortly.

If deconstruction can be said to be 'after' itself from the very start, it is because of its *Ursprung* in repetition, which is to say, in a process that is both irreducible and aporetic. For how, after all, can a *repetition* be at the origin of anything? It is no accident that the name of Husserl comes up in this context, for it is in his reading of Husserl that Derrida first elaborates what might be called the *constitutive ambivalence of repetition* for his work (which had not yet acquired the name of *deconstruction*). In his study of Husserl's attempt to arrive at an ideality of thought that would transcend linguistic and semiotic signification—*La voix et le phénomène* (1967)[7]—Derrida shows how the key phenomenological categories of 'ideality' and of 'living presence'

---

7 English as *Speech and Phenomena And Other Essays on Husserl's Theory of Signs*, 1973. Future references are given in the body of the text using the abbreviation *VP*. [My translations—SW]

depend upon a process of *repetition* that can never be fully present to itself (which is to say, can never be fully *alive*). Identity, in short, depends upon repetition, which, however, in turn presupposes something like identity. That is the aporetical insight in which Derridean deconstruction *originates*; and it remains an aporia whose ramifications his writings have never ceased to explore and to articulate in the most varied ways.

Perhaps the most accessible general statement of this irreducibility of repetition and of its consequences can be found in 'Limited Inc a b c...',[8] the text that Derrida wrote in 1977 in response to a polemical attack by John Searle. In his reply to Searle, Derrida elaborates what he takes to be the underlying characteristic of writing, of language and of articulation in general: 'the structure of iterability'. A certain iterability—the *possibility of being repeated*—Derrida argues 'is indispensable to the functioning of all language, written or spoken [...], and I would add, to that of every mark' ('LI', 53). That is to say, in order to be apprehended or identified as such—and every signifying element must be *identifiable as such* in order for it to signify—every signifier or 'mark' must be re-cognizable, re-peatable. It never can present itself simply once. Taking this argumentation one step further: in order to be *cognizable*, an element must be *re*-cognizable as the *same*, which in turn presupposes a process of *com-parison* and *repetition*. It must be compared with earlier instances of itself in order to be recognizable *as a self*, as an identity.

This process of repetitive comparison, out of which self-sameness emerges and which it therefore must *pass through*, introduces an element of *heterogeneity*, of *otherness*, into the constitution of the same. The question, however, now becomes:

---

8   Derrida, *Limited Inc*, 1988. Future references are given in the body of the text using the abbreviation 'LI'.

precisely what is the role of this heterogeneity in the process of repetition that is presupposed by every identification and by all identity? Derrida's response to this question is that the alterity presupposed by all repetition can never entirely be absorbed into the identification of the same. There will always, he argues, be something left over, a remainder, *un reste*:

> Iterability supposes a minimal remainder [...] in order that the identity of the *selfsame* be repeatable and identifiable *in, through,* and even *in view of* its alteration. For the structure of iteration—and this is another of its decisive traits—implies *both* identity *and* difference. Iteration in its 'purest' form—and it is always impure—contains *in itself* the discrepancy of a difference that constitutes it as iteration. The iterability of an element divides its own identity a priori, even without taking into account the fact that this identity can only *determine* or delimit itself through differential relations to other elements and that it hence bears the mark of this difference. It is because this iterability is differential, within each individual 'element' as well as between the 'elements', because *it splits each element while constituting it*, because it marks it with an articulatory break, that the remainder, although indispensable, is never that of a full or fulfilling presence: it is a differential structure escaping the logic of presence or the (simple or dialectical) opposition of presence and absence [...]. ('LI', 53) [Last italics mine—SW]

What Derrida calls, in French, *le reste*—here translated as 'remainder'—can be said to 'escape the logic of presence' because, paradoxically, it does not merely come *after* that which is identifiable—the 'mark' or 'element' that it is said to 'split'. It *at the same time* comes *before* it. For it is precisely this vestige or remnant—which is to say, precisely a certain *aftermath*—that makes possible identification and hence everything

identifiable (mark, element, signifier, sign, etc.). This is why, in
the passage just quoted, Derrida writes not merely that the differential dimension of iterability *splits* each element but that 'it
splits [it] *while* constituting it'. What is decisive in Derridean
deconstruction is this *while*, which indicates why the process
being elaborated here ultimately 'escapes the logic of presence',
which is to say, logic as it has generally been elaborated in
Western philosophy. For the dynamics of iterability replaces a
logic of presence by what might be called a graphics of *simultaneity*, in which, for instance, what comes after also and
simultaneously comes before. In this sense, the 'break' brought
about by the differential nature of iterability can be said to
'intervene from the very moment that there is a mark'. On the
one hand, then, it comes 'after' the mark; it is its left-over, its
reste. And yet, on the other hand and at the same time, Derrida
can insist that this break 'is not negative, but rather the positive condition of the emergence of the mark'. Which is to say, a
certain *coming after* emerges here as also the condition under
which anything can *come to be* in the first place. If, however,
what *comes to be* only does so by *coming after*, the most precise
way to describe this paradoxical kind of event is as a *coming-to-
pass*. Deconstruction does not simply take place. It does not simply come, stay a while and then depart. It *comes to pass*. It
arrives only *in passing*, or inversely, it is only in passing that it
arrives.

If, from a logical point of view, this may sound like a more
or less sterile paradox, once we place ourselves in the so-called
'real' world of temporal and historical transformations and
alterations, it becomes far more plausible and familiar. What
such coming-to-pass suggests is that a text—which can also be
regarded as a model for *all articulated reality*, independently of
whether it is empirically inscribed or not—only comes to be in
terms of a certain *repetition*, that is, in terms of what it repeats

and of what repeats it. But this is only half the story: for what it repeats and what repeats it are in turn split in the very same way, that is, they are no more self-present than the texts they repeat or that repeat them. Repetition cannot ultimately be *anchored* in a past present that is repeated. It comes to pass rather as the effect of a powerful movement that can only be known through the traces it leaves behind, which is to say, through its *wake*.

In this sense, the deconstructive notion of iterability is both related to what is known today as *reception theory* and yet also very different from it. It is related to it by its tendency to decenter the text and to make it legible in terms of its aftermath. But to equate this aftermath, in the sense of iterability, with an actual 'reception' describable in empirical terms would be to resubmit the graphics of simultaneity to the authority of the logic of presence in the form of the consciousness or self-consciousness of the so-called 'reception'. The very notion of *Rezeption* presupposes that there is a self-identical work that can be *rezipiert*. Or rather, that through the process of reconstructing how a work is 'received', or how it intends itself to be received, its identity can be reconstructed. By contrast, the *constitutive break* introduced by iterability is incompatible with the traditional notion of the *work*. This is one of the reasons why Derrida emphasizes from the start the notions of *text, writing* or *trace*. For these terms are far less closely associated than is 'work' with the claim to self-contained meaningfulness. Both a work and a text, it may be argued, only come to be in the aftermath of their reception; but their respective ways of being remain radically divergent. For even if it is argued that the work only comes to be in and through its reception, its *being* is still generally construed according to the logic of presence. It is understood as being self-identical, even if that self-identity requires a response in order to be actualized. But the dynamic of a text is construed by deconstruction less in 'ontological', or in 'aesthetic', terms than in those relating to language and movement, since the ambivalent effects of iterability—of its graphics of simultaneity—are more accessible when speaking of language, and in particular of *inscription* or of *transcription*, than when speaking of being or of art. This is why it is more appropriate to speak not of the being of a text but of its *coming-to-pass*.

The notion of iterability also suggests why one of the salient traits of Derridean deconstruction—one it shares with the different but related work of Paul de Man—is that it involves *close and highly complex readings of singular texts*. This is what distinguishes Derridean deconstruction both from ordinary philosophy and from anything like a 'pure theory', a mode of thought that Derrida—once again, like de Man, although from a somewhat different angle—never ceases to call into question.[9] This suspicion of the 'theoretical' is a corollary of the insight into the iterable structure of thought and of language. For if all identification inevitably involves a process of repetition in which the dimension of heterogeneity can never be fully reduced or absorbed, then the *calculated confrontation* with texts that themselves have in one way or another already explored and engaged the ambivalence of this repetition will be the best way of articulating that heterogeneity, as well as of avoiding the naiveté of saying the same thing as though it were something entirely different.

This consideration explains two facts that are often misunderstood: first, why it is that *reading* constitutes a major, and

---

9   The philosophical origin of this suspicion of philosophy is doubtless ancient enough; but its more recent model is Heidegger, who, from *Being and Time* on, defines his own 'ontological' analysis by demarcating it from the essentially contemplative, 'theoretical' mode of thought that dominates modern philosophy.

indeed essential, element of deconstruction, although the latter is often held to be something like a general theory and although general theories usually do not attach decisive importance to the process of reading; and second, why such readings have never claimed to be readings in general, concerned with any kind of text, but rather have manifestly preferred to read texts of a certain kind or cast, texts in which, generally speaking, the ambivalent aspects of iterability play a singular role.

Thus, on the basis of this criterion, texts and contexts will be of more or less interest depending upon the way and the degree with which they are concerned with the ambiguities of iterability, although one must hasten to add here that the fact that such concern is more *explicitly thematic* does not at all mean that it is more significant or more elaborate than in texts where such concern is less obvious. There can therefore be no established, incontrovertible canon of iterability. Iterability is what allows canons to be instituted, but at the same time it opens up the structural *possibility* of their destabilization and transformation. The reason for this can be stated with relative simplicity: since what is at stake in iterability is precisely a certain *otherness*—which, to be sure, in the process of repetition and of comparison is always tending to be reduced to the same—the direct focusing upon such *otherness* amounts to a contradiction in terms. For to *focus* upon otherness, in the sense of making it a *theme* or an *object* of one's attention, is, paradoxically, as Nietzsche once observed, to *identify* it *as other* and thereby to turn it into the same.

The consequence to be drawn from this paradox—namely, that to seek to identify, thematize, as I am doing here, or even *to name* the *other* or the element of heterogeneity *as such* is in a sense already to appropriate it and thereby to deprive it of its alterity—is that alterity intrudes in deconstructive readings not *as such* nor *in general* but rather in terms of the *singular*, the *odd*,

of what does not *fit in*. And yet, what is 'singular' is not simply
unique, for the singularity involved here is not that of the individual but the after-effect, the *reste*, of iterability.

   One form this singular *reste* assumes is that of the *double*.
The figure of the double is one of the most persistent leitmotifs
in Derrida's writings, from the early studies of Husserl and *Of
Grammatology* until today. And the double, of course, is closely
associated both with the Freudian (and Heideggerian) motif of
the *uncanny*, *des Unheimlichen*, as well as with a certain relation
to death. The double is the ghostlike manifestation of *iterability*,
which, as we have read in the passage cited from Derrida,
'splits' each element while at the same time 'constituting' it in
and through the split. If we include the 'self' or the 'subject'
among the 'elements' to which Derrida refers—and since he is
referring here to all *articulated* beings, there is no reason not to
do so—then we can say that the double, the *Doppelgänger*, is the
most direct manifestation of this splitting: the *splitting image*,
one could say, of the *self*. The paradoxical twist, however, is
that according to the deconstructive graphics of simultaneity,
any identity, including the self or the subject, is constituted
only in and through this split, this doubling. Commenting on
Husserl's notion of the 'ideality of meaning (*Idealität der
Bedeutung*)', Derrida observes that the linguistic reality of the
first person pronoun, 'I', must be intelligible independently of
the living presence of the person who uses it; and he concludes:
'My death is structurally necessary for the "I" to be pronounced' (*VP*, 108). In other words, insofar as the sense of self
and of subjective identity depends upon the functioning of linguistic markers such as the pronominal 'I', the very utterance
which, more than any other, appears to express the living presence of the speaker simultaneously confirms his or her poten-
tial absence. Paradoxically, the pronoun 'I' can therefore be
described as 'structurally testamentary' (*VP*, 107). It can be

noted in passing that this is the Derridean, deconstructive rein-scription of Heidegger's *Being-toward-Death*, which constitutes the most intimate, 'ownmost' (*eigenste*) possibility of *Dasein* as that being for which the meaning of being is always in question or at stake. Except that what is at stake in this reinscription is not a mode of being as such but reinscription itself: articulation as iterability.

The name and work of Heidegger are yet another of those 'ghosts' that have constantly haunted Derridean deconstruc-tion from the start. The ghost of Heidegger, no less than that of Joyce, 'is always coming on board' the deconstructive vessel, inflecting its course and imposing its wake. Heidegger plays *Flying Dutchman* to Derrida's *Vaisseau Fantôme*. The very pro-ject of a deconstruction of the Western philosophical tradition is decisively indebted, as Derrida himself has often stated, to Heidegger, who in *Being and Time* describes his own work as a *Destruktion* of Western metaphysics. As always, however, when passing from one language to another, one has to be very care-ful about reading too quickly. In this particular case, it is very easy for an English-speaker to assume that Heidegger's term '*Destruktion*' means simply the same as 'destruction'. The only problem with this assumption is that had Heidegger simply wanted to say 'destruction' in German, he would almost cer-tainly have used a different German word, namely, *Zerstörung*, which is far more common than the latinate word, *Destruktion*. This is a classical example of how the 'meaning' of a word is not necessarily identical with its linguistic 'value', as Saussure emphasized, since the latter is determined first and foremost by the relation of a word to other words, whereas the *meaning* of a word is generally understood referentially, as expressing a meta-linguistic concept. Thus, the fact that Heidegger's use of *Destruktion* entails a concomitant, if implicit, rejection of the word *Zerstörung* argues against simply translating the term by

its English cognate and apparent equivalent, *destruction*, since
the difference between the more common term and the less
common one is thereby lost. Rather, as Heidegger's discussion
of the term in Section 6 of *Sein und Zeit* [*Being and Time*] makes
quite clear, *Destruktion* means something very different from
simple *destruction*:

> If the question of Being is to acquire a certain transparency
> with regard to its own history, what is required is a loosening
> of a congealed tradition and a dissolving of its established con-
> cealments. This task we understand as [...] the *Destruktion* of
> the traditional substance (*Bestand*) of classical ontology *toward*
> the originary experiences in which the initial and hence guid-
> ing determinations of being were attained.[10] [Last italics
> mine—SW]

You will have noticed that the use of *Destruktion* here by
Heidegger is doubly *transitive*. It involves not merely a certain
relation to something that is to be destroyed but also and at
the same time a *movement* 'toward' those 'originary experiences' through which Being was initially determined. A tradition that has congealed and that is now simply taken for
granted is to be cast in a different light, so that the questions of
how it came to be and at what cost it consolidated itself can be
raised. With this in mind, it would be a grave mistake to
understand *Destruktion* as purely or primarily negative or simply destructive:

> The *Destruktion* must not be understood *negatively* as involving
> the doing away with an ontological tradition. On the contrary,

---

10 Heidegger, *Sein und Zeit*, 1953 [My translation, here as elsewhere—SW].
    Being and Time, 1962, §6, 44. Future references are given in the body of the
    text using the abbreviation *BT*.

it seeks to indicate the positive possibilities of this tradition,
which also means placing it within its limits. (*BT*, §6, 44)

The Heideggerian *Destruktion* involves, first of all, a *stripping away* of the petrified premises of an interpretation that has
long since come to *take itself for granted*, in order then to reveal
how such self-evidence, rather than being merely self-identical,
dissimulates a *response to other* 'more originary experiences'
that it has sought to obscure and efface. Thus, Heidegger's
Destruktion involves a process of *delimitation*, in the double
sense of that term. *Destruktion* retraces the *enabling limits* of the
Western approach to being and reveals them to be a boundary
that not only *includes* certain experiences but also *excludes* others—if not, indeed, a certain experience *of* the other. In a
Nietzschean vein, one could say that the Heideggerian
Destruktion strives to reveal how Western metaphysics has
sought to efface that to which it attempts to respond.

In this sense, the Heideggerian *Destruktion* redefines the
notion of *enabling limit* itself. A limit does not simply mark out a
space *within which* something can take place; it does so only by
excluding other possibilities and other questions. Those exclu-
sions, and the alternative possibilities they imply, are what
Heidegger's *Destruktion* seeks to render legible once again.

Despite its name, then, Heideggerian *Destruktion*, like
Derridean *deconstruction*, is not primarily destructive or negative, much less nihilistic: '*Destruktion* does not assume a negative stance towards the past; its critique is aimed at the "today"
and at the prevailing way in which the history of ontology is
treated...' (*BT*, §6, 44).

The implication of such a project of *Destruktion*—that is, of
delimitation—is that the past is neither dead and gone nor simply
alive, waiting to be discovered by an empathetic present. The
implication (already to be found in Hegel) is that the more the

past is taken for granted by the present, the more it blindly determines the future. What might be required in order *not* to take the past for *granted?* First and foremost, it might require the present to rediscover its own *heterogeneity* by becoming more sensitive to the way in which the past exists not merely as a derived form of the present, as a present which 'is' no more, as a *past present.* The past might be approached not simply as a weak or deficient mode of the present but rather as a dimension and function of that iterability which belongs as much to the future as to what we commonly think of as the present. Iterability belongs more to the future and to the past than to the present because it never comes full circle, never comes to rest in a simple, straightforward identity. What iterability entails is not a simple return of the same but a process of alteration and transformation that involves difference no less than identity. For instance, the difference between *Destruktion* and its iteration as *deconstruction.* Derridean deconstruction in a certain sense 'repeats' the Heideggerian *Destruktion,* reinscribes it; but in so doing, it transcribes and alters it, in part deliberately, but also in ways that no deliberation can fully anticipate or control.

The very term, 'iter*ability'*—as distinct from simple iter*ation* or repetition—is constructed, as Derrida reminds his readers, in order to emphasize that what is at stake here is not a self-present reality, not a fact, but a *possibility.* Not just any old possibility, to be sure, but one which 'pertains, *qua possibility,* to the structure of the mark as such' ('LI', 47) and which, in so doing, renders all articulated marks themselves more *possible* than *real,* in the sense of their never being fully, exhaustively and

---

11 It cannot be insisted upon too strongly, however, that such a delimitation of determinability is not simply the 'opposite' of determination, not simply in-determination or indeterminacy. Rather, it always entails an *excess* of concrete determination, an *over-* or *hyper-determinability.*

definitively *determinable*.[11] But it would be more accurate perhaps to say that the very notion of reality is thereby transformed. The 'real' begins to emerge as an *after-effect* of the possible rather than as its actualization or implementation. And
the possible begins to look more like the *origin*—the *Ursprung*,
the primordial *crack*—of the 'real' than like its deficient anticipation. In a Derridean style, one could say that *possibility defers
the real,* instead, as previously thought, of *deferring* to *it* (that is,
submitting to its authority).

Seen in this perspective—which is that of what Derrida calls
différance—iterability splits the mark into a past that can never
be fully rendered present and a future which is always about to
arrive. Past and future are thus no longer construed as a simple
polarity. They overlap. It is *because* the past, through iterability,
can neither be fully excluded from the present nor fully absorbed
into it that there *is* anything like a *future*. For the future *is* that
part of the past that *remains after* any determinate iteration or
repetition. In short, *the future is what remains of the possibility of
the past*. But by virtue of that same dynamics of iterability, the
future itself will only come to be in coming to pass. What is
called the *present* is this *coming-to-pass of the future*.

After Deconstruction, then, far from simply relegating deconstruction to the past once and for all, can also be read as
announcing the future of deconstruction. After deconstruction,
we can no longer read the word 'after' as determining a simple
frontier that could be definitively crossed, a border that might
be left behind or a univocal, irreversible temporal or historical
relationship.[12] If we really, seriously, intend to place ourselves
after deconstruction, we must understand that the frontier that
separates the 'after' from the 'before' is no longer a simple, self-

---

12 On this question of border crossing, see Jacques Derrida, *Aporias*, 1993.

identical line. It is rather the edge of an iterable mark that cuts
both ways. What comes *after* deconstruction is also and simultaneously *placed before it:* placed before the questions it raises
and the ambivalences and ambiguities it retraces. In this sense,
we can say not merely that our situation today is *after deconstruction* but that deconstruction is also *after us.* That does not
mean simply that deconstruction has yet to come, that it has
not yet arrived—although I suspect that Derrida would have
no trouble endorsing both of these assertions (since deconstruction *as such* can never be fully present). Rather, the phrase
'after us' also suggests that deconstruction is *pursuing us.*

It is curious and remarkable how, again and again, what I
have referred to as the ambivalent *graphics of simultaneity,*
which violates the more traditional logic of identity, is far more
thoroughly articulated in spontaneous, colloquial English (or
American) expressions than in professional and technical discourse. Here, the expression 'to be after' makes explicit the etymological, and indeed logical, paradox that what is 'after' is
also and at the same time *behind* and *before...* Everything
depends not simply upon the perspective but upon the *way* in
which one regards the position from which one judges.
Deconstruction suggests that we must learn to look out of two
eyes, not in the same direction but in two different, and indeed
divergent, directions at once. For in being 'behind' us, deconstruction is also and at the same time *after* us: *pursuing us from
behind* but also *waiting for us to leave*—in short: *coming-to-pass.*

We are, then, doubtless *after* deconstruction; but deconstruction is also and no less *after us.* It is *behind* us, but that is
small source of comfort for it is also *before* us, summoning us to
appear *before* it, before the questions it raises, the figures it
traces, the types of readings and writings that seek to negotiate
with the paradoxical 'law' of iterability and to retrace the
strange history it entails. In the wake of deconstruction, we

awaken to the fact that what it names is our *splitting image.* Our title, 'After Deconstruction', challenges us to *recognize* this *split* less as a *loss* than as a *chance*: the chance of opening our discourse and our horizons to what has hitherto been excluded from them. It is the chance that something *else* might still come to pass.

But that 'coming-to-pass' can turn out to be an 'event' of a rather surprising kind, more like a forgetting that haunts us than a memory that we 'have'. In Joyce's other great novel, *Ulysses*, Leopold Bloom is haunted throughout the day by a word that returns, again and again, but whose meaning he can never quite recall. The word is *parallax.* 'After Deconstruction' reminds us that the predicament is not Bloom's alone, since, to vary Hölderlin's celebrated verse, it is not just 'King Oedipus' who has 'one eye too many'.

Deus Ex Media

Interview of Samuel Weber by Cassi Plate on Arts National's weekly film, video and television program *SCREEN*, broadcast July 16, 1992 on Radio National, the Australian Broadcasting Corporation:

Cassi Plate: 1992 marks the centenary of the birth of the German-Jewish philosopher and critic, Walter Benjamin, who, 56 years ago, wrote one of the first major analytical essays about the newly emerging art form—film. This essay, 'The Work of Art in the Age of Mechanical Reproduction', explored the complex phenomenon of mass culture and is still constantly referred to in the area of cultural criticism today. His work was commemorated last month with the visit of an American academic, Professor Samuel Weber, who gave a lecture in Sydney and Melbourne entitled 'Mass Mediauras, or: Art, Aura and Media in the Work of Walter Benjamin'.

The papers last week carried the story of an eight year old child asking his mother if the world was black and white when she was little. 'Why do you ask?', she replied. 'Well, all the pictures of you when you were little are black and white, the old movies are black and white and so is our old TV set. When did the world become coloured?'.

One of the first responses to film in the '30s was the criticism that it was mere distraction, not art. Walter Benjamin on the other hand saw film as opening out and helping us deal with the industrialized world around us.

I asked Samuel Weber about the effect of film on people in its early days...

Samuel Weber: One of its more important effects was to raise questions about the way people perceived the world, or rather, about the way most people *thought—and think*—they perceive the world. Generally, people see the world in terms of sequenced perceptions that they take to be continuous, i.e. causally interrelated. One scene or image or perception is felt to follow more or less necessarily from that which came before it and to lead, with equal necessity, to that which follows. The very term 'world' is generally understood as implying such continuity. In its relatively early stages, film played precisely with such presumptions, showing that they were in fact nothing but suppositions which by no means necessarily corresponded to the reality of the perceptual process. Thus, you might have two successive scenes in a film in which it was raining, and this would lead the viewer to infer that there existed a close temporal or spatial connection between the two scenes such that the second was held to follow more or less immediately upon the first. The inference of such continuity was then shown to be arbitrary, a construction of the perceiver, eager to establish transparently meaningful relations between disparate perceptions. Such constructions thus indicated more about the perceiver than about the perceived. Film, in playing with such inferences, their unreliability but also their symptomatic significance, referred at least implicitly at the same time to its own status as a construction. But what assures us that perception *outside* the film theatre is any less constructed or symptomatic? In its earlier years, film exploited the fact that perception is largely constructed behind the backs of the perceivers, as it were—or should one say rather, behind their *eyes*? There are traditions and conventions of perception, just as there are traditions of thought and other forms of behavior. Film, which itself involved a certain break with traditional art forms (however much it was influenced by them, especially at first), exploited the relatively naive faith placed by many people in the 'objectivity' of their perception of the world.

One of my favorite instances of film calling traditional perceptual certitudes into question can be found in the films of Fritz Lang generally and in his first Hollywood film in particular: *You Only Live Once*. The hero, played by Henry Fonda, is on trial for murder. After the trial is over, there is a scene that begins with a close-up of Fonda's face wreathed in smiles. We immediately infer that he has been acquitted. But the scene goes on, and the camera pulls slowly back to reveal that the face is in fact a photograph on a mock-up front page of a newspaper. Above the photo there is a huge headline announcing Fonda's acquittal. We still believe that we are looking at the result of the verdict, even though we now realize that what we are seeing is a journalistic representation and not reality itself. But as the camera continues to pull back, another face comes into view. Once again, it is that of Fonda, only this time it is scowling. And under it, we read the single word: 'Guilty!'. Finally, as the camera continues its traveling shot, Fonda's face (photo) comes into view for a third time, this time impassive, and above it the headline: 'Hung Jury!'. At last we realize that we have been looking not at reality, or even at a direct representation of it, but at a newsroom wall, where the editor is nervously awaiting the call of his reporter on the scene. We have been looking at three mockups of the front page of a newspaper, ready to go no matter what the result of the trial...

Cassi Plate: The three possible outcomes.

Samuel Weber: Exactly. The film here plays on the fact that the viewer is constrained to supply elements of a context that is not given, is not self-evident; and it shows by implication how much we generally have to take for granted about what is

going on outside our field of vision spatially, but also temporally, and how ready we are to make assumptions concerning
continuities, logical connections and the like—assumptions
that can easily be mistaken.

Cassi Plate: Another significant thing that people commented
on was the fact that film, unlike previous cultural forms,
reached mass audiences and was infinitely reproducible. What
were some of the particular effects of its mass character?

Samuel Weber: One of the things it seemed to do, which was
of particular interest to Walter Benjamin, was to call into question many of the most basic categories that had been used to
study works of art and the aesthetic medium up until the 19th
century—above all, the category of the *original masterwork*. If
we go to museums in order to see the original work of art, the
situation of film is quite different: there is no original in that
sense. From the very beginning, film was made to be reproduced, replicated, distributed and shown in many places at a
time. In this fact Benjamin saw not just a technical change but
a transformation in the attitude toward and experience of what
we call 'art'. By going out and meeting its audience at least
half-way, works of film, photography and the other reproductive media were operating in a way quite different from traditional art works. Their value was no longer identified with their
uniqueness or their originality, or at least not as had been done
previously. It didn't make as much sense, let's say, to try to see
the 'original' of a film as in the case of a painting by
Rembrandt. The relation between original and reproduction
was thus radically altered.

Cassi Plate: So it lost its uniqueness because it was reproducible. But still, film had an incredible, electrifying effect on

the audience. For example, when people would look out a window, they would see a street scene as just a street scene. Put a camera on that street scene, project it on a wall and it somehow has an extra special effect.

Samuel Weber: One of the reasons for that 'special effect' has to do with the difference in the way perception actually proceeds and the way people generally think about it. Perception tends to be taken for granted. We think that we 'open our eyes' more or less the way we open a window to look outside. It's our path to reality; and since we have to depend upon what we see (and hear) in coping with the various challenges and dangers that we must continually confront and anticipate in order to survive, we don't like to think of the process as being any more complex than opening a door or a window. Or as any less reliable. Setting up a camera to film a street scene doubles our own perceptive experience of that scene, but it does so in a way that is rather uncanny. Because we see, or rather, don't see but experience that vision is not something self-evident, that it depends upon a vast apparatus that we don't and can't see and that we therefore cannot easily evaluate, much less control. If you generalize this situation and think about its implications for the way most of us have to relate to reality in our everyday lives, its implications are prodigious—and, I think, unsettling. Film, radio, television—all have this kind of unsettling implication, precisely because they simulate, or reproduce, the process of what we call 'sense-perception', upon which we depend to navigate through our everyday existences.

It is this relationship to our apprehension of reality that distinguishes these media from the more traditional forms of art. Take theatre. Its apparatus and site seem clearly separable from everyday perception. We believe that we can separate its fictions from our realities. In the theatre we see real people acting on a no less real stage, and their reality seems clearly distinguishable from the roles they play. The actors have real names, they are physically present, they wear costumes, there is a stage set. We don't doubt that we know when the representation begins and when it is over. With film, too, there is a separation of the theatre from the 'outside world', but the proximity of its representations to our everyday process of perceiving is such that we can no longer be confident about distinguishing what is fiction, what is supposition, what is construction and what is 'objective reality'.

Thus, film doubles the reality of everyday perception, our visual and auditory perceptions, while at the same time revealing them to be full of suppositions and even projections. This cinematic duplication of reality thus tends to render the latter uncanny: both all too familiar and all too strange. At the same time, what cinema was able to reveal about everyday perception effectively cast doubt on the ability of the latter to serve as a reliable means of controlling reality. You can and do walk out of the darkened film theatre into the light of day, but that light is blinding rather than simply transparent. You still have to rely on your 'own two eyes and ears'. But after having experienced the ways in which film can play games with those senses, their reliability can no longer be taken for granted. This may be a theme that is as old as Western philosophy, but it was surely never as *widespread* as in the age of cinema. Cinematic representation demonstrates that one's bodily senses are not simply one's 'own'. This is why I suspect that film has a structural affinity to uncanny motifs calling into question the integrity of the body and its senses—long before *The Terminator* came along.

Cassi Plate: So in a sense it heightened the subjectivity of people's experience?

Samuel Weber: It heightened the sense of subjectivity, but perhaps even more, it *transformed* it, because prior to film that sense had depended very much on the conviction that the subject could accede to a stable place from which it could 'view', and if necessary 'confront', the challenges of 'reality'. What film tended—and even today still tends, in an ironic way—to thematize is the suspicion not just that such a position may well turn out to be inaccessible to human beings but that the desire or fantasy of acquiring that kind of control may well have very serious and destructive consequences.

Cassi Plate: Was it also that film was coming about at a time, too, when people's lived experience was undergoing extremely rapid change? The world about them was changing very fast; and film seemed to be able to throw that change back at them or reflect the very changes which they were feeling outside the cinema.

Samuel Weber: No doubt. But I would see the phenomenon of 'rapidity' as, in part at least, a temporal correlative of the *overall complexity* that film was revealing to be at work in what for most people had been considered to be a relatively straightforward and reliable process of perception. In order to interpret the data of our senses, we require frames of reference which are not given in those data. We therefore, at every moment, are required to make decisions, to rely upon presumptions or even to invent new ones, and none of this is 'covered' by 'reality', since what we call *reality* is itself a result of those assumptions and the way they enable us to structure the perceptive data. When the relationship between that data—which, as I have already said, is itself not simply 'given' but the materialization of other assumptions and categories—and the interpretive frame required to transform data into perception is no longer self-evident, when it no longer functions in what appears to be a 'spontaneous' manner, then the question of time in turn is no longer self-evident: it emerges, as it were, as a factor to be taken into account on its own. I suspect that this contributed to the sense of 'speed' that was increasingly imposing itself from the mid-19th century on. In addition, of course, the acceleration of the pace of transportation and communication also played a decisive role, as has often been noted. But I mention the first factor because it seems to me to have been less emphasized. Changes in the technology of transportation and communication could only become as powerful as they were by transforming the ways in which perception and self-perception operated. I think that this is important to remember even—and especially—today, if one hopes to understand the power of 'the media' and how it enables them to transform the world.

Cassi Plate: If we move into television, we face a whole new change in the way that people are viewing. Generally speaking, they are viewing television in a much more private space and often individually. What sort of changes has the technology of television brought about? What do they indicate about people's relationship to that medium and the way it is affecting their lives?

Samuel Weber: I would approach that question on the basis of what I have already outlined concerning the changes brought about by film and its relation to what might be called, not without a certain irony, the general 'perception of perception'. If film heightened a sense of the uncanny unreliability of everyday perception and hence of our notion of 'reality', which depends so heavily upon perception, then television (and before it, radio) continued and intensified this tendency. Think of the panic caused by Orson Welles' famous broadcast of *The War of the Worlds* on Halloween of 1938, narrating the arrival of

Martians in New Jersey. With the economic disaster of the Great Depression and the approach of the Second World War, there was reason enough to be anxious—which is a reminder that the media never work in a vacuum but rather exploit, deliberately or not, the existing social environment. But they are particularly effective in manipulating anxiety because of their unsettling effects upon our ways of perceiving the world. With the advent of radio, and then of television, the reliability of our perceptual access to the 'world' tended to become increasingly dubious.

Cassi Plate: Why is that?

Samuel Weber: Because there was even less possibility for an individual to be able to distinguish representation from reality than there had been with film. The idea that there are stable, self-evident limits separating the perception of reality from that of fiction had already been strongly undermined by the cinema. With the coming of radio and television, such a dividing line became even less evident. The television or radio audience can never be entirely certain whether what it is seeing and hearing is a reproduction, and hence potentially fictive, or whether it is 'live'. You must depend upon information that stands in no verifiable relationship to what you are seeing. That is perhaps most uncanny when you hear a program about someone who is dead, and that person's voice is broadcast and is as 'real' sensorially, as 'present', as those who are speaking 'today' and who are alive. You have to take the word of the media about the status of what it is transmitting. You can no longer rely upon the evidence of your 'own' two eyes and ears. Of course, such reliance was always questionable, but never was it as demonstratively so and never did it involve as great a dependence upon a technological-economic apparatus as it does today.

But this is also why all attempts to grasp the effects of the media in terms of a 'global village' miss one very important point, namely, that however much television brings people together, it does so only at the cost of introducing—or confirming—an irreducible distance and separation in all of their relations, not just to each other but to themselves, to their—our—'own' two eyes and ears. And hence, to their—our—'own' bodies. In short, what the media bring closer is a certain separation, a certain distance.

Cassi Plate: It's almost a contradiction in terms. To bring distance closer is not actually making the distance less, it's making us more aware of the distance.

Samuel Weber: More aware in certain ways, less aware in others. The more people depend upon the media for their contacts with the outside world, the stronger the sense of separation and of isolation will be—not simply because of the contents of what is shown on television but because of its equivocal ontological status. If separation and uncertainty are indelible effects of the media, people can react very differently to these effects. Inasmuch as they feel anxiety, people can seek to deny such separation, for instance, or at least its implications. This is, I suspect, one of the reasons that sitcoms, soaps and the like are so popular. By representing 'ordinary people' living average lives and facing familiar problems, they tend to reassure viewers and help them forget the more uncanny aspects of television transmission: the fact that we are dealing with phenomena that are much closer to ghosts and phantoms than to what we think of as 'real' people. Since, however, the 'realness' of people is far more phantasmatic and uncanny than we are generally willing to concede, it is entirely appropriate that the fictional figures of television, dressed up in banal everyday roles, tend to usurp the roles of their 'real-life' counterparts, as the much publicized encounter of Vice President Dan Quayle with 'Murphy Brown' demonstrated.

It is hardly an accident that the new heroes of television should be domestic types. For isn't that one of the distinctive aspects of television, in comparison with film? With cinema we are, or were, still dealing with a collective, public medium. Television, by contrast, is largely a domestic medium, at least in terms of its reception. It has replaced the hearth at and *as* the centre of the household. If we keep in mind the uncanny reality that television transmits, then we can see that the entry of the television set into the home was something like that of the Trojan horse into Troy. At the heart of the most intimate, supposedly most secure sphere of human existence, we find the uncertain reality of the television screen. People don't go out any more to see a film, they watch a video of it at home on their set. Film survives today—to the extent that it survives at all—strictly as an apanage of television, from an economic point of view at least. To be sure, television confronts the domestic household with 'realities' that it could never otherwise have 'seen'; at the same time, however, that 'confrontation' reaffirms the isolated, dependent immobility of the television audience. The television audience 'counts' above all as statistics in the ratings. The fact that television itself takes great pleasure in 'mobilizing' its viewers—whether as charitable donors in telethons, as participants in 'reality shows' (significant enough name!) or as knowledgeable fans of sports or of soaps—is itself a reaction to the fundamentally *immobilizing* influence of the medium.

To sum up my response to your question: I suspect that people are 'aware' of the ambivalent reality of television, but since they are ill-equipped to cope with its more unsettling effects or to exploit its more exhilarating ones, they have a difficult time

finding an alternative to it. And I am not certain that there is
one available, at least not in our societies as presently constituted. This is why the general attitude toward the medium is an
ambivalent mix of familiarity and fear, awe and contempt.

Cassi Plate: Do you think you can use to describe that feeling,
say, the difference in the coverage of the Vietnam War two to
three decades ago and the coverage of the Gulf War? Do you
think we've seen a different relationship to television in the
way that television has presented those two wars?

Samuel Weber: Absolutely. The ambivalent nature of and attitude toward televisual reality can help to indicate some of those
differences. The Vietnam War, as we know— those of us at least
who are old enough to remember the reporting of it—showed,
for example, a great deal of physical destruction, a great deal of
bodily mutilation. The destructiveness of war was brought
home over a period of years in very concrete, bodily terms, however remote those bodies initially were. The military, in planning and executing the Gulf War, learned a great deal from the
problems it ran into during the Vietnam conflict. And much of
what it learned was related to television. The result was that
what we were confronted with in the Gulf War was an event
that, from the very first, was organized with television in mind,
a bit like a show, which is also the way it was presented by the
networks. A show with a beginning, a middle and an end. In
between, there was just enough dramatic tension about the outcome to hold the audience breathless. From the very first, a tight
narrative-dramatic structure was established, as opposed to the
endless meandering of the Vietnam War.

But above all, the Gulf War was organized in such a way as
to exploit the tendency of television to *decorporalize* the vision
that it is transmitting. What television does, as I understand it,

is to transmit not so much images, as people generally think, but rather *vision*, which is something quite different. Television, as the name suggests, transmits the power to see at a distance. But in so doing, it necessarily *detaches* the power of seeing from our experience as individuals who are situated in bodies. What television does is to allow us to participate in an experience of seeing that is not subject to the spatial-temporal limitations of the individual body. One, if not the most important, of these limitations, perhaps even the enabling limit of the body, has to do with its mortality, its finitude. Television, in this sense, is not just the medium of phantoms and of ghosts. It is also that of the Holy Ghost, for what it promises, or appears to demonstrate, is a vision that sees all without being anywhere in particular and which hence is by implication immortal and divine. That's why there is something deeply shocking in viewing a film taken by a cameraman in a war zone who, while shooting, is hit and falls, perhaps even dies. All that is left is a series of images that are suddenly blurred and destabilized. It is a moment of truth, an instant that breaks through the otherwise smooth flow of images; but its shock is immediately transfigured and transformed into mere titillation when the network takes over, rescuing the viewer, as it were, from the encounter with death. The global TV network is thus the manifestation of immortality today, and hence also quite literally the deity of our age.

There is a scene in the reporting of the Gulf War that sums all of this up quite well. It is one of the most vivid scenes of the war, one which television itself foregrounded through incessant repetition. It showed a missile 'homing in' on its target, a cement building, with no windows, apparently some sort of warehouse or bunker. The television camera was situated in the nose of the bomb; it served both to guide the missile to its target and to transmit information and images back to the base and ultimately through the networks to us. So television was part and parcel both of the *event* and of its *transmission and reception* (the latter, of course, comprising one of the most important dimensions of that 'event'). As the missile approached its objective, the target grew larger and larger and became a distinguishable object. One could see a slit in the concrete, and it was precisely this gap that the missile was aiming at. At the moment of impact, the screen went 'dead', i.e. black or grey, for an instant; and then, after a second or so, the television anchorperson reappeared, in the reassuringly familiar network newsroom. The target had presumably been hit and destroyed. But what had been shown was a vague image growing ever more discernible as an object, satisfying the desire of viewers to identify what they were seeing, even if the outcome of such identification was the disappearance, and implied destruction, of the object. And, of course, of whatever was 'behind' it. But that we never saw. When you are invited to play God, you don't want to be worried about such banal terrestrial things as mutilated bodies. *Chi si pasce di cibo celeste, non si pasce di cibo mortale.* The televisual reporting of the Gulf War thus offered its viewers an exhilarating spectacle of 'Command and Control', one that magnified but also repeated the more ordinary gesture of 'zapping' through which the TV viewer demonstrates his or her freedom of choice (and of elimination, as the word also indicates).[1]

Cassi Plate: So in that example we become the camera lens which becomes the bomb, but we never see the mutilated bodies inside once the destruction's happened?

Samuel Weber: That's right. We never see such bodies, but that doesn't mean that they cease to exist. On the contrary,

---

1 For a more elaborate discussion of this episode in the context of the reporting of the Gulf War by U.S. television, see Weber, 'The Media and the War', *Alphabet City*, Summer 1991, reprinted in *Emergences*, 3/4, Fall 1992.

sometimes what we don't see can be all the more *there* for us, precisely because we aren't sure *where* it is. It's hard to tuck something unpleasant away or put it in its proper place once and for all if it can't be found. So the longer-term effects of the reporting of the Gulf War may not be as obvious or as one-sided as one might think. But that has to be left an open question.

Cassi Plate: So we've sort of been turned into a machine even watching that?

Samuel Weber: Into a machine, or rather, into a *deus ex machina*. For the viewer is invited to identify with the power of the military as well as with that of the medium, while at the same time harbouring an uneasy sense about the nature of that power. The televisual apparatus, in all of its ramifications, presents itself as the answer to an anxiety that it both exacerbates and conceals.

Cassi Plate: Do you think that, generally speaking, you're more conscious that there's a person behind the camera in the film process than in the television process?

Samuel Weber: That's a difficult question. In the example that I gave, there *is no one* behind the camera, not directly at least. So that in television, even more than in film, it is technologically possible to separate vision from the individual body. That's why television continues and intensifies what I call the *decorporalization* of vision. This is reflected in the way the Gulf War was fought. It was a *tele-war*, fought quite literally at a distance, with the help of television cameras. That's why you couldn't have anything like Vietnam or *Apocalypse Now* with a war such as that fought in the Gulf, where the adversaries destroy each other at a distance, where tank battles take place with the two sides over 20 miles away from each other. This kind of war is much more like 'zapping' than hand-to-hand combat. Its conduct, and not just the content of its images, is intrinsically *televisual*. Like video games. Tank commanders shoot at each other by means of television, which transmits numbers as much as images.

Cassi Plate: Some of which were wrong when they shot their own tanks.

Samuel Weber: Of course. But they didn't *see that* either. Or not until later, and mostly by proxy.

[Radio sound effects of the Gulf War, fading up]

Cassi Plate: You've been listening to Professor Samuel Weber, who was in Australia recently for a series of lectures.

Catching Up With The Past

A discussion between Samuel Weber and the Weber Reading Group May 25, 1992 in the Power Institute of Fine Arts, University of Sydney:

Andrew Lewis: Let's begin by turning towards the instituting of the Weber Reading Group in the hope that these activities will give this interview some context and direction.

The group was set up ten weeks ago on the basis of a reading of your works, or at least what we could secure of them. As a project it had the aim of presenting you with a set of questions—the document which we have produced and given to you. But, at least in my opinion, the manner in which the group instituted itself did not include sufficient reflection on the process through which this document was produced nor were we able to agree on the future direction of the group. Indeed, at this moment, we are to some extent in disarray.

With hindsight, it appears that these problems accompanied the setting up of the group insofar as there was no attempt to embark upon a reading practice which differed from the 'normal' process in which 'readers' constitute themselves as 'knowers' of texts. Consequently, an authority was taken by some people over your work. Certain voices tended to make themselves heard more than others and excluded others as a result. This surprised and disappointed me given that your work seems to question the very possibility of an authoritative reading. It was this 'expertise' which mobilized an authoritative investment in the name 'deconstruction' that, in a strange turn, excluded others from participating.

Perhaps I could pose an initial set of questions. In your own work how have you encountered this problem of authority and authorship? By this I mean: is there a manner in which texts can be produced so that—regardless of the name under which they proceed—there will arrive with them a persistent questioning and transformation of the institutional practices with which they must engage? Or is any attempt to produce these texts always accompanied by the possibility—as we seemed to have discovered—that they can participate in this complicity between interpretation, authority and exclusion?

Samuel Weber: That is, of course, a very difficult question, one that I have struggled with for some time, even before I had ever heard of deconstruction. As a graduate student in the mid-'60s, I made something of a pilgrimage to Frankfurt, which was known at the time as the capital of the 'antiauthoritarian' movement of 'critical theory'. What I discovered there, however, was a traditionally organized, highly hierarchical system of teaching and research. I remember being shocked at a seminar on Nietzsche given by a young professor who was one of the brightest pupils of Adorno and Horkheimer. This very gifted disciple of 'critical theory' went through Nietzsche's text with a red pencil, as it were, separating what was good and critical from what was bad and apologetic. The seminars themselves were on a very high level but conducted in a way that left little room for any questioning of the premises of Frankfurt 'School' critical theory. At the time, I had little sympathy for Anglo-American philosophy of language and logic; but I must say that I felt embarrassed when a student who was attempting to present a paper on the subject wasn't allowed to proceed beyond the opening paragraph. Adorno insisted that its premises were loaded (which they undoubtedly were) and hence that there was no point in going any further before they had been

thoroughly discussed and dealt with. The only problem was
that the discussion of those premises took up the entire seminar. Thus, students were never confronted with the arguments
themselves but only with their opening premises and above all,
with the professor's critique of those premises. At one point
during my stay in Frankfurt, I challenged Adorno about what I
felt was a rather stifling and doctrinaire atmosphere. As a for-
eigner who had come a long way to translate his work, Adorno
granted me a degree of leeway that few of his German students
enjoyed (or probably expected). I had nothing to lose since he
was very happy that his work was finally being translated into
English by persons who had read some Hegel and Marx and
who took seriously the philosophical tradition to which he was
profoundly indebted. I asked him if he wasn't concerned about
the fact that his students didn't seem to consider it necessary to
read seriously the authors they criticized—Heidegger and
Husserl, for instance—to go to their texts with anything like an
open mind but rather seemed willing to rely extensively on
Adorno's critique of them. He reflected for a moment and
replied—at least as I remember it today—that they couldn't
read everything and that if a choice had to be made, it was better that they should spend their time reading him. I was very
disappointed by this reply and told him so. Here was a thinker
who had dedicated his work to a critique of authoritarian
behaviour and to the development of critical thinking and yet
whose institutional practice tended to reproduce at least certain of those very same authoritarian attitudes.

   Now, to a degree some constitution of authority is
inevitable, no matter how critical, questioning or deconstructive one tries to be or become. The question therefore is never
one of an absolute 'either-or' but of the *relation* of authority and
its establishment to the process by which it is brought forth and
consolidated, 'institutionalized', if you like. Thus, one could say

that the work of Adorno and Horkheimer on the one hand and Derrida and Heidegger on the other involves the more or less deliberate attempt of thinking to look over its shoulder, as it were, to hold itself open to its heterogeneity, to sensitize itself to the fact that it depends upon an alterity that is neither its property nor simply its negation. The difference, however, is that, whereas Horkheimer and Adorno insisted on construing this other in largely Hegelian terms, as the *negative determination* of the *concept* or of *identity*—'the nonidentical' is what Adorno called it in his later work—the Heideggerian, and even more the Derridean, notion of 'difference' implies a structure of language and a process of articulation that includes a practical, performative moment which, I am convinced, is where one has to start—and probably end—if one is to respond to the trace of the other, to that dimension of alterity to which thinking is so profoundly indebted.

I didn't always think this way. I remember reacting to Roland Barthes' introduction to *Signes*—my first encounter with Structuralism and with Semiotics—with impatience and annoyance at what I felt to be an overly self-satisfied and arid formalism. However, at the same time that I was experiencing what I and many others felt was the theoretical and political dead end of the Frankfurt School of Critical Theory, I was also discovering the work of Derrida and of Lacan, which appeared to me to open more promising avenues by foregrounding the question of language, theoretically but also performatively. Whereas the style of Adorno was also highly performative, it was a virtuoso performance in the creation of highly complex meanings. Derrida and Lacan, on the other hand, demonstrated through their styles of writing and reading that the condition of meaning involved a certain suspension or interruption of meaning itself. The underlying problem of the Frankfurt School of Critical Theory, as I saw it then and as I still see it today, is not, as has often been alleged, that it developed a *theo-retical critique* of society but was unable to elaborate the *political strategy* required to implement the social changes implied in its critique. This was surely true, but it was not specific to the Frankfurt School. The problem was precisely that it was con-tent to be defined as a 'School'—which is another way of say-ing that it failed to take sufficient account of the conditions and implications of its own theoretical practice and its situation as a research and teaching institution occupying a determinate place in German society. It was this failure—part of the her-itage of a certain neo-Hegelian, Marxist universalism—that blunted the critical thrust of the Frankfurt School and rendered its social and theoretical analyses *abstract*, in the very concrete sense of being *detached* from their particular practice and situa-tion, which, when they were considered at all, were construed in pragmatic terms rather than as an essential constituent of the theoretical work to be performed.[1]

But such abstraction was not limited to the neo-Hegelian, neo-Marxist Critical Theory of Adorno and Horkheimer. It was, in a paradoxical way, also characteristic of thinkers far more directly concerned with institutional questions, such as Michel Foucault and Pierre Bourdieu. The distinction between their work and that of Derrida or Lacan, for instance—but also that

---

1   Characteristic of this approach to the question of the institution is a talk from 1953, entitled *'Individuum und Organisation'* [Individual and Organisation], in Theodor W. Adorno, *Soziologische Schriften*, I, 1979, 440-456. Despite his warnings against tendencies to 'hypostasize' the historical determination of 'organisations' into eternal and static anthropological givens, Adorno him-self treats the 'organisation' as essentially an entity rather than as a process. This is one of the reasons why neither the notion of institution nor that of *institutionalization* plays a significant role in his social theory—although such a role would by no means be incompatible with many aspects of Adorno's critique of the logic of identity, as it is elaborated beginning with the *Dialectics of Enlightenment* and culminating in his *Negative Dialectics*.

of Paul de Man—is that the latter three approached questions of power and of authority through their particular practices of writing, which in turn involved a problematizing of established discursive strategies and conventions. This is one of the major reasons why Derrida, Lacan, Heidegger and, in a different way, de Man are all difficult to read, whereas the writings of Foucault are more easily assimilated. For however extensively power relations are thematized and challenged in his work, his writing itself remains largely within the parameters of conventional academic discourse and hence does not disturb such relations in their most immediate form: that of linguistic articulation. By contrast, the tendency in Derrida's writings is to foreground increasingly the performative aspects of writing and reading, in order to demonstrate how relations of force establish themselves first and foremost through symbolic practices, including, above all, the ways we read, interpret and articulate those interpretations. And the 'we' in Derrida's work—in which, as with Adorno, by the way, the first person plural pronoun is never used in a naive, self-evident manner—is always related to an historically specific set of institutions or practices, beginning with those that situate and make possible his own work: the institution of the teaching of philosophy in France, its relation to the Ecole Normale Supérieure, to Hegel through Victor Cousin, etc. (See in this context Derrida's 'The Age of Hegel', in *Glyph* 9: *Demarcating the Disciplines*, 1985.)

In this way, I began to envisage an alternative approach to the question of authority from that which I had encountered in the Critical Theory of the 'antiauthoritarian' Frankfurt School. And although it is easy enough to demonstrate that no one approach will ever entirely eliminate the aporias of authority, the deconstructive-rhetorical-performative strategy I have described seems to articulate those aporias in a manner that opens the way to further analysis and transformation.

Perhaps...

Alan Cholodenko: Following on from what you've said, Professor Weber, my question is: do you see Foucault as setting up a totalized and totalizing field of institutional power from which he would wish to set himself apart but of which he is at the same time inescapably a part, a part uninterrogated by him?

Samuel Weber: That is a very good description of what I find problematic in his work, which in a way is the same problem I found in Adorno's, namely, that it addresses the connection between discursive and disciplinary or institutional practice largely at the level of *theme* or *content* but not through what might be called a *reflective-performative problematization* of its own discourse. Foucault gives us path-breaking analyses of the relations of power and discourse but in a style of writing that does not, as far as I can tell, put its own relation *qua writing* to that power sufficiently into question. Perhaps Foucault sensed this, and that was one reason why he reacted so allergically to Derrida's emphasis on this very question. At any rate, his ill-tempered and short-sighted attempt to disqualify the problem of textuality as 'lowly pedagogy' (*petite pédagogie*) in the introduction to the Japanese translation of *Madness and Civilization* seems symptomatic of his inability or unwillingness to take seriously the implications of writing as an inevitable and significant site of the power plays with which he is concerned. This is all the more regrettable insofar as such implications are by and large consonant with many of the major themes of his work.

There was a similar resistance in the work of the Frankfurt School, although in some ways it went even further, since it included not merely the process of articulation, 'writing', but also its institutional implications and conditions. As I have already suggested, the term 'institution' did not belong to the basic vocabulary of Frankfurt School Critical Theory, which at best dealt with the problems of 'organisation'. The analysis of institutions, of their structure and history as well as of *institutionalization* as such, was left to the very 'positivists' that Adorno otherwise bitterly attacked and who he rightly felt dominated the 'institution' of German academic sociology. But Lukàcs' argument in *History and Class Consciousness*—that questions of organization (and hence of institutions) ought to be treated with the same stringency and incisiveness as the more familiar theoretical questions—never succeeded in imposing itself upon the macrological, world-historical perspective of neo-Marxism. It was as though there was a fear of getting bogged down in the rather prosaic details of the everyday struggle for power and thus losing a clear over-view of its general tendencies. This is a neglect for which Marxism has paid dearly. The Frankfurt School of Adorno and Horkheimer produced many remarkable analyses—of automation and anti-semitism, of the working class and the middle class—but there was very little reflection upon the institutional history and conditions under which the Frankfurt School itself operated. It was as if notions such as 'fascism' and 'liberalism' precluded microscopic analyses of institutional and disciplinary histories, structures and practices. And apart from Adorno himself, there was little sense of language being an integral part and medium of such problems.

That has been the contribution of Derrida, Lacan and Foucault, in differing ways, of course. What has always impressed me about their approach to this question, despite all the important differences, is that it does not permit the problem to be formulated in terms of an 'either-or'. The alternative can never be simply that of 'authority' versus 'non-authority'. I see this other alternative developed in a most interesting way in

Derrida's essay on Freud and *Beyond the Pleasure Principle*, 'Spéculer—sur "Freud"',[2] which retraces a scenario or strategy of 'making a name' for oneself: Freud making a name for himself, although it is a pseudonym, one which confuses genre and species, as it were—'psychoanalysis'. But of course one could say similar things about the noun 'deconstruction', and that is precisely the point. What is distinctive of Derrida's writing, there and elsewhere, is that it *does* what it *describes* and describes what it does, but in a way that keeps open the dimension of alterity to which I referred. For what he is doing, first and foremost, is describing or retracing a network composed of texts which turn out to be neither entirely separate from his own text nor simply a projection of it. Rather, the 'object' texts are reinscribed in a way that reveals aspects of their significance that in turn reflect (back upon) the staging to which they have been submitted. Properly read, in other words, the deconstructive reading works both ways: it reveals the alterity not merely of the texts being read but the text that is doing the reading. This puts a certain burden on the reader, since s/he is placed at the epicenter of a double bind, in which it becomes highly dubious as to whether an ultimate or definitive separation can be made between the texts engaged in the reading process.

This does not lead, however, to any sort of antiauthoritarian pathos but rather to what I would describe as the *exploration of how authority strives to impose and to consolidate itself* and how language both makes this possible and limits its success. Derrida himself has, of course, acquired considerable authority through his articulation of such readings; yet the peculiar strength of this authority—as well as of the reactions it elicits!—has to do with

---

2   Derrida, *La carte postale: De Socrate à Freud et au-delà*, 1980.

the way that his texts demonstrate—and indeed, sometimes even flaunt—the *singular* character of all authority, however general or universal the validity that it may claim for itself. The demonstration of such singularity occurs in a manner that is never entirely predictable. If a text by Derrida, or any text for that matter, is largely predictable, then it isn't very interesting. Such predictability is not easy to avoid, particularly for original and powerful thinkers, as paradoxical as that may sound, for they can easily be entrapped by the very strength of their own discoveries. This became a problem for Adorno in later years. By contrast, Derrida's work is constantly surprising me. I am surprised that he is able, by and large, to resist the kind of 'entropy' which is the other side of a certain 'consistency'. Nobody can or should want to avoid that entirely; but if you are not able to reconcile consistency with surprise, even with wonder, then you are in trouble. It's the same situation as with jokes: if the punch line gives itself away then there's not much left to laugh about. I know there are those who claim that deconstructive readings in general and Derrida's in particular always wind up with 'the same conclusions'. I think this reproach is often a projection. What it does is to make a *general claim* that leaves no place for singularity—i.e. '*all* deconstructive readings say the same thing'—and then ascribes such generality *a priori* to texts it therefore need not read. The test is always in the attention to *detail* since if singularities resist universalizing subsumption, they will be found not in general propositions but in minute and ostensibly insignificant details. This is perhaps why there is such rancor and resistance directed against microscopic textual analysis, which refuses to jump either on bandwagons or to conclusions.

Another important insight in regard to the question of authority, for me at least, has been the Lacanian theory of the *sujet supposé savoir* and of the narcissism to which it is related.

Once it is formulated in such terms, one realizes that what psychoanalysis calls 'transference' is by no means restricted to the analytical situation, although it operates in psychoanalysis in a way that generally does not obtain outside. The linking of knowledge, of *savoir*, with 'supposition' and 'subjectivity' is a line of thought that undoubtedly derives from Heidegger; and it opens up possibilities of analysis that have still to be explored, much less exhausted. Here again it turns out that the neo-Marxist critique, at least insofar as it is neo-Hegelian in inspiration, may be too shortsighted. Adorno's critique of modernity, and indeed of Western history as a whole, focused upon the 'constitutive subject' as the paradigmatic, albeit ambiguous, category responsible for the 'dialectics of enlightenment'— which is to say, both for its tendency toward emancipation and autonomy and for its inclination to subordinate all alterity to itself. Adorno, however, did not consider the category of subjectivity as such to be the problem but rather a certain interpretation of it, against which he sought to elaborate an alternative that would be more open to heterogeneity and less obsessed with appropriation. The Heideggerian analysis, by contrast, argues that the modern notion of subjectivity is itself part and parcel of the project of command and control, of controlling alterity and rendering it calculable, and that therefore it cannot serve as a point of departure for construing effective alternatives. These questions are, of course, far from settled, even and especially today; but I think that the most fruitful discussions of authority and institutionalization will have to come to grips with this debate, an encounter which up to now has largely been supplanted by polemics, whose sterility is generally in direct proportion to their volume.

Patrick Crogan: Is not the fact that Derrida has not been named to the Collège de France evidence of a certain resistance to his work there and for reasons that you have been indicating?

Samuel Weber: Certainly, it is a rather striking fact. One could also mention Deleuze in this respect. Those thinkers who are well known abroad are not necessarily honoured in their home countries. Indeed, a certain international celebrity is often cited as the symptom of a lack of seriousness, and not just in France nor only in regard to Derrida. Concerning the particular resistance to his work, which has recently taken on such spectacular forms, it is interesting to observe that, whereas in the United States Foucault has been assimilated rather easily into the academic establishment, both Derrida and Lacan have not—or rather, where they have been received, they—or those responsible for such reception—have provoked very strong reactions of rejection. The ultimate reason for this, I am convinced, is, as I have suggested, that their writing problematizes practically, performatively, immediately—and not just thematically—the accepted norms of academic discourse. And this is why you often encounter the charge of 'charlatanry' in regard to both Derrida and Lacan. Or, more politely, the reproach of a lack of 'seriousness'. Why? Because it is not considered 'serious' to use language as anything other than an instrument for the communication of meaning. What turns out to be at issue in this kind of reproach is a certain conception—usually implicit and presupposed—of the relation of knowledge and language. To insist on the performative dimension of language as a condition of its constative-cognitive operation is to call into question generally accepted norms of 'scholarship'. As a result, many in the academy—but also many outside who are in profound complicity with its division of labor—react more or less violently.

Cameron Tonkin: Professor Weber, could I ask you then a

more specific question to do with the setting up of institutions and the example provided by the Collège International de Philosophie. Do you think that there is a possibility of instituting, as I believe Derrida attempted to do with documents such as his 'Sendoffs', a certain necessity for self-reflection on institutionalization to maintain the institution at its moment of instituting? This is the problem that we were having with the reading group, as Andrew mentioned at the beginning of this discussion. Is it simply a matter of individual vigilance or is there some structural component by which...

Samuel Weber: The problem is already evident in your question: what can it mean 'to maintain the institution at *its* moment of instituting'? If you 'maintain' it, then it is no longer 'at *its* moment of instituting', which is, precisely, a *moment* of *transition*, in which something that was not there before emerges. Can a moment of emergence be *maintained*? Most recent historical attempts at 'permanent revolution' are not, one must admit, very encouraging. However that may be, even apart from historical evidence, already at the most speculative level your question folds back upon itself, as it were, and new questions (or old ones) reemerge in its folds.

When we speak of 'institutions', we are speaking not of a purely speculative situation but of determinate—and determined!—*relations of forces*, which set the scene for the move from the state of a project or a proposal to that of a more stable structure. That structure must negotiate with the existing state of affairs, since any sort of institutional 'maintenance' requires means; and these are never given easily or without conditions. In the case of the Collège International de Philosophie, one of its founding principles was that it was to have a rotating membership in order to avoid the kind of bureaucratization and inbreeding so characteristic of institutions with permanent members. Another principle, embodied in its name, was that it was to have an international, i.e. not simply French, composition and scope. The first aspect, that of rotating three-year researchers, was preserved to an extent, although there are a number of 'program directors' who seem to have become more or less permanent fixtures there. The second aspect was more difficult to realize, because it required financial means that the Collège has never been able to secure. A third aspect, this time more purely French, was achieved; it is of considerable importance, although hardly 'revolutionary': release time for a limited number of philosophy teachers working in the *lycée*—and this is the primary professional goal for most students majoring in philosophy—permitting them to pursue research interests rather than simply preparing students to take state teaching exams. This certainly does not entail a major restructuring of French educational or cultural institutions, nor might it seem very significant outside of France. But it does constitute a considerable achievement and one that continues to arouse much envy and hostility within the country, as you can well imagine.

Thus, the Collège is attempting to open up and maintain new spaces in the interstices of existing institutions, such as the system of secondary education, on an extremely small scale, to be sure. Yet this has allowed certain projects to be undertaken which otherwise would have had a very hard time existing within the established French academic division of labor. That was one of its guiding ideas, and on a modest scale it continues to pursue those objectives. Otherwise, it is not at all marked by any one school of thought or approach; and the notion of inter-disciplinarity that it embodies no longer seems particularly indebted to the work of either Derrida or Lyotard, both of whom were active in its early days. We seem to be moving into a period when there are fewer 'heroic' intellectual authority figures than during the past few decades. Part of that gap is made up, in appearance at least, by media figures, intellectuals who owe the main part of their celebrity to the ongoing need of the media to produce 'stars' and events in order to sell programs, publications, etc. In general, however, there seems to be a resurgence of traditional forms of discourse, even where what is being addressed claims to be new, critical and even subversive.

This is why there is all the more reason to study and ponder the writing experiments practiced by Derrida, Lacan, de Man. Such experiments are never simply narcissistic gestures but on the contrary deliberate efforts to open up access to a dimension of alterity that is otherwise all too easily effaced and appropriated or instrumentalized by the unquestioned use of established forms of cognitive discourse.

Andrew Lewis: Even in courses that are actually teaching Derrida, there is a way of teaching his work that is simply spreading information about it rather than allowing the students to perform Derrida in their own work.

Samuel Weber: But what would it mean to perform Derrida? Do you perform his work the way you perform a piece of music? Or a play? That is certainly not to be entirely excluded. Yet however much I stress, here and elsewhere, the extent to which deconstructive writing calls established cognitive discourse and its premises into question, I would still hesitate to describe the 'appropriate' relation to Derrida's texts strictly in terms of 'performance' (even though it is already a *contresens* to speak of an 'appropriate' relationship here). The problem with performance is that Derrida's writings are themselves already quite performative. Can a performance be re-performed?

Perhaps the difficulties here explain in part why I find de Man's insistence on *reading* as allegory and as aporia both salutary and helpful. Whatever forms deconstruction may take, it will always have to involve strong and subtle practices of reading. This is why I think that, whatever its shortcomings may have been, the Anglo-American tradition of 'close reading' had at the very least the virtue of sensitizing students to the complexities of language and to the importance of opening oneself to its heterogeneity. De Man's essay on 'The Resistance to Theory' and his earlier text on 'The Impasse of Formalist Criticism' describe this tradition very well. The pedagogy of close reading is also in no small part responsible for the reception accorded deconstruction in the United States. So much criticism has been directed at this tradition in recent years that it is time to affirm its prescience. In areas where it does not exist or where its influence is much weaker, for instance, in Germany—but also, perhaps surprisingly, in France—the reception of deconstructive styles of writing has taken place largely outside of departments of literature, with very different results. In Germany, it has been received less as a practice of reading than as a general theory of culture or society, which it certainly isn't and has never claimed to be—a significant difference with respect to theories of 'postmodernism'—notwithstanding the fact that it has important implications for our understanding of such phenomena. This is why the work of de Man, for whom the resistance *to* theory is also, and probably above all, the resistance *of* theory to its other, i.e. to reading and to language, constitutes an important supplement to, and even a corrective of, a certain 'theoreticist' reading of Derrida which would reduce his writings to a series of general pronouncements.

De Man's own relation to Derrida is interesting in this regard. De Man was one of the first to recognize the extraordinary importance of Derrida's work, even before it began appearing in book form. I doubt if you can be fully aware of the self-abnegation it must have required for de Man to salute Derrida as someone whose work was going to change the

entire intellectual scene, something he told me before I had
ever heard of Derrida. De Man himself had long been working
on many of the same texts discussed in *Of Grammatology*
(Rousseau) or 'The Double Session' (Mallarmé), with Heidegger
in the background of it all. And it must have been very difficult
for him to acknowledge that Derrida had achieved something
very close to what he, de Man, had been striving for many
years to attain. It certainly could not have been easy to do; but
de Man did not, and probably could not, hesitate in recognizing
the significance of Derrida's work. At the same time, however,
he also had certain reservations, which he tried to articulate in
an article on the *Grammatology*, published in *Blindness and
Insight*, in which he warned against the temptation of a too
teleological, too straightforwardly narrative reading of
Rousseau, one which would assimilate his work too onesidedly
to the age that, according to de Man, Rousseau had already
powerfully begun to deconstruct. Although at the time I wasn't
certain what to make of this article, as the years pass it looks
better and better to me. Not so much because it was 'right'
about certain aspects of Derrida's reading of Rousseau—I am
not sure that it was—but because it implicitly raises questions
that Derrida himself would later go on to address concerning
the status of the *proper name* (for instance, that of 'Rousseau')
and of *narrative* in regard to deconstructive readings such as
those gathered in *De la grammatologie*. The writings of de Man
and Derrida are complementary in very suggestive ways. When
you read a text by Derrida, you can be sure, contrary to the
polemics of those eager to find a pretext not to read him, that it
is never *n'importe quoi*. Everything is calculated, deliberate. You
may not like the way it is constructed, but it is carefully,
scrupulously organized. Even and especially when it looks as
though it is almost 'off the cuff', or when it seems to be a more
or less direct transcription of oral instruction. Derrida is a per-

fectionist and a strategist, and in his work very little is left to chance. In the case of de Man's writing, the situation is not as clear. It reminds me in certain ways of Lacan, whose work undoubtedly had an increasing influence on de Man (think of his late essay on Kleist, in which the theme of mutilation is of particular importance). I have long felt that de Man, in his practice as teacher and as writer, was the most Lacanian, or Freudian, or psychoanalytic of literary critics. Not explicitly, of course, but in his use of authority, in his tendency to multiply apodictic statements in a way that undermined the absoluteness of the claims they seemed to be making. His work and his person exuded the most powerful authority while—or by—at the same time calling all authority, including his own, into question.

The power of this performance and of its double bind explains in part why he has become an object of such fascination and of such bitter polemics. As Lacan says somewhere, you don't expose yourself persistently to phenomena of transference and escape unscathed. De Man's writings increasingly inscribed themselves in a transferential scenario which deeply unsettled the decorous humanism of the literary culture that has dominated a certain segment of intellectual life in the United States for over fifty years. That is why publications such as *The New York Review of Books* and *The New York Times Sunday Book Review* have expended so much time and energy attempting to disqualify his work and its legacy.

If Lacan's writing has been compared to Gòngora or to Mallarmé, de Man could be likened to Kafka: the difficulty is in understanding not the phrases taken separately but rather how they fit together. And yet common to all three of the figures we have been discussing—Derrida, de Man and Lacan—is an awareness of the fact that the question of authority can never be posed in a vacuum and that any attempt simply to deny its intricate ramifications only contributes to its power. The question therefore is more one of how authority is imposed, staged, put into play—including our relationship to it—than of how it might be done away with, purely and simply. As always, the temptation of finding 'pure and simple' solutions to problems may satisfy the impatient, but it rarely opens up anything. On the contrary: it closes down and shuts out. That is precisely why its appeal is so strong, so lasting. In deliberate, calculated staging, on the other hand, there is less of a tendency to 'act out' in the psychoanalytical sense of the term. The essence of acting out is precisely the refusal to acknowledge repetition, the refusal to 'rehearse' (in French, of course, *répétition* also means rehearsal). In acting out, something is repeated as though it were actually present. The historical dimension of repetition, of representation, is repressed or excluded in an attempt to be fully present once and for all. So to the extent that a certain sense of theatricality or even of parody[3] is kept alive, the question of authority too is kept open.

Matthew Holt: In a sense, you still seem to be holding onto, or rather 'acting out', a Platonic, 'moral' opposition between 'good' and 'bad' mimesis, that is, you appear to be suggesting that there are certain 'correct' ways of 'putting authority into play'. Isn't that just repeating...

Samuel Weber: I don't think so. What I am arguing is that you *cannot* simply separate good mimesis from bad. Mimesis is good and bad at the same time. That's why it's 'bad', why it has been considered with suspicion by moral philosophers from

---

3 I have explored the significance of parody and of the parodic for Derrida in an essay, 'La surenchère—Upping the Ante', in Maire-Louis Mallet *et al.*, *Passage des frontières*, 1994. In English as 'Upping the Ante: Deconstruction as Parodic Practice', in *Deconstruction Is/In America*, 1995.

Plato on. Because mimesis doesn't allow the Bad to be separated from the Good in anything like a binary opposition. This is
why I would resist any such attempt to establish a polarity
between two forms or approaches to mimesis. Lacoue-
Labarthe's work on 'mimetologism' and mimesis is very illuminating in this respect. He has used the notion to reinterpret the
entire history of Western thought.

Cameron Tonkin: To that extent Lacoue-Labarthe and Jean-
Luc Nancy seem to be more Heideggerian than Derridean in
that they privilege, as Heidegger privileges a history of being, a
history of mimesis.

Samuel Weber: Yes, their notion of history seems more traditionally Heideggerian than that of Derrida. But it would be
hasty to simply identify Nancy and Lacoue-Labarthe. Even
though they have published many texts together, they still
have different concerns. In recent texts Lacoue-Labarthe has
organized his work very much around the notion of 'mimetologism' and mimesis, whereas Nancy has tried to elaborate upon
a certain number of Heideggerian themes such as 'freedom',
'resoluteness' and related concerns. Nancy has also tended to
experiment with different styles of writing, which, to my
knowledge, Lacoue-Labarthe has not yet done. The task of
developing such styles remains one of the most powerful challenges of the Nietzschean, Heideggerian and Derridean foregrounding of the performative dimension of language. One of
the primary questions they confront us with is: to what extent
can, and should, new, alternative 'styles' of articulation be
elaborated?

Cameron Tonkin: Professor Weber, may I then ask a question
less about the articulation of such 'styles' than about their

reception. I was wondering about the controversy that arose after de Man's death and specifically about the necessity of an institution to explicitly negotiate its relation to the social, especially when such wilful misreadings as happened in de Man's case occur. Obviously, there isn't any structural guarantee against misreadings in and by the press. But if there is no way to stop it, how should this be negotiated?

Samuel Weber: It has to be negotiated with the means available. In this particular case, those means are unfortunately quite limited; and part of the purpose of the 'wilful misreading' of de Man's work is precisely to justify that limitation and to heighten it if possible. Concerning the subject of deconstruction generally and de Man in particular, it has for a long time now been practically impossible for anything but the most viciously simplistic sort of polemics, masquerading as moralizing, to be published in *The New York Review of Books* or *The New York Times Sunday Book Review*. Any text even remotely informed about deconstruction, willing to engage its complexities, is simply not 'fit to print' as far as those two publications are concerned. The discovery of de Man's collaborationist articles provided a welcome occasion to continue and to justify such practices of censorship and to intensify a campaign that had been underway in those reviews and elsewhere for many years *before* those articles came to light. It is unfortunate that in the United States there are, apart from these two publications, relatively few journals that reach beyond the specialized disciplines, beyond the academy, to attain a more general 'literate' public. The purpose of the press campaign was, and is, to delegitimize deconstruction within the university as well as outside it. It is essential to analyze the situation in which such polemics, such misreadings, occur and to disseminate such analyses as much as possible. The extremely abstract and self-serving moralism that masquerades as historical or political analysis in many of these more recent polemics has to be taken seriously and analyzed as a symptom. The pleasure in playing judge and pronouncing verdicts, the barely concealed joy of being able to condemn unqualifiedly, the relief at no longer feeling obligated to read writings that precisely problematize such joys and desires—these are gestures that require analysis and discussion. By 'discussion', however, I mean something other than the kind of debating society style often practiced in the English-speaking world. I think one has to get away from the idea of 'convincing' people of one thing or another and think more in terms of articulating genuine questions and problems and responding to them. 'Negotiation' does not go on in a vacuum or in a context defined by two adversaries. Rather, it presupposes highly particular situations that reflect more complex relations of power. The analysis of writing and speech in *Of Grammatology*, for instance, is concerned more with the distribution of power than with self-contained entities or phenomena. That's why the 'Of' is there in the title and why *Of Grammatology* is not simply the effort to construct a new and better grammatology.

Now in attempting to analyze a situation, where does one begin? You begin, as Peirce says, there where you're at. In some sense, that says it all. The problem, of course, is finding out just *where* you *are* at. To do that completely you would have to be God. Since it isn't easy to be God, one generally prefers to *play* at being God, and for this one doesn't have to be at all consciously religious—in fact, it undoubtedly helps not to be. The traditional notion of truth as *adequatio intellectus et rei*, for instance, a notion that underlies our equally traditional conception of knowledge, is arguably a secularized, worldy version of the divine. As long as knowing seems a self-evident category for us—as long as we believe in grammar, as Nietzsche

put it—God is not dead. This is why one of the most interesting
issues to emerge in recent years—to reemerge—has been the
question of *decision*. And this is also why it took thinkers deeply
immersed in the history and problems of Christian theology—
Kierkegaard, and then Carl Schmitt and Heidegger—to demonstrate its significance. 'Decision' is the name which comes to
designate the mysterious, enigmatic process by which general
rules, laws and concepts are 'applied' to individual events.
Originally a legal thinker, Schmitt was fascinated by the
process through which judges arrive at verdicts. Like Kant in
the Third Critique, he wondered whether there was any general system or principle that guaranteed the applicability of laws
to particular *cases*, given the inexhaustible and unpredictable
heterogeneity of the 'real' world. And, like Kant, he came up
with a response that was far more problematic than he himself
realized: what he called 'decision'. In deciding, there is a leap
from what is known and general to what is unknown and singular. This leap or gap can be more or less obvious, but it is
always there. Kierkegaard called it a 'moment of madness'; and
Schmitt tried to construct a systematic theory of jurisprudence,
and indeed of political sovereignty, upon it. Reading his texts,
it's sometimes hard to 'decide' whether he has succeeded in
theorizing madness or whether the theory itself has gone mad.
Doubtless a bit of both, and for good reason. This is why it is so
necessary, but also so difficult, to negotiate with lucidity.
Nevertheless, when you negotiate, you should always do your
best to 'examine' the situation in which you find yourself as
carefully and as thoroughly as possible in view of the power
relations it entails, the tendencies and resistances at work.
None of this, however, will ever entirely eliminate that leap of
decision—Mallarmé's *coup de dès*—that both traverses and
opens the 'hermeneutic circle' to alterity and to chance.

    What this implies is, among other things, that students

such as yourselves would do well to learn how to deal with such conflict situations as effectively as possible, not just out of pragmatic considerations but because such pragmatic factors are themselves necessarily constitutive of any performance, in the strong sense of the term. And, as has often been observed, deconstructive reading and writing must be particularly attentive to their own performative—or transformative—dimension. Graduate students tend either to ignore this aspect of their profession or to treat it in a merely instrumental manner. They should, however, learn to see this as a challenge to develop rhetorically aware strategies of reading and writing that would be neither metatheoretical nor narrowly practical. When I say 'strategies', to be sure, I don't mean a simple synonym for 'methods' but rather ways of ferreting out the singularity of a situation or an event, be it a 'text' in the conventional sense or another kind of happening. It is precisely the degree to which writers succeed in achieving such singularity that determines the transformative power of their texts. Again, the writings of Derrida and of de Man seem to me exemplary in this regard, although by no means unique.

Freida Riggs: Professor Weber, you've been describing to us Derrida's work and what we should strive for. Could you tell us how you place yourself in terms of that work and what 'decisions' you have taken in relation to it?

Samuel Weber: I have never had enough distance from my work to feel very confident or comfortable speaking about it. All the more so in the case of the question of 'decisions' that may have affected it. You notice that I hesitate to say 'made', because I am not certain that we really 'make' or 'take' decisions. I think it more likely that they make or take *us* in certain directions, the important ones at least. But one memory that comes to mind in response to your question is my initial reaction to the first text of Adorno that I read, or rather tried to read, in German. My German was still pretty rudimentary at the time—I was a first year graduate student at Yale that year; it was 1962, just thirty years ago, the year of the Cuban missile crisis. I was trying to read Adorno's essay on Balzac, which, as far as I could follow it, impressed me enormously. So I 'decided' to translate the essay. It seemed relatively straightforward and simple in its language, for Adorno anyway, and I thought its translation wouldn't present too many difficulties. The illusion didn't last for very long, however, only until I tried to translate the very first sentence: '*Kommt der Bauer in die Stadt, so sagt ihm alles: verschlossen*'. And right then and there, at the very start, I was startled to discover that I was stumped: how, after all, should one translate '*Bauer*'? The dictionary definition, 'peasant', seemed almost a foreign word in English, in American English at least, because this country had never really known—or admitted to knowing—'peasants', only 'farmers'. That at least was the closest commonly used word in what we call 'ordinary language'. The fact remains, however, that there is quite a difference between a *peasant*—and, of course, Adorno was 'translating' the French *paysan*, as in *les Paysans de Paris*— and a *farmer*, since the latter usually is a landholder, whereas a peasant rarely owns the land he works. I found myself faced with an impossible alternative. It was as if *I*, in my role as translator, suddenly found myself in a situation very much like that of the *Bauer*—peasant or farmer—to which Adorno, quoting Maupassant, was alluding. I was the peasant, and the *Stadt* or town into which I had come was the German language itself; or rather, even worse, French being translated into German. Those languages seemed hermetically closed to me, *verschlossen;* and yet at the same time they *spoke* to me about their very inaccessibility, just as Adorno had written: '*so sagt ihm alles: verschlossen'*. It was the call of this *Verschlossenheit* that summoned my curiosity. No wonder I continued trying to translate Adorno and that I finally wound up writing a dissertation on Balzac. In this way, my encounter with Adorno's German was an encounter with my 'own' situation encountering an alien language and literature. But this hall of mirrors did not simply reproduce the same picture: it mirrored something that had not been visible before in my self-portrait or self-understanding, something which then turned out to be very Balzacian. In any event, the 'decision' to seek access to some of those closed doors has undoubtedly imparted a certain *direction* to my work and life. But a direction does not necessarily have to lead to the fixity of a position. For better or worse, I at least am not aware of anything like a single or unified position emerging from what I have written. However, I do think I see a number of interrelated directions.

Gillian Thomas: I think one of the things that struck us about your work in relationship to Derrida's was the clarity of your writing. I've been wondering whether that has to do with the fact that when you're writing in English at least, we as English-speaking readers don't have to suffer the problems of translation or whether there's a conscious decision on your behalf to eliminate some of that obscurity that sometimes comes through in Derrida.

Samuel Weber: There we are again, back at 'conscious decisions'. As far as I can tell, there was a little bit of both. As my encounter with Adorno suggests, I have always been attracted to what I would call incisively hermetic texts and styles of thought, like the farmer, or peasant, who comes to town—or is it the city?—and discovers that everything is 'closed' to him. 'Everything says "closed"', as Adorno puts it, literally. That town is not merely 'language' in general but the interface of several languages: the one we call 'native' or 'maternal', the one that we are born into—or out of—and the others that we encounter on the way (in my case, German and French, primarily). So—I have always been drawn to secrets, and I have engaged them in a rather peculiar way, not simply to 'crack the code', as it were, but also to get closer to that *other secret* at the heart of what was closest, which in the case of language is the 'native tongue', in my case English. At the risk of demonstrating an obscurity that would belie your question, or rather my answer to it, I would say that yes, I have always felt the need to find ways of making the complex and esoteric as simple and straightforward as possible. I guess that has something to do with the notion that thinking, and the work of the intellectual, should ultimately not simply isolate but also, and perhaps above all, bring together. But it should do so only by opening itself to the secret, to that which has hitherto been kept secret, enigmatic, and which in its secrecy and secretiveness has determined our lives. Opening oneself to the secret, however, is not to destroy it but to transform it, to rediscover it at the heart of what seems self-evident, self-explanatory. The relationship of languages to one another is something very mysterious, enigmatic, not least of all for those who would like to believe that there exists a single reality independent of language and of its heterogeneities.

I must add, however, that I do not find Derrida particularly 'obscure'. It's rather a question of habituation. Very often, what seems 'obscure' is the result of linguistic practices which are unfamiliar in one cultural context but which may have a long history in a different one. A discursive tradition marked by the poetry of Mallarmé, for instance, allows certain kinds of moves to be made which would be impossible in other languages. Such differences pose a particular challenge to any pro-

ject of 'translating', including the sub-project of 'understanding' or 'reading'. I have always looked for and been stimulated
by the challenge of translating the unfamiliar into a more
familiar language and thereby transforming the latter. But if
there is a pedagogical concern with clarity in my writing, it is
first and foremost because I myself want to understand the
texts to which I am responding. In any case, this desire or
imperative or whatever it is is not simply a matter of choice.
Which is why I said earlier that I consider it more accurate to
speak not of making or taking decisions but of being taken—
even overtaken!—by them. A decision, in the strong sense at
least, is often something that catches up with you. You have
fairly little to say in the matter—no more than trying to choose
freely whether or not to laugh at a joke. You don't have much
choice in the matter. It either happens or it doesn't.

Patrick Crogan: Baudrillard describes the relief of that. You
can accept yourself as an object, accept your objecthoodness.

Samuel Weber: Yes, there's relief, no doubt, but there is also
the sense of an ongoing struggle and a feeling of ambivalence.
'Accepting', as I understand it, doesn't mean curling up and
going to sleep; it means what it literally meant in Latin: *taking-
up* or *taking-on*, like a runner in a relay taking over the baton.
Except that you never know for certain where the race is leading or when it is over. That's why writing, as a process, seems
so paradigmatic. You can 'decide' to move in a certain direction, in a certain way, make an outline, do your research and
all the other preparation you want. The actual process of writing, however, almost always leads somewhere other than
where we expect. I say this without evaluation, since that
'other place' can turn out to be a blind alley, just as in more fortunate cases, it can also turn out to be an opening. It's both

exhilarating and intimidating. I think that's the real reason why I often advise students to work with an outline. Not because I think you can really decide in advance where you are going to go but because you can then discover just how little you knew where you were going.

This question of writing is particularly important in France, not just as a theoretical question but as a practical institution. One of the reasons why the French have produced some of the most prolific and provocative writers to have engaged the subject of writing may well have to do with the importance of writing in the French educational system. In French schools and universities students write constantly. If you have ever been in a French university course, you will have noticed just how much note-taking goes on and how generally assiduous it is. This is in part a European tradition; but it is of particular importance in France—as opposed to Germany, for instance—since the French student must pass written exams each year in order to be promoted. Also, the French system of competitive qualifying examinations involves a large percentage of written work—no multiple choice or computer punch-cards to my knowledge, not yet anyway. The result is that French students learn through writing; and in the process they also learn to define themselves by their writing to an extent that is difficult to imagine elsewhere, or at least in the United States. You often have the sense that French intellectuals are addicted to writing, the way some people become addicted to jogging. If you miss a day you feel guilty. So you see that the French were hooked on writing long before Derrida came along and revealed it to be one of the paradigmatic drugs of Western thinking in general.

Gillian Thomas: Does Derrida usually sit and write longhand or does he just talk into a microphone and then give it to somebody else?

Samuel Weber: My information on this is strictly limited to what has been written on the subject, which is as reliable or as unreliable as you can imagine. But I seem to remember that he began using machines—typewriters, then computers, possibly dictating machines—fairly early on, which may be just as well, especially when I think of the time I had to devote before then to deciphering certain of his letters. But a far higher percentage of French academics—and not just academics, once again—prefer to write by hand than by machine. Writing, and language in general, play such a determining role in French socialization that they have resisted mechanization far more effectively than in the U.S. where mechanization and technology have long enjoyed greater social acceptance and prestige. Just think of the signature in France and in the English-speaking world, or rather in the U.S. (I don't know how it is in Australia). In the U.S. you are often asked to 'sign legibly', especially on checks or official documents—which is to say, where it *counts*. In France, by contrast, the signature serves primarily to distinguish the signatory. It must be distinctive, like Saussure's signifier. It is a mark of *distinction* (think of the title of Bourdieu's book). It is not supposed to communicate or represent anything, least of all the proper name.

Lisa Stefanoff: I am approaching some of these questions from what remains in this country as anthropology. One of my concerns about how deconstruction has been received in this discipline is that it has set the scene for an institutionalized theory/practice split, which is difficult for those who continue to practice anthropology as a study of cultural difference. On the one hand, there are those who consider deconstructive readings unimportant with respect to anthropology; and on the other hand, there are those who have instituted a metacritical discourse which has almost made 'anthropology' into a practice of *reading* ethnographic texts. To this extent there has been a devaluation of the *writing* of the very encounter with alterity, and it is this very encounter with alterity which is one of the important philosophical questions that deconstruction has thrown into play and which is only very rarely being engaged with in ethnographic contexts.

Samuel Weber: It is probably because I am not very familiar with current anthropology or 'ethnography'—and obviously the way one names the discipline is already extremely significant—that I have difficulty understanding why the valorization of the problem of writing, of articulating the encounter with alien cultures, should necessarily have to be *opposed* to the non-literary aspects of that encounter. To interpret deconstruction as instituting or aggravating a cleavage between practice and theory is to misinterpret it in an unnecessarily unproductive manner. The Heideggerian tradition—to which deconstruction is so profoundly indebted, however much it may transform that tradition—is one that seeks to rethink the relationship between theory and practice rather than taking it for granted or assuming a metatheoretical position. This is even more evident in the writings of Derrida, which, as I have already remarked, sought from the very beginning to demarcate their project from anything like a meta- or general theory (as, for instance, in his debate with Searle in *Limited Inc*). The imperative of writing, the emphasis on the non-reductive nature of textuality, should indicate that a deconstructive approach is not to be equated with any sort of contemplative, theoretical stance. One could say that the issues are already embodied in the alternative names used to designate your discipline itself: *anthropology* denotes the science of the *anthropos*, of Man, whereas *ethnography* designates the study of groups or 'peoples'. These are two quite different ways of naming, and of construing, the encounter with alien cultures.

If deconstructive readings can have a certain significance for ethnography, then, it is less in terms of any particular cognitions that it might contribute—and it is important to insist on the fact that deconstruction is concerned *primarily* not with the production of *knowledge* but with the process and practice of *articulation*—than in demonstrating how and where the question of the other impinges upon established forms of discourse, whether cognitive or not. When ethnographers 'confront' an alien group, they never do so in a vacuum, of course, but rather through the highly predetermined perspective of their particular language and discourse, through the traditions in which they are formed, etc. Since such factors are never 'innocent', I would have thought that the more ethnographers are aware of the extent to which hidden constraints, presuppositions and practices preform their approach to the 'other', the better able they would be to *leave room* for—and hence take into account—the alterity of the peoples they are seeking to study. This can be done only to the extent that the investigator is able to put himself or herself into question, which is to say, to the extent one is aware of alterity at work in one's relations to oneself, to the traditions that delimit one's possibilities of experience, etc. Only by realizing *that* and *how* the other is never simply out *there* but at the same time very much with us and within us can we hope to accede in some measure—and we are always speaking here of a more or less, never of an absolute: you can never accede fully to the other—to an alien people in their specific difference. To contribute to this is, however, something very different from claiming metatheorical status. In fact, it is as far removed from that as possible, since it problematizes one's *involvement* in rather than one's *detachment* from heterogeneous processes.

Again, although it is not my field and I can therefore not

speak directly to the issues you raise, I can recount an experience related to the questions you are asking. I was asked to review a book manuscript written by an ethnographer and dealing with Indonesia. Despite the fact that I knew even less about Indonesia then than I do now (which is little indeed), the publisher wanted my opinion because he thought that the book might be of interest to readers concerned with critical theory. I liked the book very much and my only suggestion was that the author write an introductory essay tying together the different essays collected in the volume, bringing out some of their underlying connections and making more accessible the general arguments implied by the individual chapters. The author responded by writing an introduction, one which, however, turned out very differently from what I had had in mind in making the suggestion. There was no mention of the rich theoretical literature that I knew the author had read. Instead, the ethnographer told the story of how he had participated in a play given by townspeople whom he had come to know. He had been asked to act precisely because of his being foreign, and this required him to speak a language, or languages, not his own, before a large public. What emerged from this anecdote was a complex picture of the situation in which the author, as ethnographer, found himself. If you want to find out more about it, you can read the book, *Solo in the New Order*, by James T. Siegel. Needless to say, this introduction, which mentioned practically no theoretical texts, pulled things together in a far more effective way than any sort of metatheoretical reflection could ever have done. And I suspect it was not entirely fortuitous that the story he told involved a theatrical performance, since the sort of involvement with alterity exemplified by the situation of the ethnographer is also powerfully at work in the theatre. Now I don't know if Siegel—who was a student of Clifford Geertz, I believe—is an isolated case in your discipline or if similar tendencies are taking

place more generally in it. In any case, for deconstruction to be
effective, something unexpected, unpredictable, has to *happen;*
and in that happening, the theatrical underpinnings of theoretical knowledge come to the fore.

Lisa Stefanoff: That is happening. But it has nonetheless led to
a theoretical puritanism: that all that anthropologists can now
do vis-a-vis 'ethnography' is to reinscribe texts. This project has
come to define the productive limits of what I nonetheless in
some regards believe are the more innovative and challenging
movements within the discipline. This is a troubling situation.

Samuel Weber: I can see how that could be a problem. But
you should remember, and perhaps remind others, that
Derrida's concern with textuality and his concept of the text
have never been limited to *actually written, empirical documents.*
Textuality was and remains a figure that designates the *other-
directedness of structures of signification,* where 'other-directed-
ness' should be understood here in a profoundly non-psycho-
logical sense. Deconstruction entails an approach to the other
as articulation and to articulation as other. This is easy to state
in general terms, as I am doing now; but its ramifications are
many and complex. Thus, what we think of as *lived experience*
involves textuality and reading no less than do books. That has
to be true of field work as well, since neither the *field* nor the
work can divest themselves of interpretation, of deciphering
and of decision in the (aporetical) senses already discussed. And
these processes all belong to those studied and put into play by
deconstruction. It is only if one believes that there exists a
directly intuitive or perceptual access to the other—be it an
alien group, an individual, a text or a non-verbal event—that
one can accuse deconstruction of being a barrier or an impedi-
ment to the advancement of knowledge. The real obstacle, as

far as I am concerned, is the widely held and propagated belief
that what we call 'reality' or the 'world' on the one hand and
'language' and 'text' on the other are mutually exclusive phenomena and that therefore to speak about a text is not to speak
about the real world, and vice versa. This sort of naive belief is,
in various forms, very widely held, even in academic circles;
and it contributes to the social isolation of intellectuals by placing them outside of reality, at least insofar as they are concerned precisely with language. Here, as elsewhere, one cannot
be suspicious enough of simple(minded) oppositional thinking,
of arguments based upon mutually exclusive polarities, such as
theory and practice, or their cousins, activity and passivity.

Alan Cholodenko: But to speak of a deconstructive practice
for me articulates with the idea that deconstruction, as distinct
from Deconstructionism, involves processes that are always
already in play, so that at the same time that one is talking
about voluntaristic activities, there is always this other side to
be acknowledged—that deconstructive processes, regardless of
your will, decision, act, etc., will always be acting on you. So if
deconstructive processes are processes of the world, then voluntaristic activities of deconstructive character would be those
which would accord with these processes. To say that an individual practice would be isomorphic with deconstruction is to
say that it would be isomorphic with the world's acts.

Samuel Weber: I agree that deconstruction names both a
response to and an *articulation of* processes which in no way can
be attributed simply to *individuals*, whether construed as subjects, self-consciousnesses, wills or what have you. 'Individual
practice' is determined as a response to such processes, but it is
determined in a way that makes the very term 'individual'—if
you take it literally at least—a misnomer. The only reason that

the 'isomorphism' to which you refer is both possible and necessary is because, as Novalis once put it, the *in-dividual* is in fact highly *dividual*. This is why the term that has tended to impose itself in this context is *singular* rather than *individual*. The singular is what doesn't fit in to the established modes of identification; it is precisely not autonomous and self-contained, characteristics often associated with the individual, although both terms imply a certain uniqueness, a certain non-substitutability. Also, *singular* is used more as an adjective than as a noun, whereas *individual* tends to suggest more of a person or an entity of some sort. For these reasons I prefer to speak of *singular* practices rather than of individual acts, since the notion of *act* often carries with it the implication of *actualization*, in the sense of fulfilling or making-present, and thus is once again more closely bound up with a logic of identity and of identification. Of course, as has often been noted, *act* can also signify performance in a theatrical sense, which is far more compatible with a deconstructive approach. What is important therefore is not so much the term used but the way it is used and how that affects the connotations usually attached to it. This relationship—between the particular use of a term and its preexisting general connotations—is certainly one of the most exemplary sites of the isomorphism to which you refer.

Alan Cholodenko: I was wondering if you might want to comment on something that was said to me a few years ago, that American academics have resisted deconstruction and one reason for that resistance was because of Paul de Man's wartime journalism and the issues around that. Would you care to comment?

Samuel Weber: Well, it is difficult to speak of 'American academics' as a whole either resisting or embracing deconstruction.

There seems to have been more interest in deconstruction in the United States than in many other countries; and indeed, the reaction against this has therefore been quite strong as well. A considerable amount of quite promising work is going on in the United States as a result of the encounter with deconstruction; and it is against this background that the de Man 'affair' has to be seen. As I have already said, the discovery of the collaborationist journalism of the young Paul de Man and the prominence given it in the media simply continued a process of rejection that was already well under way long before the articles in *Le Soir* were rediscovered. In many cases, the incident served merely to supply fresh ammunition to a moralism that had hitherto been at something of a loss about how to respond to a challenge it neither understood nor wanted to understand. For those who were capable of *reading* de Man's texts, as opposed to being simply fascinated by the person or the aura, it was clear how much of his later work was indeed an effort to interpret and analyze the wider implications of what he had done during the early years of World War II. One has to remember that the positions taken by de Man in 1940-1942 were also extremely attractive to a large number of people at the time, including some of the most brilliant and creative intellectuals, and that if this was so, it cannot be understood by being disqualified as moral turpitude or mental lapses, which is all that the polemical moralizing that we have seen has to offer by way of explanation.

Such tendencies to historical simplification in the name of (a certain notion of) history—attempts which seek to construe historical and political phenomena as expressions of individual (or collective) wills and values—are part of the problem they claim to attack. There is a *complicity* between certain forms of individualism, moralism and liberalism on the one hand and the cognitive ideal that dominates much academic work on the other which de Man (along with Derrida and Heidegger) explored and interpreted. The attempt to disqualify de Man, first as a person and then as a critic, is the liberal-democratic form of censorship. Certain texts are not to be read, the issues they raise not to be taught, the questions they pose not to be thought about—that is the bottom line of the 'de Man affair'. Which, of course, is not to say that the articles in *Le Soir* should not be read or written or spoken about. To the contrary. Much can be learned from them. But the conclusions to be drawn are necessarily going to be complex and have little to do with the simplistic binarism of the moralistic-juridical question—guilty *or* innocent?—that has informed much of the 'debate'.

Keith Clancy: What interests me is whether you would like to comment on the seemingly obligatory investment that contemporary thought has in '*l'affaire Heidegger*', given that much of your work ('Deconstruction Before the Name' and 'The Debts of Deconstruction' especially) is concerned with questions of justice and of debt? What becomes of critical-juridical reason when someone like Heidegger is called to render reason for what Lacoue-Labarthe and others have called, a little euphemistically, his 'political misadventure'?

Samuel Weber: Well, in a way I have already been discussing that, implicitly at least. One aspect of the interest that, as you rightly say, is invested in such controversies is the attempt to reduce complex issues to moral questions involving only the acts of individual persons. If we speak about 'Heidegger' at all, it is because of a vast number of extremely difficult texts. The texts and events associated with his Freiburg Rectorship and his continued political involvement with the National Socialist regime are part of the 'work', to be sure, but they hardly provide a simple key that would enable one to avoid engaging the complexities just mentioned. The fact that Heidegger accepted the position of Rector at the University of Freiburg in 1933, the fact that he was a member of the Nazi party and other 'facts' of this sort hardly relieve us of the obligation to engage the texts he wrote before, during and after that period. And yet that is precisely the message that some of the more extreme 'critics' would have us believe. The fact that de Man wrote for the collaborationist *Le Soir* for several years in Nazi-occupied Belgium and that his writing of that time incontestably demonstrates a fascination with the prospect of a Nazi hegemony in Europe does not provide a key to everything he wrote thereafter. It is precisely the tendency—the desire—to establish simplistic equations and identifications that contributes to the fascination to which the young de Man, and many others at the time, succumbed, and which once again has reemerged today.

So, on the one hand, the ostensibly political scandals of de Man and Heidegger serve to reinstate what the work of each calls powerfully into question: the status of the individual and of the subject. But on the other hand, such scandals also dramatize problems and stimulate interest in them. I suspect that much reading and rereading has gone on as a result of these controversies, and that is all to the good. Of course I am referring to genuine reading, which is a difficult, time-consuming and often uncomfortable, often exhilarating process, in which readers open themselves to the alterity of the text rather than just projecting preconceived notions upon it. Such reading is far less spectacular than the polemics celebrated in *Newsweek* or *The New York Review of Books*. But its effects may turn out to be more important in the long run.

Gillian Thomas: You're saying there's a time to read Heidegger, and I'm wondering why the time is now. Why is there a renewed interest in Heidegger's work?

Samuel Weber: Yes, I think that is on the agenda today, more significantly, perhaps, than all the talk about postmodernism and poststructuralism and all the other *posts* and *neos*. The reason this reading is urgent is that a certain development or articulation has gone about as far as it can go productively without going back to its origin, to its past, without trying more seriously 'to catch up with its past', as I put it (and which, to be sure, is an impossible undertaking ever to accomplish fully: when you fully 'catch up', you're no longer there—you're past...). If it is true that much of the most innovative work done in the past three decades has involved in one way or another what might be called the 'problematization of representation' in all its forms—aesthetic, political, epistemological, linguistic, etc.— then I think that movement has gone as far as it can without going back to what is doubtless its origin, not chronologically, of course, but structurally. And that origin is largely to be found in the work of Heidegger, whose writings raise the question of representation in the context of a long history of Western thought. It is in Heidegger's texts that we find the most powerfully systematic attempt to *delimit* this problem of representation, which is to say, to interpret its conditions, its ramifications, as well as possible alternatives. And I am quite convinced that whatever thinking claims to be innovative today, whether it is concerned with questions of gender, of postcolonialism or of multiculturalism, can only benefit by accepting the challenge of confronting its categories and concepts with the thought and texts of Heidegger. Above all, Heidegger's effort to rethink the subject-object dichotomy that structures so much contemporary thinking is of particular interest. Fortunately, it has today become possible to reread Heidegger in a way quite different from what was done previously, and this is not the least merit of the work of Derrida, Lacoue-Labarthe, Nancy and others.

Gillian Thomas: And following on from Heidegger...

Samuel Weber: 'Following on...' A very apt remark and locu-
tion. We always are *following on* or *in* the wake of something
that has come to pass, that has marked us and the textual
structures that make up our world. We are *followers,* even if we
are fortunate enough to take the lead in the ways we follow.
This is in fact one of the most interesting motifs in Heidegger's
rethinking of the questions of time and of history. He allows us
to think that our past, in a certain sense, is still *before* us, and
that therefore we have considerable catching up to do, especially given the time allotted us. This is why it is dizzying to think of
our future as the dimension through which we try to catch up
with the past. It is why we tend to cling to what are ostensibly
more stable phenomena, like *proper names*: Heidegger, Derrida,
de Man, and countless others. You name it. But it makes a difference whether those names serve as end points or as points of
departure, or perhaps even as *places* where you catch your
breath before setting forth once again.

Andrew Lewis: Thank you for your thoughts today and
thanks very much for your visit to Australia and the opportunity you've provided all of us.

Samuel Weber: It's been a real pleasure for me as well.
Thank you.

*The Weber Reading Group, instituted by Andrew Lewis and
Cameron Tonkin, included in addition: Rodger Allen, Alan
Cholodenko, Keith Clancy, Patrick Crogan, Allison Gill, Matthew
Holt, Pauline Moore, Freida Riggs, Richard Rushton, Lisa Stefanoff
and Gillian Thomas.*

Goings On

Discussion between Rex Butler and Samuel Weber, conducted
in Brisbane, June 2, 1992:

Rex Butler: At the end of your lecture on Benjamin, people
were asking you how you would apply your arguments about
the aura to some actual artistic practice. Now, one of the things
you stress in your work is the performative or aesthetic aspect
to theory, the way theory is absolutely singular, cannot be generalized. On the other hand, as we know, theory also wants to
be absolutely universal, to speak of everything. To begin, could
you say something about these two sides to theory and how a
theory might be 'applied'?

Samuel Weber: Let me begin by taking up certain parts of
your question that seem to me somewhat problematic. First of
all, I don't think one can argue—and I hope I haven't done
so—that 'theory is *absolutely* singular' or that it 'cannot be generalized'. Theory, as you quite rightly say, is impossible to separate from a certain tendency toward generalization, if not uni-
versalization. In this sense, the notion of 'application' is an emi-
nently 'theoretical' notion, implied in the subsumptive character of the theoretical enterprise itself. To construct a theory is to
construct a scheme that subsumes individual phenomena
under general concepts, be these understood as empirical or as
transcendental. If it is valid, a theory has to be 'applicable' to
the phenomena it purports to explain. Now, although it is true
that the question of *how, whether* or *to what extent* such subsumption and such application take place has been a constant

source of concern in the history of Western thought—for instance, in the medieval debates between 'nominalists' and 'realists'—the question takes a significant turn when it becomes identified by Kant with the aesthetic. In the *Critique of Judgment* this question becomes: is a transcendental theory of aesthetic judgment possible?

In the process of responding to this question—or more precisely, already in the process of articulating it—something emerges that could be described as the *aporia of the singular*. The domain in which such aporetic singularity manifests itself is precisely that of manifestation itself, of phenomenality. The world of appearances, so argues Kant, contains an unlimited number of phenomena that resist subsumption under familiar concepts, rules and laws. How do we deal with such phenomena, how do we 'bring them under' the known, how do we appropriate them? Insofar as this problem of aporetic singularity poses, or rather, *imposes* itself in the domain of what traditionally is called 'perception', the term 'aesthetic' can legitimately be associated with the challenge of the singular to traditional 'theory' and its procedure of subsumptive appropriation. But only—and this is my point here—if it is remembered that the 'aesthetic' thus marks a certain dilemma in the traditional understanding of *theory*. 'Aesthetics', in the wake of Kant, implies a theory but also defies it.

The ambiguous, even ambivalent, notion of 'aura' elaborated by Walter Benjamin in his effort to rethink the aesthetic in the light of modern technologies of representation is very indebted to this Kantian tradition. For Benjamin, 'aura' designates the phenomenal effect of an original that resists all processes that would dislocate it by having it take place at more than one place at one time. Since, however, even the most immediate perception entails a minimal dislocation of the *perceptum* by the *percipiens*, aura itself already implies a certain separation: the irreducible distance that separates the observer from the observed, which difference is necessary for the original to be apprehended. But aura, as a sort of *emanation*, also entails a continuum. The perceived object *emits*, as it were, an aura, a *glow* that is both part of the object and yet also no longer part of it, since the aura is *taking place*—i.e. *transporting place*—elsewhere, whereas the original is defined as that which can only be in *one place* at *one time*, not in many places simultaneously.

The aura, then, is the visual manifestation of the fact that a perceived entity, no matter how original—self-identical and autonomous—it is construed as being, can *exist* qua apprehended entity *only* insofar as it *ek-sists*, that is, only insofar as it *goes out* of itself, *leaves itself* in a certain sense *behind*, *takes leave* of itself in order to become apprehensible by another. The 'original', in short, can only *be* insofar as it *comes to pass* in and as its aura.

This aura doesn't simply reproduce the essence of what it leaves behind. It *is* something else again. What it leaves behind and yet still transports (leaves behind *because* it transports) is precisely a certain *singularity*. But that singularity is something quite different from the *self-identity* with which we (thought we) started. The singularity of a phenomenon is precisely something constituted by and through that ineluctable *taking-leave* that allows it to appear and to be perceived. Singularity, in short, is constituted as the *aura* of itself. It *is* only insofar as it *comes to pass*.

Now it is clear that anything like a theoretical discourse that seeks to confront this ambivalent coming-to-pass of singularity is going to have to be extremely suspicious of any notion of 'application'—whether it be that of 'applied psychoanalysis', for instance, or of 'applied grammatology'. *Application* is very difficult to construe outside of a logic of subsumption. This is also why, for instance, Heidegger, in *Being and Time*, specifically and repeatedly distinguishes his project—whether understood

as that of constructing a 'fundamental ontology' or that of a
Destruktion (i.e. *delimitation*) of Western metaphysics—from
traditional *theory*. Heidegger's entire thought is an effort to
rethink the relation between the particular and the general so
as to leave room for the heterogeneity of the singular, which in
Being and Time, for instance, is associated with the *Jemeinigkeit*,
the 'each-and-always-mineness' of *Dasein* (*being-there*). In the
case of *being-there*, Heidegger's investigation insists upon the
irreducibility of one's involvement in the world, in respect to
which the modern subject-object dichotomy appears as a
defensive and derivative conception. One of the leitmotifs of
Being and Time is that the theoretical apprehension of the world
derives from an involvement that cannot be understood in
strictly theoretical terms. Hence, the titanic effort of Heidegger
to develop a new language to articulate this other, existential
structure—even though it turns out that this 'new' language is
also frequently quite common and fairly 'old'.

In this sense, it is understandable but not quite accurate to
assimilate Heideggerian thought or Derridean deconstruction
to the very notion of theory that they have tried to delimit and
to transform, and this for reasons very closely associated with
the question you are asking—that is, with the relation of the
universal or general on the one hand and the singular on the
other. I am not certain that the best way to explore the 'performative' dimension is to approach it in terms of the applicability
of a theory.

Rex Butler: To rephrase the question so that we may think
about it another way, it is interesting that Derrida in his own
work often emphasizes the empiricity of his own starting point
or, as in his debate with Lacan, reproaches the other for forgetting the empirical nature of what he is saying: in Lacan's case,
the fact that fiction is narrated and not the simple presentation

of truth. And yet, on the other hand, Derrida's own work does not proceed empirically but by a strange 'doubling' of its author. That is to say, when he criticizes the philosophers of logocentrism, for instance, he never takes seriously their contingent flaws as though these could not be corrected. Rather, he at once perfects their various systems and shows that these perfected systems have not merely a contingent limit, dependent upon their authors' failings, but an *absolute* one. In his debate with Lacan, again, he will point out certain empirical failings in Lacan's analysis; but he will also say of it that it is in a way perfect and that he can only repeat it, make the same 'mistakes' himself.

Samuel Weber: I don't find the same emphasis on the 'empirical' in Derrida's work that you do. Rather, there is more emphasis on the notion of 'singularity', as distinguished from the universalizing tendencies of the concept and the system. If I can therefore reinterpret your question by replacing 'empirical' by 'singular', I wouldn't agree with what I take your remark to imply or presuppose: that Derrida—whether in his reading of Lacan or elsewhere—is less interested in the singular than in the universal. To focus upon the structural tendencies of an interpretation rather than upon what you call its 'contingent flaws' is not the same as sacrificing the singular to the universal. The singular is not the same as the individual or the personal, or the simply contingent, for that matter. It is not situated 'this side' of a certain generalization, before it, as it were, but *beyond* it. The singular is that which is *left over after* all the powers of generalization have been exploited to the fullest and their potentialities both realized and exhausted. The ability to achieve this kind of saturated generalization from the particular is what distinguishes Derrida's reading of Lacan, or his other readings, from a mere series or accumulation of isolated criticisms or observations that remain safely removed from that which they are criticizing. The singular can only emerge as something other than the merely idiosyncratic or illustrative *after* the general has been allowed to deploy its resources upon the particular. Whereas the particular is always more or less an integral and integrating *part* of the general, the singular disintegrates. It *is* that which doesn't *fit in*, and its force is in direct proportion to the power of the general that it resists.

Hence, what I am referring to as the 'singular' inevitably implies a certain generality. On the other hand, general, systematic constructions are themselves always more or less singular. For instance, Lacan's reading of 'The Purloined Letter', however paradigmatic it is intended to be—a point Derrida stresses, alluding to its position at the beginning of the *Ecrits*— is still, need it be said, highly specific despite or because of its generality. That is why the question of the transcendentality of the signifier can be posed so powerfully in regard to this text. In problematizing this issue, Derrida is at the same time problematizing his own origins, since his work comes, in part at least, out of a movement in which the notion of the signifier plays a very important role. In calling attention to the *narrative frame* as paradoxically something that never entirely 'is' what it claims to be—a self-enclosing, delimiting line separating inside from outside, self from other—Derrida adds a new dimension to what had previously been associated with the 'singular'. He is increasingly calling attention to the 'performative' aspect of 'framing', as distinguished from its merely 'constative' function. It is ironic, of course, that no one was more adept at *exploiting* the performative resources of discourse than was Jacques Lacan. But it is also true that in exploiting those resources he sometimes resorted to cognitive positions that his practice tended to call into question.

What I think has to be remembered, however, is that

Derrida's concern with singularity cannot simply be *opposed* to the generalizing aspects of his writing. Rather, it is the *result* of them. At the same time, the relationship of singular and general is not a static one. Singularity cannot be opposed to generality in Derrida's work because the two cannot be definitively *separated*. Notions such as '*différance*', 'supplement', 'iterability' and the 'rest' do not have an unchanging, universal truth-content, however much they may resemble traditional concepts. Not only do they emerge out of the readings of particular texts and writers but their ramifications and implications remain a function of specific situations. Although they may transcend any particular set of texts and writers, they cannot pretend to any sort of permanence. In this sense, their generality is generative rather than universal. They are *traces* of a space of singularity that they seek to reopen. Derrida's reinscription of the supplement, in Rousseau and elsewhere, can open up perspectives that lead in unpredictable directions. But it cannot or should not have as its end-result a generalized theory of supplementarity.

Of course, most of us are also involved in *teaching*; and the process of teaching necessarily involves a considerable element of *repetition*. But even then, the repetition is not simply the return of the same. For the question there is: the same for *whom?* For students discovering these texts and issues, the question of the 'supplement' is something new and different. But one has to be careful not to confuse the role of teacher with the role of writer. They are intimately related, but they are not identical. Nevertheless, the task of distinguishing what is 'new' from what is the 'same', what is 'general' from what is 'singular', is always necessarily and structurally dependent upon the situations and contexts in which we are ineluctably involved. In other words, however abstract and unchanging, however 'universal', this question of the universal and the singular may seem—or for that matter, that of the 'empirical' and its other:

the 'theoretical'—it is itself anything but simply universal: its generality is inseparable from its singularity.

Rex Butler: To think about the problem even another way, when Derrida attacks a tradition like logocentrism, obviously his analysis of it—and indeed, his entire philosophy—at once completes it, perfects it and shows that it is impossible, has a limit from the very beginning. And this in a way would render redundant any empirical attempt to investigate this tradition's limits within a kind of history, its actual mistakes, as though these had some real meaning any more. This leads me to wonder why, despite its best efforts, deconstruction has not entered into an alliance with history in a true disciplinary sense, why no one can write deconstructive history. I do not think one can underestimate the universalizing logic of deconstruction, which seems to make the investigation of actual facts, despite its very profound recognition of empiricity, slightly unnecessary.

Samuel Weber: The only reason I can see—and it is an important one—why deconstruction should 'make the investigation of actual facts' or 'empirical attempt[s]' at investigating 'within a kind of history' 'slightly unnecessary' is because there *can* be no investigation of actual facts that would be strictly empirical, actual or factual—i.e. that would not be indebted to a whole series of conceptual and categorical presuppositions and premises regarding the way in which the 'actual', the 'factual' and the 'empirical' are delimited. Here again, I think it is useful to go back to Heidegger: the respect for certain aspects of empiricity that we both agree is in some way at work in the writing of Derrida is, in some ways at least, a continuation of the Heideggerian motif of 'facticity' elaborated in *Being and Time*. For Heidegger, one of the constitutive dimensions of being-there (*Dasein*) is the 'fact' that it always 'finds itself' in a situation that Heidegger describes as 'thrown' and which he associates with what he calls 'facticity'. In such 'facticity' of existence, the 'fact' is not simply a 'given' that will associate with other 'givens' to form a body of *data*, which in turn will furnish *material* for the progress of cognition. What sets off Heidegger's notion of 'facticity' from the 'factual' in the more familiar sense is precisely the way in which it *resists* being inserted into a chain of causal explanation. The *factical*, as distinct from the factual, marks the defining limits of an irreducible *heterogeneity*. The 'fact' of the matter, as Heidegger elaborates it in *Being and Time*, is that being-there *comes to be* only by finding itself in a situation that is, first, not of its own making, and second, not simply reducible or retraceable to an original cause or goal that would make it intelligible as a transitional phase. Just as (what is often called) the empirical might be said to mark a limit-condition of heterogeneity for Derrida, so for Heidegger the *factical* marks a limit-condition of *Dasein*.

Now, if the empirical or the factical therefore have the effect of imparting a moment of alterity to any point of departure we might establish, this is going to have consequences for the way in which 'history', including historical analysis and interpretation, is construed and conducted. First of all, it can no longer go without saying that 'history' is to be understood as a movement made intelligible by its origins, goals or subjects. Even more, the writing and study of history cannot presuppose as self-evident the *temporal-narrative* structures that furnish the discursive framework of such archaeo-teleological intelligibility, for instance, the mutual exclusivity of what we call past, present and future.

One of the major projects of Heidegger was to delimit the suppositions of traditional notions of temporality in order to elaborate alternatives. Summarizing and vulgarizing, one could say that he sought to call into question a position that conceived of time as a dimension of subjective self-realization, of control and of calculation, a notion of time based on the 'present', to which he contrasted a notion of temporality based on the 'instant' (in German, *Augenblick*). The difference, as I understand it, would involve a conception of time rooted in the notion of the *present, Gegenwart,* which would support an understanding of *being* in terms of *beings* qua *entities*, in contradistinction to a conception of temporality as *Augenblick*—literally, *eye-glance*—which would support a conception of being as *turning-point* rather than as self-present *state*.

From this it is clear that it cannot be *easy* to write what you have referred to as a 'deconstructive history'. It does not, however, follow that it cannot be done. What *is* required, however, is a rethinking of the concept of history in the light of the Heideggerian and Derridean problematizing of the established concepts of time, causality and subjectivity. It requires a rethinking of the significance of death and of finitude as well as of language. It requires finally—'finally', that is, as far as this response is concerned (there are, to be sure, many more factors to be considered than can be mentioned in the course of this discussion)—renewed meditation on the role of *repetition* in regard to a history no longer construed in terms of totalization or progress. Your own preferred notion of 'doubling' would be as pertinent here as, for instance, the related phenomenon of the 'uncanny'. A deconstructive history would have to leave far more space for the uncanny than has hitherto been done, I suspect. It is entirely possible that what emerges from this kind of rethinking will no longer be 'historical' in the way that many have traditionally used that term. But if 'facts' and the 'empirical' are understood as being inseparably bound up with the heterogeneous, then a deconstructive history would involve the effort to *respond* to their appeal rather than trying—or pretending—not to listen.

Rex Butler: But do you think that this kind of asymptotic thinking of the other, and of the other that allows this other— the asymptotic logic of your paper on Benjamin where you speak about the 'setup' allowing us to question the setup and the 'aura' allowing us to think the aura (which is why the aura does not simply disappear in Benjamin, because it is what allows us to think it and to think even its disappearance)—do you think that this asymptotic logic, which is not a logic and not a model, has become, strangely enough, the final logic and model for all thought? And might we from this perspective see deconstruction as the final version of a whole series of 'doubling' logics that have marked Western thought from the very beginning? That is to say, Derrida allows us to look back and see how each great thinker works by a set of hypotheses that both totally encapsulates the thinker who comes before him in the tradition of thought and shows that what he is saying is impossible, or possible only for a reason completely outside the system he sets up. To attempt to criticize a thinker like Hegel, for instance, one would have to work through this 'method'— and one can see someone like Bataille, in thinking the laughter, the play, the empiricity, the 'nothing' excluded to allow the perfection of Hegel's system, proceeding in this way. Perhaps today Derrida's is that perfect system, but in a way beyond Hegel's because it already takes into account the possibility of its 'doubling', the thinking of that 'other' excluded to ensure that its other is always the same. There might be no way of thinking 'outside' or 'beyond' Derrida except in the very terms he gives us. Derrida's system might be a kind of 'nothing', but against it we cannot any more think that 'nothing' excluded to make it possible. This might be why one feels a kind of panic that there is nothing more to be thought, that we can only repeat him. One might think here of Derrida's own article on copyright, where he says deconstruction must be inventive if it is to be anything; but in this very programming of invention or the singular, it might be said that deconstruction is precisely robbing us of it. ·

Samuel Weber: I suspect that the 'panic' to which you refer is based upon an 'all or nothing' approach to what is 'new' and what is not. After Derridean deconstruction has made its mark—but also after Heidegger—it is much more difficult to think of the New as being simply opposed to the Old. But the sense of panic that this difficulty might initially provoke should not blind us to the fact that the logic, or more accurately, the *graphics,* of exclusion exposed by deconstruction also opens up perspectives and above all *leaves room for the other* in a way that hitherto was difficult to do. In this context, I think that it is relevant to recall that Derrida's writing is as much about *responding* to the appeal of the singular as it is about *inventing* it. Writing in a way that is responsive to the singular is hardly compatible with 'that perfect system' to which you refer. Deconstruction delimits the aporetic conditions of systematicity as such; it does not, however, remain fixed upon the system in a negative or even dialectical way, as its inverted mirror-image. If Derrida's texts are hard to go 'beyond' or get 'outside' of, it is surely because they complicate the relationship between inside and outside, before and beyond, to the point that these terms no longer designate the mutually exclusive, self-identical poles of a binary opposition. Rather, they are literally *com-plicated,* folded into and over one another. I don't see where or why this must produce a movement that is 'asymptotic', as you put it.

The problem seems to be in conceiving of a 'movement' once it is no longer oriented by a goal and an origin, an end and a beginning. Thus, if one surveys the subjects of Derrida's seminars over the past few years, one comes up with titles that seem, at first sight, to have little in common and to lead nowhere in particular: witnessing, the secret, cannibalism, friendship—to name just a few. And yet, although they do not add up to a goal-directed movement, and hence are also not really asymptotic, they open up a number of interrelated avenues of research which converge and criss-cross with one another. So I see a situation marked neither by asymptotic movement nor by essentially static 'doublings' and redoublings but rather by the increasingly dense elaboration of interrelated issues and projects. And what distinguishes this network is that its approach almost always proceeds by way of the reading of individual texts. The text is for Derrida, and for deconstruction, at least as I understand it, the irreducible repository of that 'factical', 'empirical' heterogeneity that we were discussing earlier. Since texts can only be acceded to—indeed, only really *exist*—in being read, reread and rewritten, and thereby in being *transformed*, Derrida's insistence upon dealing with individual texts rather than addressing general questions directly concretizes that *responsibility to the singular* that constitutes the ethical imperative—if there is one—of deconstruction.

Rex Butler: To think about your work on Freud in this context, it is interesting to note a kind of movement in his project from the empirical towards an hypothesis that cannot be refuted. The intriguing thing about your analysis in 'It' and *The Legend of Freud* is that you are able to trace a trajectory throughout his successive series of speculations whereby the possibility of his theory being empirically disrupted becomes more and more remote. And this is part of that strange ambivalence you note there. For instance, his theory of anxiety not only involves an empirical threat to a person but a threat to the theory of anxiety itself, which is anxious about its own outside—an outside that could be thought of as the empirical. I find the work in 'It' and *The Legend of Freud* very interesting on a meta-theoretical level: a theorist of anxiety, which is a theory about the threat of the 'other', anxious about the threat of some 'other' upsetting his theory of anxiety...

Samuel Weber: Isn't this the case in the most immediate way in *Beyond the Pleasure Principle*? Freud there is reacting to 'empirical' evidence that calls into question the simplistic notion of pleasure through the fact of traumatic neurosis and through the fact of the traumatic repetition of experiences that could not possibly have been pleasurable. It is interesting to observe how he takes what is obviously an empirical fact (not, of course, a purely empirical fact since it is mediated by the psychoanalytical institution and perspective) that intrudes upon a psychoanalytical expectation or even axiom, or at least upon an expectation that he feigns to have about pleasure being a direct motivation of psychic activity, and then through that essay refuses to explain it away, or rather, goes through an elaborate staging of possible explanations which he himself then refutes (apparently with great pleasure). You see, Freud could just as well have done what he did in *The Interpretation of Dreams*, where he knows very well that there are anxiety dreams but says nevertheless that such dreams do not alter the fact that pleasure is still the main determining factor behind psychic life and, in particular, behind dreams. He does not take this line in *Beyond the Pleasure Principle*. Now, this in a certain sense could be said to be a response to an empirical intrusion into the theory or a deliberate refusal to allow the theory in its existing state—for obviously, he is now dealing with an established theory and institution, even if it is one in a state of constant transformation—to explain away the fact of anxiety or the fact of trauma. My interpretation has been that he is reacting against a certain institutionalization, a certain entropy. In the earlier texts, such as the book on dreams, he is still staking out ground and defending the coherence of his theory; but once it has been secured, he has to defend, as it were, the empirical disturbances of the theory from the theory itself, in order to keep psychoanalysis in movement. And you recall that one of his favorite phrases was precisely 'the psychoanalytical *movement*'.

Rex Butler: Your work is often about institutionality and about those singular names that found institutions. What is interesting here is that one could begin to speculate that the kinds of names that allow their institutionalization are those names standing in for a body of work that institutes, strangely enough, these kinds of 'doubling' theories. Freud, for example, can only be known as a name that is able to be applied to a number of different things when he can come up with a theory that is no longer empirical. Does this sound right to you?

Samuel Weber: I think there is a great deal in what you say. It reminds me a bit of Foucault's remarks on the use of proper names to designate an intellectual institution—Marxism, for instance—as distinguished from the anonymity of more traditional scientific disciplines. Foucault, if I remember correctly, wrote of a 'lack' or deficiency, from the strictly cognitive point of view, that allowed and necessitated the use of proper names to designate what was otherwise not entirely self-contained or self-identical. But I think one goes a step further in replacing that notion of 'lack' with that of 'doubling'. It is difficult to contest that what we usually think of as being 'empirical' is hardly adequate to account for the movement of duplication, redoubling, mirroring, repetition, reproduction and any of the other terms one wishes to attach to the notion of 'doubling'. One could argue, however, that the notion of the 'empirical' is itself not entirely homogeneous or simple. On the one hand, it is understood as entailing a realm of *self-identity*, of things and data and phenomena that exist independently of thought. On the other hand, if one looks closely at this initial determination of the 'empirical', one sees that it is closely linked precisely to a certain *otherness*. The empirical is also thought of as that which is not simply the product or projection of a subject. But since this 'non-subject-created' aspect is not sufficient to determine the 'empirical' positively (except perhaps for a dialectically inclined mode of thought), this differential-heterogeneous element is generally grasped as merely the sign or expression of an underlying self-identity. Thus, one tends to assume—at least in the Anglo-Saxon world—that the 'empirical', to which we are supposed to accede through our senses, antedates those senses both chronologically and ontologically. This assumption considers the *heterogeneous* aspect of the empirical as though it were ultimately nothing but the phenomenal by-product or after-effect of *identity*, of *homogeneity*. Thus, the moment of *alterity* that is inseparable from and perhaps constitutive of the 'empirical' is subordinated to that of *identity*. This process could be described as one of 'doubling': the empirical other redoubles itself as the *same*—this is what Derrida has described as *iterability*. But such doubling is highly paradoxical, even aporetical, for it *brings forth* what it is generally understood to *presuppose*: the 'same', the identical, the One, and moreover, it brings it forth *as other*. There's a German expression, one which Benjamin quotes, that says it quite compactly: *Einmal ist keinmal*, 'once is nonce'; and it is probably not fortuitous if what it describes is the attempt of desire to attain fulfillment.

Now what makes this extremely ambivalent movement—which situates alteration and transformation at the very heart and origin of the emergence of identity and sameness—possible, if indeed it is possible, is intimately bound up with the practice of *naming* and with the equivocal structure of the *proper name*. That name turns out to be no less duplicit, or split, than the 'empirical'. On the one hand, it gestures toward a singular, self-identical entity, to which it claims to refer, at least insofar as it is a 'proper' name (or noun); on the other hand, every name also participates in the distinctive relays and networks that constitute language and in this sense it is entirely determined by its differential relations to other elements of the language. It is probably symptomatic that Saussure's course begins—at least in its published version—with the effort to demarcate the signifier, as he understands it, from the name, because the name, in a certain sense, is the absolute other of the signifier. And yet, as absolute other, it is not entirely absolute, since it still maintains a relationship—of exclusion—with that from which it detaches itself. This is why some of the most interesting, and significant, events in language involve the conflating or confusing of proper names with generic nouns. Such conflation and confusion haunts all names, however 'proper' they may try to be, insofar as names are expected to assist in the process of identification. Names are haunted because the signifier is the double, the *Doppelgänger* and the revenant of the name, always menacing it in its property and its propriety. And this is no less true of generic nouns than of proper names. Traditionally, this has been described as the menace of ambiguity, of 'homonymy' (Aristotle) to the univocality of the word. Such a menace has implications both for the existence of individuals and for that of institutions and organizations.

What one should not lose sight of is that all these effects of doubling involve alterity as much as they involve sameness. Doubling is not merely 'more of the same'; it also entails an *excess* of the same, of the *same-becoming-other*, if only to be recuperated once again. Reduced to a formula, this process can quickly become quite sterile; but the fact of the matter is that it does not operate exclusively or primarily at a formal level. As a process involving alteration, it has more to do with *deformation*.

That is precisely the point, and that is also what saves it from mere solipsism. The role of doubling in deconstructive readings is therefore quite different from the circular movement of reflexivity, which is determined by an identical point of departure and arrival.

Rex Butler: You talk about that violent founding act that makes an institution possible. Now, this violent act might be like one of these 'doubling' hypotheses that comes from nowhere, is not derived from any observation, but after which the immanence of the world is divided into two. For example, after the hypothesis of that 'frame' which allows Lacan to say what he does in his 'Seminar on "The Purloined Letter"', there is now Lacan and there is Derrida's explanation which 'frames' him. Do you think that this kind of speculative hypothesis might be that violent initiating act of which you speak?

Samuel Weber: To begin with, I am not sure that I understand what you mean when you assert that the 'doubling' hypothesis 'comes from nowhere'. The doubling to which you refer is, to be sure, never entirely reducible to what was there before; but qua double can it be said to come from nowhere? Does a shadow come from nowhere? What of the figure of the 'supplement', for instance? Or *'différance'*? Or 'iterability'? They involve a certain *violence* only because they *violate* the integrity of what claims to *come before*. Such violation, however, involves a relationship to *something*, even if that something turns out to be quite different from what it claims to be. You cannot violate 'nothing', or can you? In regard to the specific instance to which you refer, what I think you underestimate is the singular power—however enigmatic it may be—of *reading*. Derrida 'reads' Lacan's text, even if one may well contest that reading. If we are talking about Derrida here and now, it is because of the strength of his readings and of the writings through which they are articulated. Now, 'reading', however imaginative and innovative it may be, can never simply abrogate its relationship—and indeed, its *indebtedness*—to *another text*, to something else, which is not simply 'nothing'. Derrida 'frames' Lacan (in all senses) by demonstrating—and it is a demonstration that *can* be discussed, contested, perhaps even refuted—*how* and *where* Lacan's 'Seminar on "The Purloined Letter"' ignores or avoids the question of the frame, and above all, of its own frame, the enabling condition of its own authority.

The question, of course, is whether such avoidance itself is entirely avoidable and if not, whether the demonstration of such unavoidable avoidance can ever suffice to establish an 'institution'? I am not certain about the answer to this question, just as I am not certain that it is either possible, necessary or desirable that deconstruction become an institution. There is enormous pressure to move deconstruction in this direction, if only because it is, to a large extent, situated within areas—such as that of the university—where legitimacy is often measured in terms of institutional standing. The best way to resist such pressure is to keep transforming what is called deconstruction, never allowing it—or its practitioners—to rest on their accumulated laurels (real or not). On the other hand, such transformation—and I return to the point raised earlier about its relation to others and to 'nothing'—can never be simply arbitrary inasmuch as it continues to be oriented by the problems and questions and analyses that have emerged, for instance, by a certain interpretation of what you call 'doubling' and what I would prefer to call 'repetition' (although the two terms are complementary and doubtless both necessary).

To return briefly to the final part of your question: it seems to me that Derrida's gesture in 'framing' Lacan tends not so much to initiate an institution as to undo one—that of the psychoanalyst as transcendental subject, if you like. Deconstruction 'is' the movement of this undoing, which is why it cannot and should never hope to become an institution, as psychoanalysis has tried—with differing success—to be. To be fair, however, it should be noted that psychoanalysis has had to make itself into an institution since it could not develop its practices in any of the existing institutions, whereas deconstruction, which found something of a 'home'—however precarious—in the academic institutions, has not been forced to carve out a social space of its own in order to survive. Not yet, anyway.

Rex Butler: My 'objections' here against deconstruction can only be asked in a Sophist-like manner. I can only use the logic of deconstruction itself against deconstruction. That is to say, my objections, though perhaps true, might also be inconsequential. But might this be to think that the 'doubling' of the world by deconstruction is likewise inconsequential, that a theory that cannot be tested at once changes everything and nothing?

Samuel Weber: Again, I am not certain that I can agree with your assertion that the effects of deconstruction have been or have to be 'inconsequential', for reasons that I have already indicated. The 'doubling' of the world by deconstruction is not merely a reproduction of the same, it opens up spaces of transformation and therefore also new perspectives and avenues of investigation. I am speaking not merely of the 'spaces *between*' the actual 'doubles', if one can refer to them that way, but also of the spaces 'within' the individual members of the 'couple'. What perhaps allows these spaces and perspectives to look 'inconsequential' is the fact that their dimensions and ramifications can no longer be fathomed by the criteria hitherto used to measure consequences, that is, in terms of what the American pragmatists used to call cognitive 'payoffs'. It is a slow, gradual process, which, in the age of the Quick Fix, already serves to disqualify it in the eyes of some. But the transformations that have been initiated or promoted or accelerated by deconstruction cannot be judged in terms of 'all or nothing'. Deconstruction neither 'changes everything' nor 'changes nothing'. Its effect and significance cannot be evaluated in terms of 'either/or'. Don't forget that it is not a proper name nor does it designate a monolithic movement. It involves a sensitivity and effort to respond to the singular alterity of language, wherever this may be found—and that means, in principle, *everywhere*. Or, as you would probably prefer to put it: nowhere. *Ça revient au même*: It comes down to the same, although the same re-turned is no longer simply itself but rather significantly different. And although it is true, as you say, that this difference cannot be 'tested', it *can* be *put to the test*. That is what is going on all the time, all around us. The mode or modes of reading and writing that we call 'deconstruction' are constantly being put to the test, not so much by polemics that bear little relation to what they attack but in less spectacular ways, in projects that are less evident because they are often quite deeply involved in very particular issues and areas. The effects of deconstruction will, I suspect, make themselves felt in the years to come not only in broadly synthetic works but also, and perhaps even more, in highly focused practices or performances.

This said, however, 'performance' should again not be understood to deny the 'reality' of power relationships that characterize the world in which we work and live. We have to make judgments, 'take' decisions, evaluate situations. But such efforts are not simply means to an end independent of them. They are caught up in what they seek to grasp, discern, transform; and that involvement can perhaps best be described in terms of the relation of 'performance' and 'play'. Does such a

theatrical perspective take reality too lightly? Or, on the contrary, does it do justice to the complexity—and indeed, to the
ambivalence—of our involvement in the world? In any case, I
think that theatricality excludes both radical skepticism and
radical dogmatism as possible responses to such involvement.

Rex Butler: Is this why one could make some connection
between anxiety, the gift and the question of aesthetic judgment? They are all after-effects of a certain something that we
can never be sure has actually occurred, although we have to
assume that it has. So that even when you speak in your article
'Ambivalence' about the confrontation with the new work of
art as though it is this thing you bump into, it is not, strangely
enough, as though this 'bumping into' precedes one's coming
to terms with it. One's having bumped into it is in a sense an
after-effect and a pure fiction of one's having come to terms
with it.

Samuel Weber: 'Having come to terms with it'? If the phrase
is to be understood as 'having come to blows with it', I can
agree. For it is not as though the matter has been settled, once
and for all. After all, we still are left with the sense—fiction or
fact—that *something has happened.*

Rex Butler: Can we think here of Lyotard's famous question: *is
it happening?*

Samuel Weber: The present participle certainly takes us to the
heart of the question. It is the temporality of a presence that is
never simply present, self-identical, closed, but rather happening, over and over again. Doubling and repetition are both participating in the uncanny partiality of the present participle.
Something is going on, coming to pass...

Postface

In May 1992 Samuel Weber—Professor of English and Comparative Literature at the University of California at Los Angeles and Director of its Paris Program in Critical Theory—took up the invitation from the Power Institute of Fine Arts at the University of Sydney to be its third Mari Kuttna Lecturer on Film. The Kuttna Lecture was created by Madame Barbara Gré in memory of her daughter, Mari Kuttna, who had taken First Class Honours in English at this University and pursued a career as film reviewer in England until her untimely death in 1983.

This book comes out of Professor Weber's visit to Australia to deliver the Kuttna Memorial Lecture. While in Sydney Weber not only presented the Kuttna Lecture—'Mass Mediauras, or: Art, Aura and Media in the Work of Walter Benjamin'—but also conducted a weekend of seminars during which he delivered three further papers: 'The Unraveling of Form', 'After Deconstruction' and 'Television: Set and Screen'. And, on his ensuing trip to Melbourne and then Brisbane, he not only repeated some of the lectures presented in Sydney but added a fifth: 'Objectivity and its Others'. Feeling that these lectures formed a coherent entity of sorts, Weber was receptive to the idea broached by the Institute that they be published as a book, to which would be added one interview he conducted while in the country—by Cassi Plate for the ABC Radio Arts National's *SCREEN* show—and two discussions—one with the Weber Reading Group, composed of postgraduate and undergraduate students in the Power Institute, the other with Dr Rex Butler of the Department of Art History, University of

Queensland. As well, it was decided by Weber to add his essay, 'Upsetting the Setup: Remarks on Heidegger's "Questing After Technics"', to facilitate the reader's understanding of his treatment of Heidegger and technology in the other essays.

Samuel Weber is not only a leading thinker across the disciplines of literary theory, psychoanalysis and philosophy today. He occupies a unique role as disseminator of the culture of not one but three countries and in their very own languages. Paul de Man wrote of him: 'Weber is probably the only person in his generation who is equally at home and directly informed about contemporary literary theory and its antecedents in Germany, France, and the U.S. His theoretical interest in psychoanalysis serves as a viewpoint from which a powerful combination of philosophical, linguistic, and political concerns are brought together in an uncommonly productive dialectical interplay'.

Professor Weber grew up in New York City and took both his undergraduate and postgraduate degrees at Cornell University, where he trained under de Man in Comparative Literature and wrote his PhD, subsequently published as *Unwrapping Balzac: A Reading of 'La peau de chagrin'*. Before taking up his present post at UCLA in 1989, he taught at Johns Hopkins University, the University of Minnesota and the University of Massachusetts/Amherst, as well as held Visiting Professorships in a variety of departments in numerous universities in France and Germany. Furthermore, in 1977 Weber was Co-founder and Editor of the journal *Glyph*; between 1983 and 1985 he was Associate Member of the Collège International de Philosophie in Paris, and from 1985 to 1989 was Program Director; in 1991 he served as Professeur associé at the Ecole des Hautes Etudes en Sciences Sociales in Paris. And, as a cognate activity, he served as Dramaturg on Wagner's *Parsifal* and *Ring* at the Frankfurt Opera House between 1985 and 1987, on Strindberg's *Dream Play* for the

Stuttgart Schauspiel in 1987, on Genet's *Balcony* for the Düsseldorf Schauspiel in 1988-1989 and on *The Magic Flute* for the Ludwigsburg Festival in August 1992.

Professor Weber has authored such major texts as the already mentioned *Unwrapping Balzac* (University of Toronto Press, 1979), *The Legend of Freud* (University of Minnesota Press, 1982), *Institution and Interpretation* (University of Minnesota Press, 1987) and *Return to Freud: Jacques Lacan's Dislocation of Psychoanalysis* (Cambridge University Press, 1991). A significant activity has also been translating: he translated (with Shierry Weber) the essays of Theodor Adorno in the book *Prisms* (MIT Press, 1983), as well as Jacques Derrida's *Limited Inc* (Northwestern University Press, 1988). He has also edited the book *Demarcating The Disciplines*, written the Introduction to Daniel Schreber's *Memoirs of My Nervous Illness* and written the 'Afterword' to Jean-François Lyotard's *Just Gaming*. A prolific contributor of articles to journals of contemporary critical theory, Weber is presently preparing a book on the work of Walter Benjamin for Harvard University Press.

One of the world's foremost theoreticians of 'deconstructionist bent', as Wlad Godzich characterizes Weber in his 'Afterword' to *Institution and Interpretation*, Professor Weber in his work articulates—and at the same time disarticulates—at the least the three 'disciplines' already mentioned: literary theory, psychoanalysis and philosophy. His first book—*Rückkehr zu Freud: Jacques Lacans Entstellung der Psychoanalyse*—which he wrote in German and published in Germany in 1978, introduced the work of French psychoanalyst Jacques Lacan to German readers and that of the structural linguist Ferdinand de Saussure to other than specialized linguistic circles in Germany. (This book, in an expanded second edition, was published under the same title by Passagen Verlag, Vienna, in 1990 and by Cambridge University Press in 1991).

His second book—*Unwrapping Balzac* (derived from his PhD)—is one of the earliest instances of the poststructuralist study of literature. Written before but published after Roland Barthes' *S/Z*, it implicitly mounts a challenge to an idea fondly held by Barthes at the time, upsetting his set up of a clearcut opposition between Balzac and the tradition of the realist novel on the one hand and Flaubert and literary modernism on the other. Weber mounts that challenge through a reconsideration of Balzac's work as already exhibiting features usually assigned exclusively to that of Flaubert. Such an attack on simple oppositional thought is characteristic of Weber's insistence on the complex conflictual dynamics—the agonistics—at work across cultural forms, institutions and interpretations.

In his next publication, *The Legend of Freud*, Weber develops the theme of the 'uncanny' nature of Freud's work, 'uncanny' because Freud, the thinker of the 'uncanny', would find his work unable to stand outside the effects of the 'uncanny', thereby making his efforts to institute scientific interpretation against speculation both necessary and necessarily doomed to failure. Taking the case of Freud's interpretation of the dream work as *Ent-stellung*, that is, as a form of dislocation, displacement, disfigurement, etc., Weber argues that, while that interpretation and its interpreter would wish to stand apart from the dream work process itself, the process inescapably forms a part of, involves itself with, them, making interpretation itself partake of the ineluctably speculative.

And in *Institution and Interpretation*, Weber engages in a sustained speculation on the conflictual dynamics of institution and interpretation, marking those dynamics between institutions and interpretations, within any institution and its interpretations and within instituting 'itself' and interpreting 'itself'. What is marked here for Weber is a complex splitting, doubling, dislocating, displacing, disseminating, etc.—the setting apart of that instituting act from that instituted form of which it is at the same time a part. Such an ambivalent dynamic between instituting act and instituted form—their simultaneously being apart from and a part of each other—means that, as with psychoanalysis, any philosophical, or rather 'deconstructionist', interpreting of interpretation must be alert to its own enabling and disenabling conditions and limits, as well as to the debts it assumes, including to assumption itself.

Insisting on the ineluctable fictionality in all interpretation—the necessity for society, both inside and outside the university, to 'admit and accept the fictionality of what it assumes to be real, as well as the reality of its fictions', as he puts it in his essay 'Ambivalence'—Professor Weber has himself fashioned an ongoing body of speculative essays, a complex weave of texts engaged precisely in thinking the necessity of its going(s) on.

Alan Cholodenko
Sydney, July 1995

BIBLIOGRAPHY

Selected Bibliography of Books and Articles by Samuel Weber in English

'Upping the Ante: Deconstruction as Parodic Practice', in *Deconstruction Is/In America*, ed. Anselm Haverkamp, New York University Press: New York, 1995.

'*La surenchère*—Upping the Ante', in Maire-Louis Mallet *et al.*, *Passage des frontières*, Editions Galilée: Paris, 1994.

'Taking Exception to Decision: Walter Benjamin and Carl Schmitt', in *Enlightenments: Encounters between Critical Theory and Contemporary French Thought*, eds. Harry Kunneman and Hent de Vries, Pharos: Kampen, Netherlands, 1993. Also in *Commemorating Walter Benjamin*, Special Issue of *diacritics*, vol. 22, nos. 3-4, Fall-Winter 1992.

The Parallax View', *assemblage* 20, Special Issue, ed. Mark Wigley, April 1993.

'The Media and the War', *Alphabet City*, Summer 1991. Reprinted in *Emergences*, 3/4, Fall 1992.

'In the Name of the Law', in *Deconstruction and the Possibility of Justice*, ed. Drucilla Cornell *et al.*, Routledge: New York & London, 1992.

Return to Freud: Jacques Lacan's Dislocation of Psychoanalysis, revised and expanded version of German original, trans. Michael Levine, Cambridge University Press: Cambridge, 1991.

'Deconstruction Before the Name', *Cardozo Law Review*, vol. 13, no. 4, December 1991.

'Genealogy of Modernity: History, Myth and Allegory in Benjamin's *Origin of the German Mourning Play*', *MLN*, vol. 106, no. 5, April 1991.

'Criticism Underway: Walter Benjamin's *Romantic Concept of Criticism*', in *Romantic Revolutions*, ed. Kenneth R. Johnston *et al.*, Indiana University Press: Bloomington & Indianapolis, 1990.

'On the Balcony: The Theater of Technics', in *Bild-Sprache: Texte zwischen Dichten und Denken*, eds. L. Lambrechts and J. Nowé, University Press of Louvain: Louvain, Belgium, 1990.

'The Vaulted Eye: Remarks on Knowledge and Professionalism', *Yale French Studies*, 77, 1990.

'Upsetting the Set Up: Remarks on Heidegger's Questing After Technics', *MLN*, vol. 104, no. 5, December 1989.

'Theater, Technics, Writing', *1-800*, Fall 1989.

'The Monument Disfigured', in *Responses: Paul de Man's Wartime Journalism*, ed. Werner Hamacher *et al.*, University of Nebraska Press: Lincoln, 1989.

Introduction to D. P. Schreber, *Memoirs of My Nervous Illness*, Harvard University Press: Cambridge, Massachusetts, 1988.

'The Foundering of Comparative Literature', in *Aspects of Comparative Literature*, eds. Clayton Koelb and Susan Noakes, Cornell University Press: Ithaca, 1988.

Institution and Interpretation, University of Minnesota Press: Minneapolis, 1987.

'Laughing in the Meanwhile', *MLN*, vol. 102, no. 4, September 1987.

'Caught in the Act of Reading', *Glyph* 9: *Demarcating the Disciplines*, 1985.

'Literature—Just Making It', Afterword to Jean-François Lyotard and Jean-Loup Thébaud, *Just Gaming*, trans. Wlad Godzich, University of Minnesota Press: Minneapolis, 1985.

'The Intersection: Marxism and the Philosophy of Language', *diacritics*, vol. 15, no. 4, Winter 1985.

'Taking Place: Toward a Theater of Dislocation', *enclitic*, vol. 8, nos. 1-2, Spring/Fall 1984.

The Legend of Freud, University of Minnesota Press: Minneapolis, 1982.

'Translating the Untranslatable', Introduction to Theodor W. Adorno, *Prisms*, trans. Samuel and Shierry Weber, MIT Press: Cambridge, Massachusetts, 1981.

Unwrapping Balzac: A Reading of 'La peau de chagrin', University of Toronto Press: Toronto, 1979.

'It', *Glyph* 4, 1978.

'The Divaricator: Remarks on Freud's *Witz*', *Glyph* 1, 1977.

'Saussure and the Apparition of Language: The Critical Perspective', *MLN*, vol. 91, no. 5, 1976.

'The Sideshow, or: Remarks on a Canny Moment', *MLN*, vol. 88, nos. 4-6, 1973.

REFERENCES

In English

Aristotle. *Metaphysics, The Complete Works of Aristotle: The Revised Oxford Translation*, ed. Jonathan Barnes, Princeton University Press: Princeton, 1984.
_____ . *Physics, The Complete Works of Aristotle: The Revised Oxford Translation*, ed. Jonathan Barnes, Princeton University Press: Princeton, 1984.

Benjamin, Walter. 'On Some Motifs in Baudelaire', *Illuminations*, trans. Harry Zohn, Schocken Books: New York, 1968.
_____ . 'The Work of Art in the Age of Mechanical Reproduction', *Illuminations*, trans. Harry Zohn, Schocken Books: New York, 1968.
_____ . 'Theses on the Philosophy of History', *Illuminations*, trans. Harry Zohn, Schocken Books: New York, 1968.
_____ . *The Origin of the German Tragic Drama*, trans. John Osborne, Verso Books: London, 1977.
_____ . 'Central Park', *New German Critique*, 34, Winter 1985.

Cavell, Stanley. 'The Fact of Television', in *Video Culture: A Critical Investigation*, ed. John G. Hanhardt, Smith/Peregrine: Layton, Utah/Rochester, New York, 1986.

De Man, Paul. 'The Rhetoric of Temporality', *Blindness and Insight*, 2nd ed., revised, University of Minnesota Press: Minneapolis, 1983.
_____ . 'Anthropomorphism and Trope in the Lyric', *The Rhetoric of Romanticism*, Columbia University Press: New York, 1984.

Derrida, Jacques. *Speech and Phenomena And Other Essays on Husserl's Theory of Signs*, trans. David B. Allison, Northwestern University Press: Evanston, 1973.
_____ . 'Two Words for Joyce', in *Post-Structuralist Joyce*, eds. Derek Attridge and Daniel Ferrer, Cambridge University Press: Cambridge, 1984.
_____ . 'The Age of Hegel', *Glyph 9: Demarcating the Disciplines*, 1985.
_____ . 'Limited Inc a b c...', *Limited Inc*, Northwestern University Press: Evanston, Illinois, 1988.

_____ . *Aporias*, trans. Thomas Dutoit, Stanford University Press: Stanford, 1993.

Doane, Mary Ann. 'Information, Crisis and Catastrophe', in *Logics of Television: Essays in Cultural Criticism*, ed. Patricia Mellencamp, Indiana University Press: Bloomington, 1990.

Esch, Deborah. 'No Time Like The Present', unpublished essay.

Feuer, Jane. 'The Concept of Live Television: Ontology as Ideology', in *Regarding Television: Critical Approaches—An Anthology*, ed. E. Ann Kaplan, University Publications of America and the American Film Institute: Frederick, Maryland, 1983.

Heidegger, Martin. *An Introduction to Metaphysics*, trans. Ralph Manheim, Doubleday: Garden City, 1959.
_____ . *Being and Time*, trans. John Macquarrie and Edward Robinson, Harper and Row: New York, 1962.
_____ . 'Overcoming Metaphysics', *The End of Philosophy*, trans. Joan Stambaugh, Harper and Row: New York, 1973.
_____ . 'The Origin of the Work of Art', *Poetry, Language, Thought*, trans. A. Hofstadter, Harper and Row: New York, 1975.
_____ . 'The Age of the World Picture', in *The Question Concerning Technology and Other Essays*, trans. William Lovitt, Harper and Row: New York, 1977.
_____ . 'The Question Concerning Technology', *The Question Concerning Technology and Other Essays*, trans. William Lovitt, Harper and Row: New York, 1977.
_____ . *Nietzsche:* vol. I: *The Will to Power as Art*, trans. David Farrell Krell, Harper and Row: San Francisco, 1979.
_____ . *The Principle of Reason*, trans. Reginald Lily, Indiana University Press: Bloomington, 1991.

Kafka, Franz. 'The Cares of a Family Man', in *The Metamorphosis, The Penal Colony and Other Stories*, trans. Edwin Muir, Schocken: New York, 1988.

Kittler, Friedrich. *Discourse Networks 1800/1900*, trans. Michael Metteer, with Chris Cullens, Stanford University Press: Stanford, 1990.

Lacoue-Labarthe, Philippe. *Heidegger, Art and Politics*, trans. Chris Turner, Basil Blackwell: Oxford,1990.

Plato. *The Republic*, trans. B. Jowett, Modern Library: New York, 1982.

Siegel, James T. *Solo in the New Order*, Princeton University Press: Princeton, 1986.

In German

Adorno, Theodor W. *'Individuum und Organisation'*, *Soziologische Schriften*, I, Suhrkamp: Frankfurt am Main, 1979.

Benjamin, Walter. *Ursprung des deutschen Trauerspiels*, Suhrkamp: Frankfurt am Main, 1963.
_____ . *'Das Kunstwerk im Zeitalter seiner technischen. Reproduzierbarkeit'*, *Gesammelte Schriften*, I/2, Suhrkamp: Frankfurt am Main, 1980.
_____ . *'Goethe's Wahlverwandtschaften'*, *Gesammelte Schriften*, I/1, Suhrkamp: Frankfurt am Main, 1980.
_____ . *'Über den Begriff der Geschichte'*, *Gesammelte Schriften*, I/2, Suhrkamp: Frankfurt am Main, 1980.
_____ . *'Über einige Motive bei Baudelaire'*, *Gesammelte Schriften*, I/2, Suhrkamp: Frankfurt am Main, 1980.

Fuld, Werner. *Walter Benjamin: Zwischen den Stühlen*, Fischer Taschenbuch: Frankfurt am Main, 1981..

Heidegger, Martin. *Sein und Zeit*, Max Niemeyer: Tübingen, 1953.
_____ . *Der Satz vom Grund*, Günther Neske: Pfullingen, 1957.
_____ . *Nietzsche*, Bd. I, Günther Neske: Pfullingen, 1961.
_____ . *'Wozu Dichter?'*, *Holzwege*, Klostermann: Frankfurt am Main, 1963.
_____ . *'Die Zeit des Weltbildes'*, *Holzwege*, Klostermann: Frankfurt am Main, 1963.
_____ . *'Die Frage nach der Technik'*, *Vorträge und Aufsätze*, Günther Neske: Pfullingen, 1967.
_____ . *'Die Überwindung der Metaphysik'*, *Vorträge und Aufsätze*, Günther Neske: Pfullingen, 1967.
_____ . *Der Ursprung des Kunstwerkes*, Reclam: Stuttgart, 1967.
_____ . *Metaphysische Anfangsgründe der Logik im Ausgang vom Leibniz*, *Gesamtausgabe*, Bd. 26, Klostermann: Frankfurt am Main, 1990.
_____ . *Grundfragen der Philosophie*, *Gesamtausgabe*, Bd. 45, Klostermann: Frankfurt am Main, 1976-1994.

Kafka, Franz. *'Die Sorge eines Hausvaters'*, *Sämtliche Erzählungen*, Fischer: Frankfurt am Main,1981.

Kant, Immanuel. *Kritik der reinen Vernunft*, Felix Meiner: Hamburg, 1956.
_____ . *Kritik der Urteilskraft*, Wissenschaftliche Buchgesellschaft: Darmstadt, 1983.

Kracauer, Siegfried. *Das Ornament der Massen*, Suhrkamp: Frankfurt am Main, 1962.

Reichel, Peter. *Der schöne Schein des Dritten Reiches: Faszination und Gewalt des Faschismus*, Hanser: Munich, 1991.

Walter Benjamin 1892-1940, ed. Rolf Tiedemann et *al.*, *Marbacher Magazin* 55, 1990.

In French

Derrida, Jacques. *La voix et le phénomène*, Presses Universitaires de France: Paris, 1967.
_____ . *La carte postale: De Socrate à Freud et au-delà*, Flammarion: Paris, 1980.
_____ . *'Différence sexuelle, différence ontologique'*, *Psyche. Inventions de l'autre*, Editions Galilée: Paris, 1987.
_____ . *Khôra*, Editions Galilée: Paris, 1993.

Descartes, René. *'Discours de la méthode'*, *Oeuvres et Lettres de Descartes*, ed. André Bridoux, Gallimard: Paris, 1953.

Virilio, Paul. *La machine de vision*, Editions Galilée: Paris, 1988.

In Italian

Franci, Giovanna. *'Oltra la decostruzione?'*, in *L'Ansia dell'Interpretazione: Saggi su hermeneutica, semiotica e decostruzione*, Mucchi: Modena, 1989.

INDEX

Names and English terms

Adorno, Theodor, 76, 169-175,
177-178, 192-193, 233:
Dialectics of Enlightenment, 172
note 1; *'Individuum und
Organisation'*, 172 note 1;
Negative Dialectics, 172 note 1;
Prisms, 233

aesthetics, 2, 4, 15-16, 23-24, 32,
55, 75, 83, 108-110, 119, 142,
155, 207, 209-210: aesthetic
idea, 28-29, 30; aesthetic judgment, 17, 19-23, 32-33, 210,
230; aestheticization of politics,
101

allegory, 93-97, 105-106, 125-126,
128

alterity, 44, 50-51, 171, 176, 178,
182, 190, 198-200, 206, 217,
224-225, 229

anthropology, 197-201

anxiety, 160-161, 166, 221-222,
230

Aristotle, 43, 70, 131 note 3, 225:
Metaphysics, 131 note 3; *Physics*,
70

aura, 76, 82-83, 85-90, 93-95, 99-
102, 104, 106-107, 204, 209-
211, 219

authority, 39, 149, 168-170, 173,
175-178, 181, 184-186, 227

Balzac, Honoré de, 192-193, 234

Barthes, Roland, 55, 171, 234:
Signes, 171; *S/Z*, 234

Bataille, Georges, 219

Baudelaire, Charles, 76, 94, 96, 100,
102, 104-106

Baudrillard, Jean, 195

Benjamin, Walter, 23, 29, 76-107,
125, 129, 131, 136, 152, 155,
209-210, 219, 224, 231, 233:
'Central Park', 96; *'Das Kunstwerk
im Zeitalter seiner technischen
Reproduzierbarkeit'* ['The Work of
Art in the Age of Mechanical

Reproduction'], 76, 82-92, 101-
102, 152; *'Goethes
Wahlverwandtschaften'*, 105;
Passagenwerk [Paris 'Arcades'
Project], 76-77; *'Über den Begriff
der Geschichte'* ['Theses on the
Philosophy of History'], 129 note
1; *'Über einige Motive bei
Baudelaire'* ['On Some Motifs in
Baudelaire'], 76, 94-100, 106;
Über Haschisch, 85 note 5;
Ursprung des deutschen Trauerspiels
[*The Origin of the German Tragic
Drama*], 93 note 9, 125 note 13,
137

bodies, 10, 34, 103, 114-117, 120,
122, 127, 134, 157, 161, 163-
166

Bourdieu, Pierre, 172, 197

camera, 89-91, 98-100, 102, 154,
156, 164, 166

Cavell, Stanley: 'The Fact of
Television', 108 note 1, 110 note
3, 117 note 8

cinema, 157-158, 160, 162: cinematic, 81, 90-91, 157

Collège International de Philosophie,
180, 232

Coppola, Francis Ford: *Apocalypse
Now*, 166

Cousin, Victor, 173

critical theory, 24, 56, 169, 171-
173, 175, 200, 233

de Man, Paul, 23, 56, 95, 104, 142,
173, 182-185, 188, 191, 203-
206, 208, 232:
'Anthropomorphism and Trope in
the Lyric', 98 note 18, 104 note
21, 105 note 22; *Blindness and
Insight*, 184; 'The Impasse of
Formalist Criticism', 183; 'The
Resistance to Theory', 183; 'The
Rhetoric of Temporality', 95 note
14